THE HOLOCAUST IN HUNGARY

AN ANTHOLOGY OF JEWISH RESPONSE

Edited and Translated,
with Introduction and Notes, by

Andrew Handler

The University of Alabama Press
University, Alabama

Library of Congress Cataloging in Publication Data
Main entry under title:

The Holocaust in Hungary.

(Judaic studies series)
Bibliography: p.
Includes index.
1. Holocaust, Jewish (1939–1945)—Hungary—
Personal narratives. 2. Jews—Hungary—Persecutions
—Addresses, essays, lectures. 3. Hungary—Ethnic
relations—Addresses, essays, lectures. I. Handler,
Andrew, 1935– II. Series.
DS135.H9H58   943.9′004924   81-1261
ISBN 0-8173-0071-6   AACR2

To the memory
of the victims of the
Holocaust in Hungary

Contents

Preface

With every passing year the pangs of grief fade more deeply into the merciful oblivion of time. As personal losses become a matter of record, the events and experiences that have been a reality for one generation are transformed into history for another. A great deal has already been written about the Holocaust: its roots and evolution, the unfathomable brutality of its perpetrators, the often incredible experiences of its victims, and its manifold short- and long-range effects, both physical and psychological. Observing the strict rules of tradition, the history of the Holocaust would have to be written as a record of public events, based on authentic official documents. Laws, decrees, instructions, orders, reports, memoranda, and speeches do indeed provide primary sources that are indispensable tools for the chroniclers of this most tragic and overwhelming epoch. Their study may perhaps lead to a fuller understanding not only of the Jewish experience in the Holocaust, but also of the ideological, political, economic, and military aspects of the age that produced the environment and mentality that with bureaucratic detachment and scientific precision devised and implemented plans for the systematic extermination of the Jews. Yet not even this impressive accomplishment of untiring and dedicated scholars can conceal the fundamental difficulty of such an undertaking. Each detail, authenticated, researched, and explained, is not an end in itself; rather, it leads to a set of new problems to be solved. For a phenomenon of such unprecedented magnitude and complexity, such bewildering physical and emotional costs as the Holocaust, it can hardly be otherwise. At the bottom of the difficulty lie two of the most frequently recurring themes that have been discussed by survivors and researchers alike: the propriety of methodologies and the legitimacy of sources of information. Who is most qualified to describe or speak about this catastrophic event in the turbulent history of the Jews? Is it the survivor, who claims that only personal experience can provide the ring of authenticity and the stamp of authority? Might the historian, who patiently gathers, carefully assembles, objectively analyzes, and painstakingly arranges the often puzzling pieces of information into their seemingly proper places in an effort to present an accurate sequence and full description of events, claim priority in consideration? What about the psychiatrist, who probes the minds of the quintessential practitioners of systematic dehumanization and scientific extermination on a scale that defies imagination, and identifies and analyzes the mental effects the Holocaust had on both those who were destined to perish and those who lived to tell about it? Or should the littérateur, who presents recollections based on personal experience and attempts to draw meaningful and lasting conclusions from them, single out his work as the true repository of the sights and sounds of the Holocaust? The choice is difficult and the verdict is yet to be reached unless the question remains, perhaps deservedly, rhetorical.

Admittedly, the search for historical truths is both a laborious and an overwhelming task. Distortion, omission, and falsification are the most often recurring nemeses of researchers, making conventional analysis and interpretation difficult. The definitive history of the Holocaust might therefore never be written. For perpetrators and victims alike, the real and the imagined were often inextricably fused. Fantasy became reality and reality was often pushed into the furthermost recesses of the mind. Yet recollections and impressions serve as a mirror of private life. They take the researchers beyond the point at which official documents cease to be of utility. They are the sole witnesses to the innermost feelings of people who in the course of a few years crowded into their lives more devastating experiences than their forefathers had faced in all the perilous journey of the nearly two-millennium-long Diaspora. Through private writings, the bearers of the tattooed numbers that transformed humanity into statistical data come to life again. They tell future generations about a twilight in history which their descendants may otherwise find difficult, if not impossible, to comprehend.

A no less pressing and disconcerting problem is created by the uncertainty that surrounds the availability of sources. The gradually depleting reservoir of posthumously published works and the survivors' oral and written accounts (their utility, to be sure, is limited and they can only supplement, not replace, official documents) greatly enhances the importance and relevance of the conventional sources of information. Unfortunately, the overwhelming majority of sources of this kind, excepting the ones in West Germany and the socialist states of East Central Europe that have been made accessible to researchers, remain hidden in closed archives. Such intransigent bureaucratic procedures have severely impeded the work of especially those researchers who hope to probe beyond the hitherto observed extremities of Holocaust history.

For a long time one of the direct results of limited access to indispensable primary sources (i.e., official documents) and one of the most protracted and exasperating features of the study of the Holocaust was the virtual absence of systematic and coordinated efforts to trace and document in depth the persecution and fate of individual Jewish communities. In recent years, however, there has been a notable and welcome upsurge of both interest and research in an effort to make up for past deficiencies.

This book is intended to shed light on the varied responses to the causes and effects of the Holocaust in one of the more enigmatic and exclusivist national Jewish communities in Europe—the Hungarian. Long isolated from the Jewish mainstream by language, assimilation, and more recently, ideological restrictions, it could produce no memorializers like Shalom Aleichem and Isaac Bashevis Singer, who made Jewish life in Russia and Poland an indelible ingredient in the universal Jewish experience. Elie Wiesel, who was born in Sighet (Hungarian Máramarossziget), a Romanian town that until the end of the First World War and from 1940 to 1944 belonged to Hungary, might have become such a memorializer for Hungarian Jewry. His perspective and range of interests, however, are supranational, and references to Hungary and her Jews in his books are thus incidental rather than inevitable.

Still, Hungarian Jews, like their coreligionists elsewhere in Central and Western Europe, who from the mid-nineteenth century had adopted the indigenous languages at the expense of Hebrew and Yiddish, became active in all aspects of national culture, gained grudging recognition, established loyalty to their national state, and formed a community of enthusiastic patriots and indefatigable achievers. They not only made themselves useful to their country—indeed it is difficult to imagine modern Hungary without Jews—but surprisingly made significant contributions to Jewish and non-Jewish causes far beyond the conceptual framework of their traditional way of life. Unlike the Jews in Russia and Poland, whose very numbers and use of Yiddish assured their status among the world's Jewry, or the Jews of Germany and France, whose national languages, unlike Hungarian, were not stumbling blocks to the outside world, Hungarian-born Jews could enter the Jewish mainstream only by leaving the constricting milieu of their native land and assimilating, socially and culturally, into adopted countries. For many people, Jews and non-Jews alike, the Hungarian origin of some outstanding figures who achieved lasting fame is still a cause for surprise. Among them are Theodor Herzl, the founder of modern political Zionism, and Max Nordau, his earliest disciple; composer-conductor Károly Goldmark; the Teitelbaums of Sátoraljaújhely, Máramarossziget, and Szatmár, the famed family of *tzaddikim;* Benjamin Szold, noted rabbi and father of Henrietta Szold, the founder of Hadassah; nuclear physicists Leó Szilárd and Edward Teller; Haganah fighter and poet Hannah Szenes, one of Israel's martyred national heroes; Johann Ludwig von Neuman, mathematician and a member of the United States Atomic Commission; Ármin Vámbéry and Aurél Stein, travelers and orientalists; Avigdor Hameiri, noted Hebrew author; Fülöp László, painter of kings and nobles; film producers Sir Alexander Korda and Joseph Pasternak; actors Leslie Howard and Paul Lukas; conductors Antal Doráti and Georg Szell; playwright-novelist Ferenc Molnár; and Ágnes Keleti, winner of five Olympic gold medals in gymnastics.

The Jewish community in Hungary has fared considerably better in documenting its experience in the Holocaust than most others in Europe. The reason for the preservation of records is that Jewish and secular interests in that country coincide and are steered to complement each other. The work of keeping the past alive is a moral and cultural compulsion of the remnant Jewish community, a living national monument to the horrors of the Holocaust. The leaders of the socialist Hungarian state have sought to establish and retain political credibility not only by institutionalizing the Marxist-Leninist approach to problems and goals, but also by a systematic reindoctrination of the people that awakens them to the abuses and inequalities of their thousand-year national history. The unmasking of the fascist past has been an important psychological weapon and ideological objective.

Materials in this volume are divided into two categories: those written before the end of the Second World War and those written in its aftermath. The division, however, represents a far more significant demarcation than the two distinct spans of time might indicate; it is indeed a veritable psychological chasm. Jewries in German-occupied Europe were swiftly and brutally exposed to the consequences of the attempt to achieve a *judenrein* Europe. But in Hungary, a nation which though an ally of Nazi Germany succeeded in retaining its territorial sovereignty and attended to the Jewish Question in a traditional wait-and-see manner, Jews were spared the horrors of the Holocaust until 19 March 1944, when their country finally was occupied by Hitler's armies. Until then, though undeniably affected by anti-Jewish legislation that restricted them to intracommunal social and cultural activity, most Hungarian Jews had stood outside any real awareness of the danger that surrounded them. As a result, their perspective was clouded and their attitude atypical of the despair that gripped European Jewries. In face of the mounting, manifold evidence of anti-Semitism, predictably missing the all but screaming clues of the catastrophe that was to engulf them, the Hungarian Jews often seemed oblivious of, or perhaps tried to ignore, the impregnable racial barrier that had been erected between them and their Christian countrymen.

The tone of the materials selected from this period is firm and its message clear. Most Hungarian-Jewish poets, writers, rabbis, and community leaders were by tradition overzealous patriots, yet deeply conscious and proudly expressive of the teachings and values of Judaism. They unremittingly stressed the varied contributions that they and their forefathers had made to the Hungarian nation, reaffirmed their consciousness of history and their acculturation by calling themselves Magyar Israelites, and placed their unshakable trust in a better future. Those few who sensed the ominous implications of the Nazis' rise to power in Germany and the start of the Second World War, and gave warning of the inevitable catastrophe, either kept to themselves or were ignored.

The experiences of eleven months (March 1944 to January 1945) destroyed the make-believe world of the Hungarian Jews. Staggering out of the charred rubble of the Pest ghetto and leaving their places of hiding, a stunned and scarred remnant groped for the fading images of reality and sanity. The task of rebuilding lay ahead. With the help of the Soviet Red Army and the architects of the new order, the Hungarian Jews succeeded in reviving their institutions and restoring their religious and cultural life. The powerful, extroversive, and optimistic drive of the prewar era was gone. Instead there was an irreversible turn inward. Men, women, and children were broken in body and spirit. Troubled by the inexplicable twists of fate that brought death to most and kept a few alive, and torn between the strong tradition of nationalism—now tainted with the horrible imagery of the Holocaust—and the promise of emigration, they were ultimately trapped by their own indecisiveness and the promises of the emerging socialist order. As restrictions were imposed on contact with Jewries in Israel and other countries, even those of ideological fraternity, Jews in Hungary became spiritually and culturally self-sufficient. Their perspective, though dutifully reflecting the vision of progress, equality, and peace prescribed by the political leadership, has basically been historical and backward-looking. Thus it was only natural that the millennium-long national tradition and, to a perhaps even greater extent, the Holocaust would emerge as inexhaustible sources for historical research, literary creativity, and communal inspiration.

Only after completing this book did I fully realize that the length of the list of individuals whose help one inevitably takes pride in acknowledging is not always in direct proportion to the degree of indebtedness. I am very grateful to two individuals for their display of generosity in this respect: Professor Sándor Scheiber, Director of the National Rabbinical Institute in Budapest, Hungary, without whose advice and encouragement no work in the history and literature of Hungarian Jewry may be undertaken, let alone finished, and my mother, who typed the manuscript and provided good counsel.

Editorial Note

The selections in this volume are the responses of those who detected the danger signals of the approaching catastrophe and those who bore the burdens of survival. They reflect the editor's attempt to provide the historian with new, hitherto unavailable sources for studying the mood and predicament of Hungarian Jews on the threshold of destruction, and the general reader with a perspective of the Holocaust in Hungary that is broader than the one which the eyewitness accounts from ghettoes, concentration camps, and extermination camps generally afford. The contributors, Jews of diverse social positions and professions, represent wide-ranging and multifarious views and experiences. Some of them—rabbis, community officials, political activists, physicians, educators, and lawyers—were close to or part of policy-making authorities and thus had access to information unavailable to the general public; others, the professional literati, captured and transmitted the spirit and images of the period. For this reason, consideration of literary excellence was at times subordinated to the preservation of historical accuracy and the transcendental freshness and poignancy of feelings. The stylistic quality of some selections is, therefore, understandably uneven.

Until the Treaty of Trianon (1920) that "maimed" her (csonka Magyarország), Hungary was a multinational state, and the adjectives *Magyar* and *Hungarian* stood for clearly identifiable concepts and practices. *Magyar* signified the dominant ethnic group, whereas *Hungarian* denoted the appurtenances of the political state. During the interwar period and following the Second World War, when Hungary, by and large, became a homogeneous state, the difference between *Magyar* and *Hungarian* was greatly reduced. In this anthology, *Magyar* is used only with respect to the proudly exclusivist self-view of Christian Hungarians, the status the Jews struggled for in the effort to gain acceptance. They strove to become Israelite Magyars, i.e., full-fledged Magyars of the Jewish faith.

The editor is responsible for the translation of all selections, the introductions identifying the authors, and the notes that provide information about those names, places, and technical terms that are not considered common knowledge. The explanatory notes which the authors had added were translated or reprinted verbatim and are set in italics.

Note on Pronunciation

Readers unfamiliar with the Hungarian language might find the following guide useful in attempting to pronounce Hungarian names and terms.

1. Stress is placed invariably on the first syllable.
2. The letter *r* is the so-called trilled *r*. It is pronounced by vibrating the tongue while touching it with the upper gums.

3. Consonants:

Letter	Sound	Example	
c and cz	tz	kibitz	
cs	ch	pinch	
g	g	golf	(even before e and i)
gy	di	Nadia	
j and ly	y	yoke	
s	sh	shop	
sz	s	skin	
ty	tth	Matthew	
zs	zh	bijou	

4. Vowels:

Letter	Sound	Example
a	aw	raw
á	i	night
i	i	pick
í	ee	peek
o	ou	source
ó	oa	moat
ö and eö	u	curt
ő	eu	French feu
u	oo	wood
ú	oo	moose
ü	u	French tu
ű	ue	French rue

The Holocaust in Hungary

Introduction

The Historical Framework

"The Jew speaks the language of the nation in whose midst he dwells from generation to generation," wrote Richard Wagner in 1881, "but he always speaks it as an alien. Our whole European art and civilization have remained to the Jew a foreign tongue."[1] Illogical and untrustworthy, as sweeping generalizations often are, Wagner's view of the late nineteenth-century Jew was completely off-target with respect to Jewries in Western Europe. Not even Jews living in countries to the east of Germany, where the peculiar characteristics of Jewish life were more likely to create a basis for it, could very readily induce such a patently unfavorable impression.

One of the Jewish communities in East Central Europe whose documentable experiences in and contributions to the state would thoroughly discredit the veracity of Wagner's observation was in Hungary. The history of Hungarian Jewry reveals a virtually unbroken tradition of service that links the stages of its development to every facet of the thousand-year history of the Magyars. The experiences of coexistence often proved to be more exasperating than rewarding. Anti-Semitism was as much a part of the national character in Hungary as it was elsewhere in Eastern Europe. The anti-Jewish attitude of the early kings of the prestigious House of Árpád, the temporary expulsion (1360–64) ordered by Lajos I (1326–82), the long-lasting laws that made the Jewish badge and the distinctive Jewish attire compulsory, the anti-Jewish protectionism of the medieval Hungarian guilds, the royal decrees exempting Christians from repaying their debts to Jewish creditors, the pogroms of the late fourteenth and early fifteenth centuries, the recurring charges of collaboration with the "infidel" during the Ottoman Turkish occupation of Hungary, the reluctance of towns to issue permits of settlement to Jews, and the infamous Tiszaeszlár ritual murder case (1882–83)—viewed against this backdrop, one is tempted to wonder how Jews could live in Hungary at all.

Surprisingly, none of the above phases of anti-Semitism proved to be a permanent obstacle to continuity in Jewish life. The survival of Hungarian Jewry attests to both the traditional recuperative ability of Jews in the face of adversity and the periodically renewed realization of the leaders of the Hungarian state of the usefulness of its Jewish residents. For every anti-Jewish act there was a decree or practice acting as a neutralizer. Thus the laws of Béla IV, promulgated in 1231, often protected the Jews of Hungary from the impact of previous legislations and illegal abuses. Lajos I expelled the Jews from his domains but was forced to recall them soon thereafter. The humiliating Jewish badge was no longer worn after 1520. The medieval guilds had no lasting effect on the feverish pursuit of unregulated trade, moneylending, and intracommunal crafts. Financial insecurity caused by royal, aristrocratic, or municipal absolutism was rectified by the periodic reaffirmation of the protective legal code of Béla IV. The charges of complicity with the Turks were offset by the heroic resistance of the Jews at the siege of Buda, by the alleged Turkish destruction of the Jewish quarter of the city, and by the massacre of more than four thousand of its inhabitants by Turkish troops. Displaying shrewd tenacity, the early Jewish traders gradually circumvented the municipal legislative acts that blocked Jewish residency in the free cities, and some of Hungary's most prestigious liberals contributed their services to win acquittal for the accused Jews of Tiszaeszlár.[2]

Though Emperor Joseph II (r. 1780–90) permitted Jews to settle in all cities except mining towns and conferred on them the right to education, the emancipation of the Jews in Hungary turned out to be a disillusioning and prolonged affair. His enlightened rule and the radical egalitarianism of the French Revolution had no lasting impact on the proud, backward-looking ruling class in Hungary. Parliament's refusal to debate the Jewish Question remained one of its more remarkable features for nearly fifty years. Buoyed by the July Revolution of 1830 in Paris and the sweeping influence of French, Italian, and German liberalism, some of the most respected Hungarian politicians rallied to support the cause of Jewish emancipation and led an inspired assault upon the enduring defenses of Hungarian conservatism. As a result, the Diet of 1840 succeeded in removing many restrictions surrounding the Jews. The struggle for Jewish emancipation, however, was slowed down by a noticeably weakening yet still determined opposition that professed intransigent ideals and employed crude methods of persuasion.[3]

The Diet of 1847–48, held in Pozsony (Bratislava), became a vital political battlefield. Liberal representatives failed to counter the violent outbursts of members of the anti-Semitic faction, who demanded that constitutional safeguards be approved to counter the periodic influx of Jewish refugees from neighboring countries, and that specific limitations regulating the number of Jews in Hungary be set up.[4] The mounting anti-Jewish hatred burst through the strict confines of parliamentary procedure. The people of Pozsony, wildly celebrating the beginning of the revolution on 15 March 1848, attacked the Jewish residents of the city. Their act was not an isolated phenomenon. Throughout Hungary anti-Jewish acts marred the beginning of the heroic struggle for national independence.

The Jews reacted to the outbreak of organized anti-Semitic atrocities with a display of remarkable psychological flexibility and determined political activism. Though many of them had become ardent nationalists, the majority, fearing the secular obligations of citizenship and the disruptive effects of

the Emancipation, moved slowly in offering voluntary gestures of unqual-
ified acceptance of the lofty ideals and ambitious goals of modern nationalism. They showed little if any interest in secular culture and were skeptical
of the advantages of social assimilation.[5] Soon liberal politicians found
powerful and persuasive allies in the Jewish leaders who were to become the
champions of Magyarization, guiding their coreligionists on the difficult path
to full emancipation. Even some of the most influential rabbis, discarding
the tradition of conservatism and ethnic separatism, exhorted the members
of their congregations to follow their example, strive for the respect of even
those Hungarians who tended to side with the anti-Semitic demagogues, and
become active and loyal citizens of the Hungarian nation: Magyar in body
and spirit, Jewish in religion.

The Magyarization of a large portion of the Jewish community was
achieved with remarkable facility. It exceeded the expectations of even the
most philo-Semitic liberals. Sermons were delivered with increasing fre-
quency in Hungarian, and Jewish schools initiated extensive programs in an
attempt to introduce a national, secular culture to their students.[6] The first
Hungarian translation of the Old Testament was published in 1840 and that
of the prayer book in the following year. The first Hungarian-Jewish calendar
appeared in 1848. In addition, a large number of patriotic organizations were
formed, such as the Hungarian-Jewish Handicraft and Agricultural Association and the Hungarian-Jewish Youth Association. A number of short-lived
Jewish periodicals in Hungarian were published in the mid-nineteenth
century.[7]

Yet the Jews' acquisition of the Magyar language, total immersion in
secular culture, and zealous participation in the manifold aspects of society
pleased only the champions of the Emancipation. For most Hungarians, the
persistent charges that Jews by nature were inassimilable aliens continued to
have a special meaning, enabling anti-Semitism to retain its popular appeal.
Conversely, many Jews were frightened and repelled by the sweeping anti-
Semitic terror that began in the shadow of the Diet of 1847–48 at Pozsony
and spread like a wildfire across the nation. They had little faith in the
desirability or advantages of Magyarization, and were skeptical of the constitutional guarantees for security and equality promised by the Jewish and
non-Jewish exponents of the Emancipation. As early as May 1848 the Central Emigration Bureau was set up at Pest, calling on all Jews to leave
Hungary and seek entry and settlement in the United States. Interestingly,
the Bureau's well-timed and impassioned propaganda campaign, notwithstanding the widespread anti-Jewish feeling, found only negligible support
in the community. Roused by the fiery sermons of patriotic rabbis and
encouraged by the sympathetic pronouncements of the revolutionary government, Jews pledged considerable sums for the training and equipment of
the revolutionary militia, and ignoring the initial refusal of the recruiting
committees to accept them, volunteered for military service.

The Revolution of 1848 provided one of the most convincing proofs of the willingness of Jews to adapt themselves to national aspirations. The most influential Hungarian statesmen, military leaders, and intellectuals paid eloquent tributes to the many efforts of the Jews in behalf of the revolution. According to Lajos Kossuth, the fiery leader of the revolution, more than twenty thousand Jews fought in the revolutionary armies. Generals Görgey and Klapka wrote admiringly of the bravery, devotion, and discipline of Jewish soldiers, many of whom were promoted to high ranks and awarded decorations. In a moving and passionate statement, Mór Jókai, one of the most popular novelists, praised the contributions of the "Hebrew race" in the defense of independent Hungary, and observed that the Jews were the only minority in the nation that had still not been granted civil and religious equality.

In a nation where Christianity and nationalism had for nearly a millennium formed a seemingly unbreakable bond of exclusive brotherhood, the emancipation of the Jews was a belated yet immensely satisfying accomplishment. It was in recognition of their enthusiastic support of the revolution that the Diet of Szeged (July 1849) voted to make it a law of the land.[8] The failure of the revolution and the ensuing Habsburg absolutism, however, nullified the decision. Only after Francis Joseph I had been forced to loosen his autocratic rule in the aftermath of the Austro-Prussian War of 1866 was the question of the emancipation of the Jews taken up again in the Hungarian Parliament. In December 1867 the Upper and Lower Houses again voted that civil and political rights be transferred upon Jews, thereby placing them on equal footing with the rest of the country's population. All laws and customs to the contrary were declared null and void. After the stormy debate in October 1895, with the president of the Upper House casting the tie-breaking vote, Judaism became a legally accepted and protected religion in Hungary.[9]

Though legal emancipation did not entail social acceptance except for members of some wealthy Jewish families who abandoned Judaism, the Jews became active in every sector of Hungary's political, economic, social, and intellectual life. Between 1866 and 1918, in recognition of their services, nearly three hundred Jews—industrialists, university professors, landowners, bankers, army officers, physicians, wholesale merchants, and parliamentary representatives—received baronial titles or forenames of lesser nobility.[10]

Reaction to the full emancipation of the Jews was not long in coming. The acts of Parliament had not by any means pleased all Hungarians. Traditional anti-Jewish feelings had for centuries been the stumbling block to the assimilation of the Jews into the society of the Magyars. With the rise of modern political anti-Semitism in Hungary, this feeling was to receive a powerful impetus. The founder and for a long time the lone apostle of this movement was Győző Istóczy, a little-known representative in Parliament, who in the early 1870s developed an ideology and an inflammatory style, both in writing and public speaking, that were to remain basically unchanged until the end of the Second World War. Istóczy's message was simple and uncompromising. The Jews were a "pure race," alien and inassimilable, though talented and enterprising. Because of the fundamental differences between Jews and Christian Magyars, the Jews would have to be removed from Hungary and resettled, with the help of the Turkish government, in Palestine, where they might reestablish their national state.[11] By the early 1880s he had a small group of followers in Parliament and a steadily growing constituency throughout Hungary. Though the National Anti-Semitic Party, which he founded, was short-lived, its platform remained firmly entrenched in both the public mind and the political system.[12]

As if to make a final effort to silence the voices of hatred, Jews plunged into the supreme test of patriotism, giving perhaps their most impressive performance. They distinguished themselves in the military service, the jealously guarded nationalist privilege of Christian Hungarians. At the outbreak of the First World War, Jewish generals, colonels, and majors were put in command of troops and soon awarded numerous decorations, many of the highest order. The leaders of the National Rabbinical Association called upon Jewish communities to offer prayers for victory. The rabbis reminded the congregants of their patriotic duty, gave their blessing to those who were called up or volunteered for military service, and exhorted others to support the war effort to the best of their abilities. Jewish soldiers repeated the achievements of their nineteenth-century forebears. In 1916, the future Charles IV paid tribute to the bravery and loyalty of the Hungarian Jews. The Archdukes Joseph and Francis Peter led the imperial general staff in unanimously expressing their praise of the Hungarian-Jewish soldiers who had fought with uncommon distinction in the bloodiest battles of the war. Nearly ten thousand of them died the death of heroes. The magnitude of Jewish sacrifices during the First World War was only gradually revealed in the interwar years. The doctors in the armed forces were overwhelmingly Jewish, Jewish communities contributed millions of crowns in war loans, and Jewish industrialists were commended for their role in the accelerated production of war materiel.

Official recognition of Jewish war efforts failed to prevent the outbreak of one of the most vicious anti-Semitic campaigns in the history of modern Hungary. Anti-Semitism, as an organized attack upon the alleged unassimilability of Jews, was never more irrational and unjustified. Its leaders worked feverishly to revive the myth of Jewish aloofness in times of national emergency. Jews, it was alleged, not only failed to participate in the struggle for victory, but even organized an internal conspiracy to undermine the will and morale of the people. Jewish suppliers of war materiel were accused of corruption and of delivering low-quality, often unusable goods. A number of anti-Semitic publicists went even beyond the issue at hand and singled out the late-nineteenth-century emancipation of the Jews as the source of all the subsequent misfortune that befell the Hungarian people. The anti-Semitic movement succeeded in collecting ten million crowns in donations for the dissemination of propaganda aimed at breaking the "Jewish control" of the nation's vital economic, cultural, and political arteries.

Faced with the danger of rekindling the spirit of Tiszaeszlár, Jewish leaders made a valiant attempt to discredit the allegations of the anti-Semites. Since the charges were based on unfounded rumors and on the malicious falsification of statistical data that were already distressingly inaccurate, the Committee of the Hungarian-Jewish War Archives was formed for the purposes of analyzing and publishing tens of thousands of pertinent documents attesting to the contributions of Jewish communities and individual Jews to the national war effort on the home front. The Committee also established the approximate number of Jewish soldiers killed, wounded, and decorated.

Its work, however, failed to make the anticipated impact upon public opinion. The flood of anti-Semitic studies and pamphlets not only ran unabated but also received an unexpected boost in the early 1920s. The National Statistical Office, which established the number of Jewish war dead at ten thousand, estimated that the relative losses suffered by Jews were less than half of those of Christians. Delighted by the obvious implications of this ominous discrepancy, the anti-Semitic press continued its attacks with renewed zeal. It met no organized resistance. The Committee was soon dissolved without making a determined counterstand. In the absence of an effective organization to represent its war record, the Jewish community was forced to limit itself to the deployment of essentially defensive tactics. Occasionally it published partial statistics and pointed out contradictions in the anti-Semitic press. Its inability to face the anti-Semitic challenge with convincing authority greatly contributed to the gradual public belief that the rumors and allegations directed against the Jews were substantially accurate.[13]

Modern Hungarian anti-Semitism received another powerful impetus in the shape of the immense implications of the Hungarian Soviet Republic (21 March to 30 July 1919). According to the anti-Semites, the Jewish origin of seventeen of the thirty People's Commissars was an unmistakable proof of the existence of an international organization of antinationalist Jewish Bolsheviks, whose avowed objective was to make Hungary an ideological and territorial extension of the Soviet Union.[14] Béla Kun, the guiding spirit of Hungarian Bolshevism, was both Lenin's man and of Jewish origin, which was for Hungarians a particularly odious combination of contemptible characteristics. Kun came to be seen as the very personification of the international Jew, the nation's most dangerous enemy.[15] In the aftermath of the Romanian occupation of Budapest that put an end to Kun's regime, the indiscriminately vengeful atrocities committed by groups of counterrevolutionary army officers closely resembled their glorified model, the bloody pogroms of the anti-Soviet Whites in Russia. Their leaders declared that such actions represented the sacred obligation of every citizen, that they were the defense of Christian Hungary.

The anti-Semitic torrent swept away the desperate attempts of Jews at self-defense. It mattered little that since 1869 Jews had played a significant role in the Hungarian Socialist movement, that its leaders, many of whom were of Jewish origin, had plotted against the regime of Béla Kun, and that Socialist parliamentary representatives of Jewish origin worked diligently and effectively for the welfare of the nation. Nor was it well known that nearly fifty Jews were executed at the order of the short-lived but ruthlessly efficient Revolutionary Tribunal, whose president, Jenő László, was himself of Jewish origin, or that of the roughly seven hundred hostages rounded up by the Communist government in the last frenzied hours of its existence, more than a hundred and fifty were Jews. But if the redeeming details were lost in the mounting barrage of anti-Semitic propaganda, the fundamental incompatibility of the philosophy and policies of the Hungarian Soviet Republic with the religious traditions and economic and cultural perspectives of the Hungarian Jews should have provided a sufficiently extenuating circumstance. Furthermore, the Communists' sweeping policy of nationalization, affecting virtually every aspect of economic life, was especially disastrous for the Jews whose position in the capitalist system of prewar Hungary had been firmly established. The Communist government held no promise for the Jews. Politically and militarily, the Communists were given no chance of survival against the gathering forces of counterrevolutionary, aristocratic-bourgeois conservatism.

The increasing popularity of anti-Semitism, however, failed to curtail the attempts of the Jewish community to remake its image. Probably out of apprehension that the Jewish origin of the most powerful leaders of the Hungarian Soviet Republic might provide anti-Semitic demagogues with an opportunity to arouse mass hysteria by raising charges of a Judeo-Bolshevik conspiracy, Jews displayed fervent patriotism and played an important role in the emergent counterrevolutionary movement.

At Szeged, where the counterrevolutionary government was formed by Count Gyula Károlyi on 19 May 1919, the leaders of the local Jewish community were instrumental in the collection of funds for the equipment and training of troops, and were among the founders of the influential Anti-Bolshevik Committee. Jewish participation in the counterrevolution was not limited to organization and fund raising. The Jewish Lajos Pálmai became minister of justice in the Arad government and was appointed minister of public welfare in the Second Szeged Government of Dezső Ábrahám. Samu Biedl, the president of the Szeged Jewish community and a founding member of the Anti-Bolshevik Committee, coordinated the fund-raising efforts of the new government. Yet in a nation where military prowess was the most highly praised human virtue, behind-the-scene activities were rarely acknowledged in public. Only military service in the national interest was recognized and admired as a truly patriotic gesture. The successful attack of a group of officers that led to the disarming of the local garrison of Red soldiers in Szeged and to the subsequent transfer of the anti-Communist government from Arad (where it had originally been formed) to Szeged was the first military victory of the counterrevolution.

Of the seventy-two officers who formed the nucleus of the emergent national army, fifteen were Jews. For a brief period it seemed that the anti-Semitic propaganda machinery was suspending its virulent attacks. Not even Father István Zadravetz, one of the most fanatical anti-Communist and anti-Semitic clergymen, raised objections to the inclusion of Jews in the various committees of the counterrevolutionary government. In 1932 Gyula Gömbös was to become prime minister, representing a coalition of anti-Semitic and extreme right factions. He was one of the architects of Hungary's *numerus clausus* law, which placed severe restrictions upon Jewish participation in certain professions. Yet even he supported the participation of Jews in government-sponsored activities. The anti-Semitic interregnum, however, proved to be short-lived; neither the patriotic gestures of the Szeged Jews nor the encouraging receptivity of the counterrevolutionary governments could sustain it.

As early as June 1919 the Jewish community of Szeged had to issue a firm declaration in which it unequivocally rejected anti-Semitic charges of Jewish disloyalty to the nation and reaffirmed the traditional patriotism of the Hungarian Jews. Following the victory of the counterrevolution, Jewish communities throughout Hungary issued a series of similar patriotic manifestos. On 28 August 1919 the leaders of the Jewish community of Pest made one of the most significant responses to the increasingly serious anti-Semitic allegations. Speaking for all of Hungary's Jewish citizens, the Pest declaration expressed joy and satisfaction over the victory of the national forces and denounced the political philosophy, the destructive economic policies, and the excessive brutality of the defeated Communist government. It pointed out that in proportion to the rest of the nation's population, the Jews had suffered the most substantial economic losses. Furthermore, the declaration was among the very few documents that called attention to one of the most perilous and unfounded generalizations that were to be hurled against Jews during most of the interwar period. It acknowledged that a large number of Communists of Jewish origin had played a decisive role in the day-to-day work of the Hungarian Soviet government. The Jewish leaders pointed out, however, that unlike the overwhelming majority of the Hungarian Jews, who had suffered as much as the non-Jewish citizens yet remained steadfast in their loyalty to the nation, these Communists had long terminated their religious affiliation and repudiated their sacred nationalist obligations in the interest of international Communism and the Soviet Union. The Jewish communities, therefore, severed with Communists of Jewish origin the ties of solidarity that had traditionally bound Jews to one another, branding them enemies of the Hungarian nation and the Jewish religion. They further ordered the expulsion of any Jew who had actively participated in the Communist regime or was known to have harbored sympathies with it from whichever Jewish community he had rejoined after the victory of the counterrevolution.

The impact of the declaration was minimal; it accomplished little beyond expounding the policy that was to form the basis of the relationship between the Jewish communities and the government. Between 1919 and 1924, the news of the bloody pogroms of the Russian Whites touched off a virtually uncontrollable war of purification in Hungary. Jews and suspected Communists were attacked in public by wildly anti-Semitic mobs and roaming groups of brutally vengeful counterrevolutionary officers, making the towns of Siófok, Tab, Izsák, and Orgovány the most tragic stations in the path of the Hungarian White Terror.[16]

Despite its ferocity, the bloody aftermath of the victory of the counterrevolution left few permanent scars on the Jewish community. Anti-Semitism remained a powerful though at times a dormant force in the interwar years. Between 1924 and 1938, however, Admiral Miklós Horthy, elected Regent of Hungary in 1920, succeeded in stabilizing his power with the help of the forces of conservatism led by Count István Bethlen, the prime minister. Horthy was also able to tone down the virulent anti-Jewish campaign.[17] Even the brief (1932–35) but potentially ominous premiership of Gyula Gömbös, one of the most consistent anti-Semites and a firm believer in the historic inevitability of Hungary's ideological, political, economic, and military alliance with Nazi Germany and Fascist Italy, failed to introduce sweeping anti-Jewish legislation. Gömbös was satisfied with pushing through Parliament a mildly restrictive *numerus clausus* law, which, aside from placing limits on Jewish professional activities, fell considerably short of the expectations of the anti-Semitic groups that had suported him.[18] Gömbös's death in 1935 and Horthy's subsequent appointment of the inconspicuous and moderate Kálmán Darányi kept the anti-Semitic factions at bay until 1938.

As the effects of the pogroms that had followed the victory of the counterrevolution gradually wore off, Jews resumed their diverse positions in virtually every sector of Hungarian society. Aside from private industry and commerce, where they were represented in large numbers, they were also found in municipal and state service. In the arts, education, and the professions their participation was especially prominent. There were nearly ten thousand Jewish land owners, a remarkable figure in view of the medieval restrictions that had for centuries excluded them from agriculture.[19] Patriotic Jews founded numerous organizations, many functioning within the framework of a steadily growing number of congregations that by the late 1920s exceeded 250 (with twice as many subsidiary community organizations) and were served by nearly 500 ordained rabbis, assistant rabbis, and teachers of the religious schools.[20]

One unique byproduct of the emancipation and assimilation of the Jews has been consistently overlooked. To the Hungarian the love of sport is second only to love of the nation, and preoccupation with the display of physical prowess and skill is proverbial. Hungary's relatively small population and the impressive record of its athletes in international competition to this day stand in a remarkable juxtaposition. Traditionally, participation in sports was not only a respected and popular fulfillment of patriotic duty, it was also believed to be as fundamentally Christian as it was unmistakably Hungarian. Though the Christian Hungarian athlete thought that sport was his inalienable monopoly, he could not prevent the emergence of his Jewish counterpart. It was one of the most visible and convincing signs of the success of the emancipation of the Jews in Hungary and of the high degree of their assimilation.

Jews had made significant contributions to soccer, the favorite national pastime, ever since it was first introduced in Hungary. Alfréd Brüll, who subsequently became president of the Hungarian Swimming Association, the Association of Hungarian Wrestlers, and vice-president of the Hungarian Athletic Association, and the Hungarian Gymnastics Association, was one of the founders of the Hungarian Soccer Association. Mór Fischer, one of the founders of the Association of Hungarian Railroad Workers, guided the entry of Hungary into international soccer competition and in 1927 became president of FIFA. Artúr Herendi was the first sport reporter in Hungary. Of the most famous soccer players of the interwar years who wore Hungary's colors, more than fifty were Jews. A number of Jews became respected soccer referees.

Perhaps the most astonishing spectacle was the emergence of Jewish athletes as a dominating force in fencing, a sport that due to its long association with soldierly virtues was inextricably fused with the origins and the greatest figures of the Christian Hungarian state. Jenő Fuchs was world champion two times before the First World War; in the 1920s Sándor Gombos won the European championship twice and János Garai won it once. Attila Petschauer was one of the most spectacular fencing champions of the late 1920s and early 1930s.

Although numerous Jewish athletes represented a variety of clubs at national and international competition, Jewish sportsmen still felt the need for an exclusively Jewish sport organization. In 1906, Lajos Dömény, one of the most active Zionist leaders, who was to lose his life in the First World War, founded the Fencing and Athletic Club. Two of its players were selected for the national water polo team, some of its soccer players were named internationals, and the members of its gymnastics team won many individual and team titles.

No less impressive had been the performance of Jewish wrestlers since the turn of the century. In a sport in which raw physical prowess and technical skill prevailed, Richárd Weisz was unbeatable as a heavyweight. Champion of Hungary since 1903 and winner in numerous international matches,

Weisz won the gold medal at the London Olympics in 1908. Tibor Fischer was Weisz's successor and repeated his achievements. Dávid Müller, the winner of every major gymnastic championship in the 1880s, was regarded as the most perfectly muscled Hungarian. He was said to be the model for the famous statue of Miklós Toldi, the fourteenth-century quintessence of Hungarian chivalric virtues and physical prowess. József Szalai was the undisputed gymnastic champion of Hungary in the 1920s and the winner of numerous international titles.

Jewish sportsmanship and organizational skill were instrumental in laying the foundations of competitive swimming in Hungary, a sport that was to become one of the most satisfying and consistent sources of national pride. Alfréd Hajós won two gold medals in the first Olympic Games of modern times at Athens in 1896. Ödön Toldi, Imre Elek, and Andor Bárány were the holders of world records during the decade before World War I. Hungary's world-famous water polo team was perennially staffed with a number of Jewish players. In 1921, while the terrorist activities of anti-Semitic army officers raged virtually unchecked, Nándor Velvárt, the winner of most of the national bicycle championships in the late 1910s and early 1920s, captured what must have been the most satisfying trophy of his career: the grand prize of the Awakening Magyars' Club, the athletic counterpart of Hungary's most fanatically nationalist and irredentist political movement.[21]

Despite the ominous manifestations of the controlled anti-Semitic movement, the Hungarian Jews clearly benefited by the peculiarly ambivalent political philosophy of Miklós Horthy. Anti-Trianonism, not anti-Semitism, was still the predominant national issue. Yet the visions of the Greater Hungary scheme and the rectification of the nation's dismemberment by the Treaty of Trianon (June 1920), which deprived Hungary of nearly three-fourths of her prewar territory, revealed a variety of temperaments and tactics. Due to Hungary's powerlessness in the international politico-military arena, the irredentists' dream remained a purely local yet combustible emotional issue. Thus the philosophy of the potentially dangerous ultranationalist clubs and societies that emerged during the formative years of the counterrevolution became the ideological foundation of a sacred patriotic duty.[22] Fanatically irredentist and anti-Semitic factions were generally neutralized by the official political philosophy of the Horthy regime. Although haunted by the spirit of Trianon and Béla Kun's legacy, the government was satisfied with retaining a basically conservative outlook on life that cushioned Hungarian society against the shocks of ideological extremism. Unfortunately, aside from its pronounced nationalism, which became the only identifiable common denominator in the political spectrum, and excepting further its proud adherence to the thousand-year national tradition of Christian values, the Horthy regime revealed inconspicuous yet often distressingly conflicting beliefs and views that reflected its inability to formulate distinct policies addressing either the doctrinaire spirit of emergent totalitarianism or the agile conservatism of the Western democracies. Hungary's traditional dislike of Russia, heightened by its fear of Communism, forced her to look in a generally westward direction. She was culturally enthusiastic but politically reserved to the point of taciturnity, while still nurturing the self-flagellant memories of Trianon.

The gradual normalization of conditions and the temporary control of extremely nationalistic patriotic organizations during the premiership of Count István Bethlen (1924–33) provided the Hungarian Jews with a seemingly effective system of protection.[23] To many pessimists, however, the policies of the government looked precariously superficial, lacking a broad base of popular support. Traditionally anti-Semitic Hungarians were embittered by the disproportionately advantageous social advances and demographic distribution of the Jews, who were considered Magyarized denizens rather than equals. The Hungarians were outraged by Jewish attempts at assimilation into every social sphere except the religious, and thus were easily swayed by the anti-Semitic accusations of conspiracy between Hungarian Jews and the Western democracies—of which they were suspicious and unforgiving—and the Soviet Union, which they feared and detested.

The prosperity of the Hungarian Jews, which for nearly twenty years contradicted the fears of those to whom the domestic policies of Hungary betrayed the signs of impending doom, was not a sensitive barometer of public opinion, which often reacted to the political and ideological inconsistencies and socioeconomic inequalities of the Horthy era. Most Jews went about proudly displaying an unshakable conviction in guaranteed security as the expected reward of their proven patriotism. Their prosperity, however, was a measure of utility, not a sign of acceptance. The spirit of the counter-revolution was as lasting and unforgiving as it was incoherent. National self-respect depended for survival upon an inextinguishably seething, blind hatred of an assorted variety of domestic and external ills.

For Hungary's political structure between 1919 and 1945, no alternatives seemed to suffice or indeed make sense. Those who were deceived by the illusion of the Jews' prosperity, and believed in their guaranteed security, failed to recognize the fundamental incompatibility of Hungarian nationalism and Jewish assimilationism. The admiral who, riding his white horse at the head of his anti-Communist troops, had taken control of Budapest, seemed to Hungarian Jews like the architect of a new order of peace, national solidarity, and reconstruction. In the outpour of blind enthusiasm they failed to realize that the new regent of Hungary was a political neophite of mediocre abilities who viewed his new realm through the distorting prism of his obsessive and uncritical admiration of Francis Joseph I, whose aid-de-camp he had been.

Miklós Horthy's ideological conviction and political acumen never left pre-1914 Vienna. Despite his high-sounding titles of regent and supreme war lord, he remained a hapless intermediary between opposing factions at home and abroad, often uneasy, indecisive, and invariably procrastinating. His inability to provide strong personal leadership and national purpose virtually assured the continuation of the power struggle that developed in 1919 between the two main factions of the counterrevolutionary movement: the measured, aristocratic conservatives of Vienna and the unruly irredentist radicals of Szeged. To the Jews of Hungary he gave the portentous choice between the selective anti-Semitism found in the Vienna group and the rabid anti-Jewish hatred felt by the radicals of Szeged. The former seemed tolerant, though not altogether harmless. Yet its anti-Semitism was a part of the old order, inspired by the restrictive influences of Christianity and the rigid exclusivism of the Hungarian nobility to which Jews had already become accustomed. The anti-Jewish hatred of the Szeged group, on the other hand, represented an outraged, virulent, and uncompromising form of nationalism that was to lead directly to the Arrow Cross coup on 15 October 1944.[24]

Still, it was not until the mid-1930s that the various Fascist factions gained influence. Though hampered by a political platform which their ideologues never managed to present in clear, concise terms, the Fascists, dominated by military officers, succeeded in making a favorable impression on the gentry, who had made the civil service their primary economic and social basis, and on the petty bourgeoisie, who were already feeling threatened by the dual menace of Jewish capitalism and Communist expansionism. To these groups the Fascists' unmitigated chauvinism, utter contempt for democracy, and abiding trust in the fundamental values of military dictatorship seemed to provide certain guarantees for success in the radical overhaul of Hungary's social and political system.

As if the demagoguery of the native anti-Semites were not trouble enough, the influx of Magyar-speaking refugees, from territories that the Treaty of Trianon had forced Hungary to relinquish to her neighbors, added an explosive element to the growing problems of the political system. The refugees were embittered and easily swayed by irredentist propaganda. They were ready to give vent to their emotions and were quick to blame the Western powers and their alleged collaborators in Hungary for their miseries. The Jews, constituting a seemingly insurmountable obstacle to their swift and orderly integration, were clearly the enemy. The refugees' allegiance was quickly established. The political platform of the extreme right envisioned the removal of that obstacle, whereas the lenient anti-Semitism of Horthy and the leading upper classes generated little appeal, as it provided no clearly identifiable program of immediate utility.

Characteristically, the unmistakable danger signals did not assuage the nationalist fervor of the Hungarian Jews. The leadership, dominated by rich and influential Jews in Budapest, did not want to be outdone in the display of nationalism by any of the non-Jewish political groups vying for national attention, and adopted a stance that had been tried before. The Alliance Israélite Universelle, based in Paris, had been asked by the Romanian Jews to intercede with their government on account of its prolonged reluctance to grant them the rights of full citizenship. Vilmos Vázsonyi (1868–1926), who as Minister of Justice and Minister of Electoral Rights in two pre-1914 governments had become the voice of Jewish assimilation, rejected an offer of similar help from the Alliance to secure constitutional protection for the Hungarian Jews against the increasingly vocal irredentist groups. Vázsonyi believed that the acceptance of the Alliance's help would have been doubly undesirable, because it would have reconfirmed not only the irredentist charge of the Hungarian Jews' international ties, but also the popular illusion of the unassimilability of Jews, by allowing a comparison of untenable justification between the still un-Romanized Jews with their thoroughly Magyarized coreligionists.

Similarly, it was superpatriotism that led the Hungarian Jewish elite to glorify Mussolini's invasion of Ethiopia. In a retrospective view of the anti-Semitism of Italian Fascism, the behavior of Hungarian-Jewish leadership may appear to have been indeed absurd, but only if one fails to take the chronological sequence of events into consideration. Following his victory over the Ethiopians in May 1936, Mussolini spoke of Italy's fulfilled dream and pledged his support for the maintenance of universal peace. Like most Italians, Mussolini still found the anti-Semitism of the Nazis distasteful. For nearly two years after the announcement of the Rome-Berlin Axis in October 1936, Mussolini resisted Hitler's pressure to introduce the racialist policy into Italy. Furthermore, the Hungarian Jews were not alone in their fascination with Mussolini. The ineptly favorable comparison between Mussolini and Moses, made by Dr. Simon Hevesi, the chief rabbi of Budapest, was no more tasteless than Pope Pius XI's description of Mussolini as God-sent before he denounced the Duce's aggressive nationalism and racialist philosophy.[25]

Not all Hungarian Jews shared the optimistic expectations and fervent patriotism of the leading assimilationists. Already in the 1880s minuscule groups espoused the zealous Palestinocentrism of the Hoveve Tzion (Lovers of Zion). Organized Zionism in Hungary, however, was beset by predictably grave problems from its inception. Though János Rónai (1849–1919), who had participated in the First World Zionist Congress in Basel (1897), worked tirelessly to organize the Zionist movement in Hungary, the reaction of the overwhelming majority of the Hungarian Jews was clearly unfavorable. Yet in the aftermath of the congress, Zionist groups were formed in Budapest and in other cities, and held a number of national conferences.[26]

It is interesting to note that during World War I, when the Hungarian Jews were in the grips of patriotism, the number of Zionist groups exceeded three hundred. Zionist newspapers—the first founded by Ármin Bokor in 1903—appeared in increasing numbers. The most influential, *Zsidó Szemle* (the Jewish Review), became a weekly publication by 1918. Though by virtue of a continued existence it achieved somewhat of a victory in the struggle for survival against the most vocal assimilationists, the Hungarian Zionist movement was also in trouble with the authorities. Because the central Jewish leadership was opposed to its activities, the Ministry of the Interior refused to sanction the statutes of the Zionist movement. The prevailing regulations, however, permitted it to function even without an official license.

In the aftermath of the fall of the Hungarian Soviet Republic, the first counterrevolutionary government suspended all groups, including the Zionists, that were operating without officially approved statutes. It was not before the end of 1926 that the Zionist organizations were revived and the Pro-Palestine Federation of the Hungarian Jews established. In September 1927 the Ministry of the Interior approved the statutes of the Zionist movement that had enthusiastically endorsed the goals of the World Zionist Organization, and called for the establishment of a program of financial assistance and cultural cooperation with the Jewish community in Palestine. In addition to its regular members, the renascent Zionist movement drew strength from those who viewed the long-range effects of Jewish assimilationism with skepticism and placed little trust in peaceful coexistence with the Christian Hungarians.[27]

Anti-Zionism among the Hungarian Jews, particularly among the community leaders, had been both deep-rooted and seemingly implacable. The Zionists' impassioned plea for the revival of Jewish nationalism and the uncompromising logic with which they defined anti-Semitism as a troublesome social disease, insisting that the cure for it would be found only in mass Jewish emigration, offended the cardinal theses of the assimilationist philosophy of the Jewish leaders who shared the optimistic nationalism of liberal politicians and steadfastly minimized or ignored the danger of anti-Semitism. The Hungarian origin of both Theodor Herzl and Max Nordau was an embarrassment, and the denunciation of Zionism began to resemble a personal vendetta against the prodigal sons.

The very timing of the First Zionist Congress at Basel (29 August 1897) was an event of portentous implictions for Hungarian Jewry. Herzl had been treading on sensitive ground. His message was a painful reminder of the infamous ritual murder trial of Tiszaeszlár (1882–83).[28] Furthermore, the publication of Herzl's *Der Judenstaat* (1896) coincided with the celebration of Hungary's millennial year of nationhood, an event that offered the assimilationist leaders a unique opportunity to reaffirm their patriotism.[29]

The reaction of the Hungarian-Jewish leaders to Zionism was predictably virulent. Civil equality, granted to all citizens of the Hungarian state, had become the cornerstone of the assimilationist philosophy of an overconfident Hungarian Jewry. The ideological structure of Herzlian Zionism rested on the failure of the Emancipation and on the inevitability of a Jewish state. To the Hungarian-Jewish leaders, who advocated that "Israelite" and "Magyar" become fused in one indivisible and sacred concept, and for whom the Holy Land was millennial Hungary and not Palestine, the philosophy and goal of Zionism were intolerable. Their religious, cultural, and political precepts were conditioned and sustained by proud Hungarocentric convictions.

Lipót Kecskeméti, the chief rabbi of Nagyvárad (now the Romanian Oradea-Mare) and one of the most influential leaders of the Jewish community, emerged as the wrathful spokesman for the anti-Zionist and assimilationist Jews. He rejected the doctrine of Jewish nationalism and denounced Zionism for advocating the concept of the Jewish race at the expense of the religious and moral sublimity of Judaism. Zionism, he wrote, was disastrous to monotheism. Jews in Hungary were the sons of the Magyar, not the Jewish, nation.[30]

Kecskeméti's scathing attack was not the final verdict of the Jews of Hungary on Zionism. Though its leitmotiv—proud assimilationism reinforced by fervent nationalism and heightened by the manifold communal contributions and individual sacrifices at home and on the battlefield—remained unchanged, the attitude of the Hungarian-Jewish leadership toward Zionism lost much of its arrogance and intransigence by the end of World War I. Zionism no longer appeared as blatantly offensive as before.

The promise of rapprochement, however, was conceived in and sustained by a peculiar, conveniently oblique perspective that fitted the mentality of the assimilationist Hungarian Jews. Instead of acknowledging the dynamic leadership of the practical Zionists who, following Herzl's death in 1904, infused the movement with the spirit of urgency and impatience in demanding the creation of a Jewish state, the Hungarian-Jewish leaders viewed Zionism through the more subtle, thus less offensive, writings of Max Nordau. Although they remained scornful of the idea of a Jewish state, the struggle of the early Jewish settlers filled them with compassion. More than a hundred communities pledged substantial financial aid and sent much-needed food supplies to Palestine.[31] Yet whatever hope the Hungarian Jews may have entertained for making Zionism more compatible with their assimilationist philosophy, it was dispelled by Nordau's abrupt political turnabout at the end of the war. Abandoning his cocoon of pacifism and intellectualism, he became a fervent and outspoken champion of the creation of a Jewish state.[32]

New avenues of rapprochement had to be found. Though they were preoccupied with domestic problems created by the Hungarian Soviet Republic and the ensuing anti-Semitic White Terror, and though they swore allegiance to the Horthy regime, which became their new standard of nationalism and the badge of respectability, the attitude of the Hungarian Jews toward Zionism grew surprisingly flexible. By the 1930s, what was to become the official Hungarian-Jewish attitude toward Zionism began to evolve. Despite the danger of charges of double allegiance, the hostility to Zionism that overzealous assimilationist religious and lay leaders had advocated since the turn of the century was gradually transformed into a self-assured yet understanding and compassionate mood of camaraderie. Herzl, who had often been described as a Viennese in an effort to deemphasize or even conceal his Hungarian origin, was identified as the Budapest-born, talented journalist who had conceived the plan of rebuilding Zion and given an intellectually and politically disparate, yet uniformly disillusioned Jewry strength, self-respect, and purpose.[33]

The interwar development of the Jewish community in Palestine also became the object of pride and admiration.[34] This remarkable change in attitude was accomplished without adversely affecting the nationalism of the Hungarian Jews. Their unshakable belief in the long-range beneficial effects of the Emancipation had enabled them to develop and retain their benign exclusivism. They could freely sympathize with the program, activities, and achievements of Zionism as it helped persecuted and disillusioned Jews. They did not, however, conceive of themselves as needing such help. In 1940, for the first time since his death on 3 July 1904, the Jewish community of Pest offered a memorial service to Theodor Herzl in the Temple of Heroes, the synagogue that was erected on the place of his birth.[35] But however generous they may have been to the struggling Jewish settlements in Palestine, and whatever complimentary terms they may have employed in describing the achievements of Zionism, the majority of the Hungarian Jews continued to maintain a distance between themselves and the Zionists, distinguishing their Jewishness from Jewish nationalism. For them dispersion, not concentration, preserved and gave meaning to the universal teachings and values of Judaism.

Despite the puzzling juxtaposition of their fervent allegiance to the Hungarian state and their awareness of the inherent anti-Semitism of the Horthy era, the conventional explanations of the fate of the Hungarian Jews rarely probe beyond the façade of national frustration and outrage in the interwar period. True, their ambitious and fast-paced upward mobility made them easy targets of the demagoguery of the anti-Semitic irredentist groups that conjured up the menace of a Jewish-Communist-capitalist conspiracy against the unjustly treated and long-suffering Hungarian people.

Moreover, the powerful grip of Jewish capital in certain sectors of the Hungarian economy and the seemingly dislodgable yet indispensable Jewish white-collar workers, shopkeepers, and professionals created widespread resentment and frustration. Thus it would be a mistake to think that without the racial anti-Semitism of the extremist Szeged group, the Jewish Question in Hungary would not have become the focus of national interest, or that the Jews would have earned the respect of the Hungarian people as a reward for their unswerving nationalism and thoroughgoing assimilation. Interwar Hungary was not only a class-conscious, backward-looking, and chivalry-loving extension of the millennial Magyar soul, it was also an overrated bastion of Christianity, devoted to the defense of traditional Christian values against the rising and menacing tide of atheistic Communism and deceitful capitalism. It was this innate, impenetrable exclusivism of the Christian Hungarians that the Jews in their patriotic zeal ignored or underestimated.

But whereas the state, bowing to priorities in the national interest yet reacting sensitively to international criticism, was forced to define and guarantee the civil equality and political rights of its Jewish residents, no such compulsion prompted the people to accept the Jews as fellow Magyars. The depth and intensity of popular anti-Semitism were overshadowed by the well-documented atrocities which the military authorities committed against Jews. Similarly, the hideous rule of the Arrow Cross Party (15 October 1944 to 4 April 1945) tends to blur the image of the brutal treatment of the labor service units. These had been organized ostensibly to perform heavy manual labor on and behind the eastern front, but in reality were intended to suffer as high a casualty rate as possible through systematic starvation, exposure to extremely cold weather, and the attacking Soviet forces. The acts of the Hungarian commanders of these battalions and their subordinates, even as early as 1942, equalled if not exceeded the better-known and publicized savagery of Arrow Cross militiamen.[36]

The recollections, oral and written, of the Hungarian Jews attest to the prevalence and variety of anti-Semitism in Hungary. Although the possibility of inaccuracy in detail is undeniable, such sources are, on the whole, significant and of permanent utility. Similarly, it is now possible to reconstruct the probable public attitude toward the Jews in the interwar period. The results of a poll taken in 1967 in a small rural area where Jews no longer reside showed a stubbornly and illogically persisting antipathy toward Jews despite twenty years of official efforts to deemphasize and discourage popular anti-Semitism.[37] How much more widespread, conscious, and deeply felt must such convictions have been in an irredentist Hungarian society in which anti-Semitism was promoted officially as one of the fundamental psychological pillars of a betrayed, frustrated, and revenge-oriented nationalism?

Still, the tragic fate of Hungarian Jewry cannot be blamed solely on the leaders of the extreme right. They were hapless champions of Hungarism, whose monotonous demagoguery concealed only superficially the inherent weakness of a political philosophy that would achieve results only under the protective security of Nazi arms. Their racial anti-Semitism was unwavering, unrelenting, and boisterously proclaimed. Hungary's inherent anti-Semitism had been nurtured, even if not on the crude scale of the irredentists' demagoguery, by the conservative aristocracy led by Horthy and Bethlen, and by their middle-class disciples.

Horthy's reluctance to support the violently anti-Jewish philosophy of the Hungarian Fascists was the direct result of his distaste for their leaders (and later for Hitler), and of his apprehension of adverse international, particularly Western, repercussions. Prime Minister Miklós Kállay (1887–1967),

Horthy's uncritical admirer, recalled that in the course of an emotional outburst on the eve of the German occupation of Hungary (19 March 1944) the despairing and embittered regent described himself as a "defender of Jews," though, in truth, he had condoned the brutal anti-Communist and anti-Jewish attacks in the aftermath of the fall of the Hungarian Soviet Republic,[38] as well as the atrocities of Hungarian soldiers against Jews in the occupied Yugoslav regions of Délvidék and Újvidék, which took place two years before the German occupation of Hungary and the subsequent coup of the Arrow Cross.

The explanation of the tragedy must also be sought beneath the façade of a small nation's desperate efforts to maintain the illusion of comfort, security, and content in the face of its irremediably stagnating sociopolitical system. Hungary was an aristocratic anachronism, struggling in the ever-tightening grip of the irreverent champions of Hungarism and in the menacing shadow of Nazi Germany. The Jews had become the victims of a fatal illusion; they fervently believed that complete assimilation and unswerving loyalty to the state that had led to constitutionally guaranteed rights, privileges, and civil equality were sufficiently convincing reasons to act and think as if they had been accepted as full-fledged Magyars, protected and respected by their countrymen.[39]

Horthy's Hungary, however, was a Christian state and its true sons were "racially" Magyar Christians. The tragic fate of those who had long been baptized for the promise of acceptance, yet perished in labor and concentration camps alongside their former coreligionists, is the most damning evidence of the chasm they failed to bridge. Yet the truth dawned on few of them. The efforts of Horthy and his followers to restrain the Arrow Cross Party greatly enhanced the soothing effects of self-delusion. Their public utterances gave hope and reassurance to the Jews, although they were not intended to serve that purpose, treacherously softening the impact of the frightening demagoguery of the Hungarists.[40]

Though the earliest wartime manifestations of official anti-Semitism in Hungary justified the worst fears of the pessimists, they still lacked the brutality of Nazi implementation. The longtime representation of the Jewish community in the Upper House of the Parliament was terminated, because it was alleged to have lacked convincing historical roots. The number of Jewish university students was drastically reduced by severely restrictive entrance regulations. Jews were to serve in the labor service units without rank, irrespective of previous rank earned in military service. Marriage between Christians and Jews was forbidden in order to protect the purity of the Magyar race. Successive legal enactments gradually undermined the position of Jewish merchants, and the Ministry of Agriculture ordered the confiscation of landed properties owned by Jews. In short, the protection of the Magyar race demanded the removal of Jews from virtually all sectors of Hungarian society.[41] Assimilation, the most jealously guarded communal achievement of a proudly nationalist Hungarian Jewry, and the only accepted perspective from which they tended to view themselves in the mirror of national and international relations, was dealt a fatal blow.

Because of their misplaced faith in the irreversibility of assimilation and the unrelenting constancy of fervent nationalism, the Hungarian Jews were at first stunned by the increasing flow of bombastic anti-Jewish official communiqués. As it soon became evident that the Aryanization of society was less well organized in Hungary than elsewhere, many Jews, particularly the more affluent ones, took advantage of loopholes in the hastily sanctioned restrictive measures of the government. They bribed state officials, who canceled or destroyed orders for immediate report to the labor service units. Many impoverished but greedy members of the aristocracy and gentry were persuaded, in return for ample compensation, to become silent partners of Jewish industrialists, merchants, and shopkeepers, and allow their names to be used to secure business licenses.[42]

The Kállay government remained remarkably resistant to the boisterous demands of the Hungarists and Hitler's stern warnings. In view of the dangerous proximity of Nazi Germany, Kállay's two-year-long (1942–44) political tour de force was one of the miracles in Hungary's modern history.[43] Hitler's ill-concealed contempt for Kállay and Kállay's pronounced anti-Nazi and anti-Hungarist stand, however, foreshadowed Hungary's loss of independence and the destruction of her Jewry.

The Jewish community reacted with determination to the narrow yet lifesaving political vacuum created by the Kállay government. Hitler's award to Hungary of portions of Romania and Czechoslovakia, an act that filled the champions of the Greater Hungary dream with enthusiasm and gratitude toward Nazi Germany, had resulted in the displacement of many Jews. The Kállay government expended much effort to assist them as well as the Jews whose livelihood had been destroyed by Aryanization. Jewish youths in particular received attention; they were shielded from the impact of enforced dissimilation after Jewish sport clubs had been suspended. In general, there was a noticeable turn inward, a desperate effort to cling to the illusive yet still comforting security of communal solidarity. Jewish cultural and artistic life experienced its last outburst of creativity and activity before the approaching inferno of Hungarism.[44]

Although described as a philo-Semite by his foes, Kállay himself shed light, though perhaps unwittingly, on the basic problem. Referring to the economically frustrated and politically irrational Hungarists, Kállay observed: "It never occurred to them that the explanation might be that the Jewish bank clerk was more industrious, the Jewish shopkeeper more resourceful, perhaps more cunning and more dependable, than his Hungarian counterpart." Then as if intending to tone down his remarks he went on: "I most definitely do not mean to assert that the Jewish members of the *petite bourgeoisie* were more gifted and capable than the Magyars."[45] Jews were

Jews, not Jewish Magyars. Only Christians were true Magyars. This distinction was the basis of the Hungarian Jews' perpetual relegation to the periphery, to which they had been condemned by an ungrateful and unyielding society.

In theory, the destruction of Hungarian Jewry should not have been an inevitable and predictable consequence of Hungary's gradual turn toward and dependence on Nazi Germany. "As far as the Jewish Question is concerned, I have been an anti-Semite all my life," Horthy was fond of saying.[46] Distrustful of both Nazis and Hungarists, he insisted that Hungary would retain the right as a sovereign state to resolve the Jewish Question independent of foreign influences and as befitted national interests. The large number of Jews in Hungary—800,000 among 14 million Hungarians, in contrast to 600,000 Jews among 60 million Germans—and their virtual control of the economic life of the country, Horthy reasoned, ruled out the German approach to the Jewish Question as tantamount to economic suicide.[47] Following Germany's victory in the war, he theorized, all of Hungary's Jews would be resettled elsewhere, provided that the legal and technical means were acquired.[48]

Horthy's views were doomed by Hungary's political orientation and precarious geographic position. Fearful of the hostile stance of the Little Entente (Czechoslovakia, Romania, and Yugoslavia) and its mentor, France, and also fearing the Soviet Union and the rapidly spreading organizations of the Communist International, Horthy had no choice but to ally Hungary with Nazi Germany, the principal buyer of her agricultural products and industrial raw materials, and therefore with the German-Italian-Spanish Anti-Comintern Pact. Moreover, Germany needed Hungary to establish unobstructed access to the Romanian oil fields and the Danube. Yet not even Horthy's repeated assurances of Hungary's firm resolve to honor her commitment succeeded in allaying Nazi suspicions. "It is gradually dawning upon them [the Hungarians] that they can't just sit in club chairs while the new Europe is being shaped, and later share in the success," Goebbels noted in his diary. "The Hungarians must risk blood if they want to get more territory."[49] To Hitler, Horthy's appointment of Kállay as prime minister was an unpardonable error. In high German circles the consensus was that Horthy and Kállay were Anglophiles, and Horthy's two sons, István and Miklós, Jr., were "Jew-loving lounge lizards."[50] The regent's ill-concealed attempts to sue for peace was, in Hitler's view, an affront that could not go unpunished. "The attitude of Hungary is perfidious and shameless," fumed Goebbels.[51] Thus it was only a matter of time before Margarethe I, the plan for the military occupation of Hungary, would be put into effect.

To the Hungarian survivors of the Holocaust the Arrow Cross era is equivalent to the final solution of the Jewish Question in Hungary. This description is only partially true. The destruction of Hungarian Jewry began shortly after the German troops occupied Hungary on 19 March 1944. Prime

Minister Kállay, whom the Germans called a swine,[52] sought asylum in the Turkish embassy. His successor, Döme Sztójay, a reserve colonel-general and for ten years Hungary's minister in Berlin, was acceptable to the Germans, whose interests he placed ahead of those of his own country. A sickly and politically and ideologically unstable man, Sztójay was prime minister in name only.[53] The new and real master of Hungary—Horthy had gradually withdrawn from taking an active part in politics and for the next four months left the Royal Palace only twice—was Hitler's minister plenipotentiary, Edmund Veesenmayer.[54] He was eagerly supported by László Endre and László Baky, two rabidly anti-Semitic under secretaries of the Ministry of the Interior, who made certain that the Germans had unlimited access to and support from the appropriate state and military authorities.

In an effort to assure that the timetable for the solution of the Jewish Question in Hungary would suffer no more delays, Weltjudenkommissar Adolf Eichmann, whose *Sondereinsatzkommando*, accompanied by Gestapo and security units, had been waiting in Linz, arrived in Budapest.[55] During the next two months Eichmann, Endre, and Baky worked out in detail the policy of making Hungary *judenrein*. The Council of Ministers voted to issue a decree ordering all Jews to wear the "Jew's star," a six-pointed star made of yellow cloth, sewn over the left breast on the outer garment. Jews were removed from professional organizations, and their telephones and automobiles confiscated. The Jewish Council was set up at the Germans' order and charged with carrying out their instructions. Hungary was divided into six concentration zones, and on May 15 the deportation of Jews from the provinces that constituted five zones—the sixth was Budapest—began. Under the advice and observation of the Germans, and supervised by Hungarian policemen and gendarmes whose methods, even in the German view, resembled "Asiatic brutality,"[56] more than 450,000 Jews were packed into freight trains and transported to concentration camps at Mauthausen, Auschwitz, and Buchenwald. On June 24 the Jews of Budapest were ordered to relocate in an area containing 2,600 houses, each visibly marked by a yellow Star of David.

Because it had generally been acknowledged that no organized effort would save the Jews in the countryside from being either massacred by SS soldiers and Hungarian gendarmes or being "resettled" outside Hungary in extermination camps or in labor service units on the eastern front or in Germany, plans were made to protect only Budapest's endangered Jewry. Members of the Jewish Council established contact with the Gestapo and the Hungarian authorities, hoping to lessen the impact of the erratic and unpredictable official approach to the Jewish Question by declaring a policy of "loyal cooperation with the Germans in matters of economy." Their work benefitted only a few wealthy Jews, and they were often accused of collaborating with the enemy.

More promising were the activities of the Hungarian Zionist Federation. Its president, Ottó Komoly, and two of his aides, Rezső Kasztner and Joel

Brand, set up the Va'adat Ezrah va'Hatzalah (Relief and Rescue Committee) and acquired a portion of the so-called Zionist money that had been collected in the United States and Palestine for helping European Jews. Following a number of clandestine meetings with Eichmann and other high-ranking Gestapo officers, the Zionist leaders secured documents exempting a number of wealthy Jews and their families from compliance with restrictions, and managed to free 1,684 individuals, who were subsequently transported to Switzerland. A similar attempt made by Fülöp Freudiger, president of the Orthodox Community of Pest, proved partially successful.

Other self-help maneuvers yielded only minimal results. Young Jews, wearing German and Hungarian uniforms, at times managed to confuse deportation procedures and rescue a few individuals. Uncommon resolve and bravery, however, did not help those who were apprehended. They were tortured and executed, as were the Hungarian-born Haganah parachutists, Hannah Szenes and Peretz Goldstein, who had been sent to aid in the rescue effort. Some members of Hungary's wealthiest Jewish families managed to reach safety in Portugal and Switzerland. Others were held hostage in the Third Reich or deported in spite of the huge sums they had paid their captors.

The most successful efforts were directed by Charles Lutz, the Swiss consul, and Raul Wallenberg, a secretary of the Swedish embassy. It was their death-defying ingenuity that saved 50,000 of the nearly 120,000 Jews who survived the war. Many were snatched from deportation camps and marching columns, while others were placed under the protection of neutral nations. It is also a matter of record that the leaders of the Hungarian churches registered protests with the authorities for the often brutal deportation procedures, and nuns and priests hid a small number of Jews until the end of the war.[57]

On June 26, in a last, desperate resort, the Jewish Council appealed directly to Horthy, imploring him to intervene. The regent was well informed. He knew of the atrocities through a secret and anonymously written memorandum that had been forwarded to him a month earlier.[58] Considering the presence of German troops, the menacing stance of the Arrow Cross Party, the lack of ideological unity within the government, and his own protracted inactivity, Horthy's resolve to put an end to the deportation of Jews was remarkable. On July 7 the regent issued Sztójay orders to that effect and made a courageous though unsuccessful attempt to replace Sztójay with Colonel-General Géza Lakatos, a former commander of the First Hungarian Army. Convinced that the Germans were still strong enough to react to such a radical change in government, Lakatos declined the appointment. Veesenmayer threatened Horthy with reprisals if he replaced Sztójay, who enjoyed Hitler's confidence and support. Surprisingly, Horthy persisted. On August 28 Sztójay submitted his resignation, and the regent named Lakatos prime minister to head a military government.[59]

This unexpected six-week-long interregnum came too late to save the Jews in the provinces, though for the Jews of Budapest, numbering less than 200,000, it was an almost miraculous respite. The infamous freight trains came to a halt, and Eichmann left Hungary late in August. From the start the new government was doomed. The Germans regarded Lakatos as unfriendly, probably sympathetic toward the English and the Americans, and willing to support the war effort only on the eastern front. They also accused him and Horthy of protecting the Jewish allies of the "Anglo-Jewish-Soviet conspiracy." On September 28 the regent, stunned by the defections of Romania, Bulgaria, and Finland, and by the seemingly unstoppable Soviet advances, secretly dispatched a team of negotiators to Moscow. On October 11 this team signed an agreement which stipulated that the Hungarians were to evacuate the areas they had acquired since 1937 and place their military forces at Soviet disposal against the Germans.[60]

Horthy's effort was destined to fail. Convinced that the army was still loyal to him, the regent operated from a narrow military base, relying only on his generals, and neglected to make adequate preparations politically. Thus his terse proclamation on the Hungarian Radio on October 15, declaring the cessation of hostilities, went virtually unheeded. Tipped off by the Germans, who had known of Horthy's secret negotiations, army officers in key positions disobeyed the orders of the Supreme War Lord, and the more than 120 Arrow Cross representatives in Parliament succeeded in declaring the proclamation unconstitutional. The armed opposition of the Arrow Cross Party and the Association of the Veterans of the Eastern Front quickly decided the outcome of this desperate effort. The Germans captured Horthy's younger son, Miklós, and forced the regent to sign a document of abdication that also appointed Ferenc Szálasi, the leader of the Arrow Cross Party, as prime minister.[61]

If March 19, the day the Germans occupied Hungary, was the beginning of the destruction of the Jews in the provinces, October 15, the date that marks the beginning of the Arrow Cross era, was the crucible of Budapest's Jewry. For hundreds of thousands of Hungarians who had been supporting the Arrow Cross movement, the transformation of the leader of the party to the leader of the nation was an achievement of historic significance. In light of the steadily advancing Soviet forces they saw the Arrow Cross coup not as a military takeover, but as the continuation of the war of self-defense, a heroic sacrifice protecting Western civilization from communism.[62]

Like Horthy's relatively benign anti-Semitism, the Arrow Cross position on the Jewish Question gave no indication of the outburst of brutality that was to become the hallmark of the Szálasi regime. Ferenc Szálasi was a disciple and admirer of Győző Istóczy, the founder of the anti-Semitic movement in Hungary. Szálasi concurred in Istóczy's belief that notwithstanding their predominance in the economy, the Jews should be settled elsewhere. The Jews, he wrote, constituted an alien racial group that had never professed brotherhood with the Magyar race.[63] Of his sweeping, often incomprehensible statements, this one, in view of the millennial history of mutual-ly beneficial cooperation between Jews and Magyars, was perhaps the least justifiable. Interestingly, Szálasi rejected anti-Semitism and espoused a-Semitism. Thus the Hungarist State, the so-called Carpatho-Danubian Great Fatherland, his ideological utopia, would be created without Jews.[64] Szálasi was more the man of an improbable future than the man of the hour. His obsession with making Hungary and Germany the cocreators of a new National Socialist Europe clouded his vision of the true state of affairs and prevented him from keeping his followers within even the most generously broad confines of civility and morality.

By October 15 the Germans had no choice, short of governing Hungary themselves, other than to accept Szálasi and other Arrow Cross leaders as the Royal Hungarian Government. Their opinion of the Hungarians did not improve. If Hitler did not think much of them as soldiers, he thought even less of them as politicians. He was obviously annoyed by Szálasi's presump-tuous utopia that envisioned Hungarians and Germans as running the affairs of a new Europe in a partnership of equals. No less disconcerting was the Arrow Cross leader's oft-enunciated conviction that the solution of the Jew-ish Question in Hungary would not be implemented in imitation of any foreign model, but rather in concert with domestic circumstances and the racial peculiarities of the Hungarians. Still, Hitler had to endure or ignore such ideological improprieties. Though the Nazi leaders wrote off the Hungarians as "corpses before they were dead," Hungary was the last buffer between the Russians and the Reich. The sudden loss of her oilfields would have been disastrous for the German defensive effort.

In the last desperate months of the Second World War Szálasi's theories turned into impracticable abstractions. The Arrow Cross utopia became a veritable nightmare. Instead of laying the foundations of a Christian-Hungarist future, the new prime minister presided over an inferno that was to destroy and discredit everything he had preached. He was determined to assure the constitutional legality of his position; on October 27 the Council of State acknowledged Horthy's abdication and on November 3, when the abdication became law, Szálasi took the oath to the Holy Crown, which legitimized him as temporary head of state.[66] Despite these efforts, the brief but bloody rule of the Arrow Cross government was in retrospect judged as a mockery of Hungary's traditionally proud and dignified system of parliamen-tary procedures. For some years émigré Hungarist writers have been trying to whitewash the handling of the Jewish Question, whereas contemporary Hungarian historians have accentuated this most disastrous failing of the Szálasi government.[67] It has often been said of Szálasi that he was a man who possessed a bewildering combination of qualities. He was a devout Catholic, yet state and church would be separated in his Hungarist state; he had a profound love for his people, yet he readily sacrificed them in the defense of a dream; and though his writings and recorded speeches are devoid of the crude and inflammatory demagoguery that was characteristic of most of his followers,[68] the flames of anti-Jewish hatred never soared higher than during his brief rule.

By October 15 nearly all Jews had been deported from the provinces. The tragic fate of Budapest's Jewry was foreshadowed by the fact that anti-Semitism manifested itself in pairs. Between 1920 and 1944, Horthy's relatively benign anti-Semitism had been challenged by the hard-line versions of the parties of the extreme right; in the Arrow Cross era Szálasi's resettlement solution of the Jewish Question clashed with Eichmann's uncompromising timetable and the uncontrollable brutality of the masses of his uneducated and undisciplined followers. Yet whatever Szálasi's true feelings may have been in this respect, the government he headed was probably no more responsible for many acts that have been attributed to it than it was for its own existence. The Germans, who had put into effect their desperate, last-stand measures, were the real masters of Hungary and thus the initiators, though not the executioners, of most of the gruesome plans that turned the last six months of fighting (15 October 1944 to 4 April 1945) into a bloody, senseless spectacle of unprecedented proportions.[69]

There was a sense of urgency in the manner in which the Jewish Question was approached by the Szálasi government. On October 16 the doors of all star-marked houses were sealed and the supplies of food and medical aid were cut. For ten days the living and the dead shared the same crowded quarters. Gábor Vajna, Minister of the Interior, declared that the solution of the Jewish Question, "even if ruthless, shall be such as the Jews deserve by their previous and present conduct."[70] However, the atrocities some Arrow Cross men committed within two days after the takeover were so hideous that Vajna, one of the most rabidly anti-Semitic members of the Szálasi government, felt compelled to issue a stern warning: "Let no one be an arbitrary or self-appointed judge of the Jews, because the solution of this question is the task of the state."[71] His words went largely unheeded. Except for 15,000 Jews to whom the neutral nations had granted documents of protection, the situation became critical for Budapest's Jewry. The government kept issuing communiqués in an attempt to safeguard the official Hungarist program: Jews were ordered to rejoin the labor service units, their status was regulated by law, they were to be removed from Hungary after the war, never to return, and mixed marriages were declared null and void. Nevertheless, it was rapidly becoming clear that the rule of the nation had little or no bearing on the law of the street.[72] Nor did the Germans act as if they had the slightest inclination to respect the decisions of the Szálasi government. On October 18 Eichmann and his *Sondereinsatzkommando* returned to Budapest and started working at a feverish pace. He may have feared either that Szálasi would make an attempt to solve the Jewish Question in accordance with his Hungarist dream, or that the atrocities of the Arrow Cross men would severely reduce the number of deportable persons.

Yet despite Eichmann's efforts the percentage of Jews removed from Hungary after October 15 was relatively low in comparison with the result of his indefatigable labors following the German occupation seven months earlier.

Notwithstanding Eichmann's formidable schedule and the repeated vows of the Szálasi government and the German High Command to defend Hungary to the last man, much of the tribulation of the Jews might have been avoided had it not been for a tragic miscalculation. On November 3, in an effort to reach and liberate Budapest before the regrouping of German and Hungarian forces in defense of it was completed, units of Lt. Gen. I. T. Shlemin's 46th Infantry Division, part of Marshal Malinovsky's Second Ukrainian Front, reached the southeastern perimeter of the capital. Unfortunately, the narrow line of the advancing Soviet forces was quickly stemmed by heavy formations of German Panzers, and thus Shlemin's gamble failed. Recently, Soviet and Hungarian military studies have revealed that Stalin had erred in pressing for attacks between the Duna and Tisza rivers and underestimated the morale of Hungarian forces fighting under German command. The failure of Shlemin's attempt necessitated not only the regrouping of Malinovsky's armies, but also an even more time-consuming delay as they waited for additional reinforcements from Marshal Tolbuchin's Third Ukrainian Front.

Thus the liberation of Budapest had to be postponed for more than three months, providing the Szálasi government additional time—half of its total existence—to defend Hungary and carry out its political program.[73] For the Jews, the difference between life and death was reduced to a distance of thirteen kilometers that the Soviets found more difficult to break through than hundreds of kilometers elsewhere. Accusing the Jews of collaboration with the "Anglo-American-Soviet conspiracy," the Arrow Cross government issued a flood of decrees in an effort to realize the Hungarist solution of the Jewish Question. It had no means of supervising or controlling the implementation of the orders. Long before the government was forced to leave the besieged capital, most Arrow Cross men started disobeying the restraining orders of their leaders regarding the Jews. Youths carrying machine guns often killed Jews on sight on the street or lined them up on the embankment of the Danube and executed them.[74] Arrow Cross atrocities were increasing so rapidly both in number and in degree of inhumanity that even the Germans turned to the authorities, complaining that the nightly executions "upset" the population. The Germans intervened, but by no means out of humanitarian concern. They were merely trying to protect their own investment in time and planning.

It was on the infamous death march to Hegyeshalom (by then not even mechanized transport was available) that the Arrow Cross men who provided armed escort beat and shot so many deportees that the obviously chagrined Germans, who had been waiting at the border for what they believed would be useable reinforcements for the so-called shovel army, could only process the survivors for transport to concentration camps.[75] These acts of cruelty soon became a source of embarrassment to the Arrow Cross government. In a memorandum submitted to Szálasi, representatives of the neutral powers observed that the deportation

> is being carried out with such ruthless severity that the whole world is witness to the acts of inhumanity which attend it (little children are torn from their mothers, the aged and the sick have to lie even in the rain under the insufficient shelter of a brickyard roof, men and women remain for days without any nourishment whatever, tens of thousands are crowded into a single brickworks, women are violated, people shot for mere trifles, etc.). . . . At Hegyeshalom we found the deportees among the worst conditions imaginable. The endless ordeals of the marches, the almost complete lack of nourishment, intensified by the constant dread that in Germany they were to be taken to the gas chamber, have brought about such a condition among the unfortunate deportees that they no longer possess human shape and lack all human dignity. Their condition may not be compared to persons afflicted by any other spiritual distress or physical suffering. The fact that they were divested of their most elemental human rights, that they were completely at the mercy of their guards—which in practice was manifested in the form of being spat on, of beatings, manhandling—and that everything including shooting could be done to them, left horrible marks on the unfortunate victims.[76]

A similar fate befell the Jews left in Budapest. On November 26 their ghettoization began. Police, following orders issued by Gábor Vajna, Minister of the Interior, herded all Jews who had been living in the star-marked houses scattered throughout the capital into a carefully segregated area within the Seventh District. Sixty-three thousand people were crowded into 293 houses, fourteen persons quartered in each room of every apartment. The quality and quantity of food the government distributed were far below the minimal nutritional value. Each person received daily rations of 690 calories, although even jailed criminals were given 1,500. Medical aid was woefully insufficient, mostly nonexistent. The periodic visits of Arrow Cross men and the constant bombardment of Soviet artillery claimed additional victims. Corpses, stacked in piles on streets and in courtyards, were left unburied.[77]

In the twilight of Hungarism, law and order eroded along with the last vestiges of realism. The Germans gave up on the Arrow Cross government. Hitler refused even to receive Szálasi on December 4, though subsequently he relented when Szálasi threatened to withhold the support of Hungarian forces.[78] Though the Germans vowed to defend Budapest to the last man, the concentration of German and Hungarian forces in western Hungary suggested other strategic alternatives.[79]

The Szálasi government slipped out of the capital, leaving it in the hands of the SS and the Arrow Cross militia, before the Soviet troops managed to surround it completely on December 24, cutting all lines of communication with the outside world and thus ending the deportation of Jews.[80] The battle of Budapest lasted fifty-three days. Its most notable features were a bloody, bitter, street-by-street sweep by Soviet troops, and the desperate but futile defensive maneuvers of the remnants of trapped German and Hungarian divisions to defy the inevitable.

Though diehard Hungarist writers like Lajos Marschalkó have long rejected the documentable losses of Hungarian Jewry as myth, calling it the "legend of the 600,000,"[81] though they have questioned the very existence of gas chambers and crematoria in extermination camps, insisting that their anti-Semitism was solely a reaction to the Jews' relentless quest for controlling the world, rather than based on hatred of their race or religion, some high-ranking Arrow Cross officials, for whom the fleeting taste of power and glory remained the sole source of inspiration in exile, have unwittingly become the most damaging chroniclers of the waning days of the system in the defense of which they had been expected to die the death of heroes. Ferenc Fiala, Szálasi's press chief, admitted that in the absence of law and order in besieged Budapest "everyone who had acquired a machine gun could become judge and executioner," and roving gangs of youths who had escaped from correctional institutions as well as members of the Budapest underworld took advantage of the prevailing chaos and anarchy and committed "grave atrocities."[82] These unsavory characters not only brandished machine guns but also wore Arrow Cross armbands, and instead of helping to defend the "Queen of the Danube" against the "Mongolian hordes," they perpetrated acts of violence with such reckless abandon and wanton brutality against Jews and those whom they branded politically dangerous that they succeeded in staining whatever military honor and dignity the defenders in a hopeless situation are customarily accorded. Moreover, had they indeed been common criminals in despair they would have fled for their lives rather than become the defenders of a lost cause. Those who became the masters of life and death, virtually within shooting range of the advancing Soviet soldiers, not only went on with their bloody, senseless rampage but actually made preparations to blow up the ghetto so that not a single Jew would survive the fall of Budapest. Remarkably, their plan was foiled by the resolute intervention of General Schmidthuber, commander of the SS Feldherrenhalle division, himself a casualty soon thereafter.

On January 18 the occupation of Pest was completed. For another thirty days the terror raged on the other side of the Danube. Arrow Cross men dragged gravely ill Jewish patients from their hospital beds, trampling or shooting them to death, and hunted down others who had lived in hiding or carried false identification documents. "In the sacred name of Christ! Fire!" ordered Father András Kun, the infamous Arrow Cross priest.[83]

On February 13 the battle of Budapest ended. Only a small remnant of Hungary's once large and prosperous Jewish community was left to tell its sad tale.

Part One
"It Could Never Happen Here"

Simon Hevesi

Prayer

Born in Aszód (Pest county) in 1868, Simon Hevesi (Handler) completed the last years of his high school education in the National Rabbinical Institute in Budapest, where he continued his theological studies. He was ordained rabbi in 1894, and following brief periods of service in small communities, he was elected rabbi of the Pest community in 1905. He became chief rabbi in 1927, a position he was to hold until his death in 1943. A skilled and effective speaker—he taught homiletics and Jewish philosophy at the National Rabbinical Institute—Hevesi was also a frequent contributor to scholarly publications and a leader in the cultural life of Hungarian Jewry. His works include Dalalat Alhairin *(1928), a study on Moses Maimonides's* Guide for the Perplexed. *"Prayer" is translated from "Ima," in* Ararát, *ed. Aladár Komlós (Budapest: Országos Izraelita Leányárvaház, 1941), pp. 10–11. By permission of A Magyar Izraeliták Országos Képviselete.*

Almighty and wonder-working God! I believe in the miracle of world history. I believe that Thou hast worked wonders with Hungary, our beloved nation, and shalt work wonders with her forever. May Thou keep and protect her and may Thy mercy, like a golden bridge, glitter over her.

Praised be Thou, O Lord, for restoring to our nation the lands that had been taken from her. We raise our countenance to Thee in hopeful trust and believe fervently that Thy justice shall not diminish. The paths of world history are tangled, but Thy justice is like the glittering rays of the sun that cut through even the densest mist of time. Oh may Thou continue to be the heavenly guardian of truth and bring a joyous, glorious, and blessed future upon the Hungarian nation. May truth and tranquility, fraternal labor, blissful contentment, and sincere cooperation flourish in this land. Grant us, O Lord, that we may share in the sacred work of building the future. Grant us, O Lord, the nobility of comprehension so that we may serve the highest truth, the glory and welfare of our land, the moral order of the world, and brotherly love with labor, endurance, sacrifice, renunciation, enthusiasm, unselfishness, and devotion. May we be allowed to witness the coming of better times, to contribute, with exemplary moral conduct and the purity of our daily lives, to the realization of a higher moral ideal in which the salvation of mankind and our nation is hidden and the brightness of which emanates from Thy sacred teaching.

Like a thirsty deer that languishes for the cool waters of a brook, our souls yearn for Thee, Helping God, our Protector in Heaven, and Ever-vigilant Guardian over earthly affairs. Blot out the memory of our tribulations and sufferings and bring relief to tormented mankind. May wisdom and understanding, intelligence and creativity, and the spirit of faith and kindness descend upon mankind so that we may enjoy the happiness which Thou hast bestowed upon it with the treasures of the universe that Thou hast created in Thy fatherly mercy. Like eternal desire and dreamlike lamentation, yearning for Thy mercy and for salvation lives in the hearts of all of us. Pardon our sins and redeem us. Merciful God, redeem mankind, the flock of Thy covenant, that lives in fear of the dark future and longingly awaits the blessing of Thy divine mercy.

Do not cast us away from Thee; do not deprive us of Thy sacred spirit. Let Thy light and bliss descend upon us so that they may guide us to Thee.

Sacred holidays are at hand; the present shall soon be past on the wings of time; the new year is upon us. We raise our countenance toward Thee. Look down upon us, O Lord! Our Redeemer! Our God! Write mankind into the book of happiness! Our Father, our King, grant us a happy new year!

Amen.

Aladár Komlós

The Tribulations of the Hungarian-Jewish Writer

Aladár Komlós (b. 1892) had aspirations of becoming a poet before he turned his attention to aesthetics and literary criticism. Like a number of Jewish intellectuals of his generation, Komlós supported the short-lived Hungarian Soviet Republic and was forced into a brief exile in Vienna after the victory of the counterrevolution. Following his return, he taught at the Jewish high school in Budapest and resumed his literary career. Though he published three volumes of poems between 1921 and 1941, Komlós also gained recognition as a literary scholar. His work Az új magyar líra *[The new Hungarian lyric poetry] (1928) is still regarded by some as the definitive study on modern Hungarian poetry. His critical essays, characterized by a finely tuned, intelligent approach and uncompromising logic, appeared in leading periodicals, especially in* Nyugat *[West], the literary journal that shaped the sociocultural outlook of writers and poets in the interwar years and left an indelible impression on him. Two of his novels,* Római kaland *[Adventure in Rome] (1933) and* Nero és a VIIa *[Nero and the seventh grade] (1935) were well received by critics and readers alike.*

Notwithstanding his dedication to Hungarian literature, Komlós remained intellectually and emotionally attached to Judaism. The brutal treatment of Jews during the counterrevolutionary White Terror and the protracted ambivalence between Budapest's assimilationist Jews and Zionism are sensitively portrayed and analyzed in Zsidók a válaszúton *[Jews at the crossroads] (1928). Komlós also wrote many essays and articles on Jewish subjects that appeared in Jewish periodicals, some of which he edited as well. In the 1950s he was appointed professor at Budapest University and elected chairman of the Hungarian Literary Society. In recent years, however, he has come under attack for being overly pacifistic and for retaining the* Nyugat *philosophy in his literary criticism. "The Tribulations of the Hungarian-Jewish writer" was translated from "A magyar zsidó író útjai," in* Ararát, *ed. Tibor Kőrösi (Budapest: Pesti Izraelita Nőegylet Leányárvaháza, 1939), pp. 127–33. By permission of A Magyar Izraeliták Országos Képviselete.*

It would not be difficult to change the minds of those who still doubt that Hungarian Jewry has produced talented writers since the First World War. We could make an impressive list of them even if we excluded the apostates, unfortunately significant both in number and talent. Yet would it be tactless if I confessed to being incapable of dispelling the doubt in my mind that there exists among our young writers those who, like József Kiss, Sándor Bródy, Ignotus, and perhaps Ferenc Molnár and Szomory in the recent past, belong to the intellectual vanguard of our time?[1]

Tamás Kóbor pointed out years ago the external reasons that even today prevent talented Jewish authors from achieving their goals: only two (since then, one) Budapest newspapers are in Jewish hands, and as the older writers fall silent the young ones cannot take their places.[2] He could also have mentioned the publishers who would spare no effort to avoid having to deal with anything Jewish. Shall I cite, as an example, that well-known firm whose director has recently exchanged his prayer shawl for a Szekler shepherd's cape, and who would not publish a work unless its author could prove, above all, and in advance, that he was born in Transylvania or is at least a Christian? No writer or literary movement has ever succeeded in this country without conscious or covert political support.

If I were not afraid of playing the role of the bad student who tries to explain away his report cards by saying that the teacher is picking on him, I could perhaps prove that the reason the names of our young writers do not glitter as brilliantly as those of their predecessors is that critics nowadays are wary of pushing young authors into the limelight of acclaim. Criticism plays a much greater role in the formulation of our views than we think. By and large, literary giants tend to appoint the stars of a period as if they were conducting a coup. This is particularly true in our country, where a few eminences can exercise power without parliamentary supervision, so to speak, because our sycophantic critics invariably approve their judgment. Unhappily, we must acknowledge that Jews are deprived of immortality nowadays in the same way they were prevented from occupying positions in county government or becoming army officers in the past.

I fear, however, that the critics are right this time. The Jewish writer of today falls by a hair's breadth below the level of excellence. Not that he was born with less intellectual energy, power of imagination, or talent than his predecessors, but talent is as much a sociological matter as it is biological. The artistic talent of Jews has for some time failed to develop to the same extent that the Christians' did. I could have the sharpest eyes, and still I would not be able to see things clearly if I observed the world standing on my head or hanging from a nail. Does the Jewish writer of today not find himself in a similarly unnatural and awkward situation, having been halfway pushed out of society and treated with envy and contempt? Does he not react to this treatment in a like manner? He becomes a sensitive observer of the culture that surrounds him rather than a continuator of the creative tradition. Jewish and non-Jewish influences converge in him, creating confusion in his mind, thus disorienting the powers of his artistic imagination to the point where the chaotic picture it produces no longer reveals what it had originally been intended to represent.

Yet even in such circumstances a strong and creative Jewish culture could have developed, had there been an understanding Jewish public to encourage the Jewish artists to give expression to its own confused and insecure state of mind and existence. There was, however, no such public. Thus in addition to inner conflict and lack of purpose, the Jewish writer had no audience on whose understanding he could rely. He was in the midst of strangers; Jewish readers did not want their feelings revealed. The Jewish writer was condemned to a limbo, feeling ashamed of his own colorless world yet unable to give an accurate representation of non-Jewish life. This is the reason that the works of even the best Jewish writers in the West usually fail in the accurate and concrete description of the environment, yet no such deficiency is detectable in the works of less talented but non-Jewish authors.

Since the war a new obstacle has been progressively paralyzing the Jewish writer: he is no longer permitted to express his views on subjects that are of general interest to non-Jewish Hungarians. No one would listen even if he tried. What is perhaps likely is that his head would be smashed in and thus he would only hurt the cause he wanted to advocate. No one is interested in his opinion. He therefore learns to keep silent, at first perhaps only out of caution, but as time goes on, also because he is no longer accustomed to formulating opinions, which he is not allowed to set down in writing anyway. I cannot say that the dialogue between Jews and non-Jews in the past was particularly lively or productive, but even this intermittent dialogue has been discontinued by now, and hope and expectation of its resumption in the near future have disappeared. Everyone is politicking around us, yet we are not allowed to understand what is being said. We are excluded from the discussion concerning the most burning questions that affect Europe, and condemned to subsistence at the periphery of the intellectual life of our age. We must observe fasting, political fasting, because our elders had feasted too eagerly. Today the Jewish writer must not shout, he may only mutter and equivocate. An extreme rightist publicist has recently reproached us for allowing our intellectual life to sink to that of a new Biedermeier. He was right. But could it be otherwise? First they bind us so tightly that we cannot even move, then they resent us for not being able to dance nimbly enough.

We can draw many conclusions from the powerful message that has recently knocked us in the head. That aggressive messianism that represented the spirit of revolution was forced into exile following the Depression. There it was reduced to despair and maladjustment and now it can no longer be detected anywhere. Artists throughout the world are leaving their ivory towers; the Jewish writer, on the other hand, is forced to retire to one made of pure aesthetics, abstract science, and the observation of the tremors of his own life. Perhaps Béla Zsolt, that unique publicist, is the only one who participates in debates, expressing his views, arguing points, and in general behaving as if the dialogue still existed and as if the other side still paid attention to him.[3] I fear that for a long time to come he will be the only significant exception. There are others, particularly among the apostates, who in the name of humanism have joined the opposition and, as the foot soldiers of public interest, sacrificed their creative talents. Yet they are hated more bitterly than their Jewish counterparts and thus will soon become a liability to their cause.

Which one is the correct solution? Not the apolitical poetry of private life or philology by any means. Even humanism is worthless if we use it for lofty but empty tirades that have no binding effect on us. On the other hand, if we drew accurate conclusions from it and tried to put them to good use we would revert to the sin of our "destructiveness" by butting into the affairs of the Hungarian people, who do not ask for our opinion. I, too, could resume politicking, but that is illegal, and I would only get my head smashed in. Yet if I did not participate in politics I would relinquish the greatest pleasure that writing provides: the chance to exert even a slight influence on the world.

Even if the general readership rejected me, one would still be there—the Jewish. Why should I not seek its acceptance? Why should I keep aloof from the only group of readers among whom my work may still be of social value and my word may still carry some weight? And yet, disregarding those of our writers who have made but occasional excursions in Jewish themes, only two writers are deeply conscious of the fate of our people: Károly Pap and Béla Zsolt.[4] It is a pity, however, that their attitudes toward Jews are quite ambivalent; the former's is filled with moral antagonism, the latter's with aesthetic hostility. Incidentally, we have writers who are Jewish, but we have no Jewish writers. I am fully aware that our predecessors flinched at the thought of becoming "denominational writers." After all, not too long ago the Jew was still regarded as a modern man who would not even hear of Judaism. It was only natural that when forced to choose between the somewhat conservatively educated but faithful Jewish readers and the more free-spirited, non-Jewish Hungarians, our most adventurous and talented writers should be reluctant to identify themselves as "denominational." But is the Jewish writer of today in the position to address the whole Hungarian nation as his forefathers had done? Can anyone possess a soul more sensitive and noble than he who rejects pretentious false pride and accepts his fate? What János Arany[5] suggested to the Hungarian applies to the Jewish poet as well:

> Let him spread his word, nation, God!
> The roaring flood washes away all,
> Destroys and brings life again:
> But in a small nation that resists such destruction
> The poet must share his people's fate,
> For death is ready to strike.

Of course, a program by itself is of little value in politics, even less in the arts. I know that our postwar generation of writers could turn out "professional" Jewish works in a style befitting devout, conscientious Jews rather than naïve lovers or brothers. Their efforts, however, will be meaningful only if both readers and publishers want and accept Jewish literature that is serious and of high quality. Theoretically, the public is always the coauthor in a process of artistic creativity, even though the real author may be unaware of its presence.

Only foolhardiness and malice would prompt a person to regard our message as an effort to promote ghettoization. The representation of Jewish life is no more a sign of ghettoization than, let us say, the description of life in France by a French writer. We want a more open and meaningful art, not self-immolation. God forbid that a Jewish writer should shut his eyes to new ideas or forget that he belongs not only to his coreligionists but to his nation and mankind as well! God forbid that he should feel close only to what is a peculiarly Jewish problem and notice only those phenomena that bear the imprint of Jewishness! Our objective is not to shut the non-Jewish world out of ourselves, but to absorb at last that which we have kept away from ourselves: the experiences of world Jewry. We are not only Jews, but also Hungarians and human beings. The matter in question is that we want to stress, more than ever, those aspects of our existence which the present situation demands of us and permits only to us. Let us be brave enough to see what awaits us; our work in behalf of our people will enrich us, too. Again we are sitting by the waters of Babylon. Let us at last take our harps off the willow trees and sing to the world the songs of Zion.

Béla Zsolt

Letter to a Well-Meaning Person

As a novelist, poet, journalist, and politician, Béla Zsolt (1898–1949) had ample opportunity to display his considerable talents. Though born and reared in the city of Komárom, he was a product of Budapest, intellectually and politically. The principal targets of his literary interests were the moral and economic deterioration of the urban middle class (A királynő családja [The queen's family] 1932), the deepening sociocultural predicament of Budapest's assimilated Jewry (Gerson úr és neje [Mr. Gerson and his wife], 1930), and the precarious Jewish-Christian relations (Kinos ügy [Distressing affair] 1935). In 1943, because of his anti-Fascist activities, Zsolt was sentenced to imprisonment by a military tribunal, and was subsequently deported by the Nazis. Following the liberation of Budapest in February 1945 he became a founder of the Hungarian Radical Party and the editor of the weekly Haladás [Progress]. Of his postwar works the autobiographical Kilenc koffer [Nine suitcases] (1947) is the most noteworthy. The following letter is translated from "Levél egy jóindulatú emberhez," in Ararát, ed. Aladár Komlós (Budapest: Országos Izraelita Leányárvaház, 1943), pp. 115–17. By permission of A Magyar Izraeliták Országos Képviselete.

My dear Sir:

Thank you for your well-intentioned letter in which you, an outsider, call our attention to the progressive increase in public annoyance as a result of the ostentatious behavior displayed by quite a substantial portion of the Jews, and to the fact that such behavior is a more dangerous cause of anti-Semitism than the ideological, political, and economic arguments which are so often hurled against the Jews. You, my dear sir, write that many of your acquaintances and friends, who were almost won over by ideas and facts, and who in matters relating to the Jewish Question tried to remain objective, soon became disheartened because they felt that the behavior of the Jews in public would discredit their standpoint. We not only acknowledge the good faith of your warning but its validity as well. We feel that the most important and urgent task of the Hungarian Jews is the consciousness of their extrinsic and aesthetic, rather than moral, shortcomings. These shortcomings are indeed such as to merit favorable comparison with what Talleyrand once said: "More than a sin, it is a shortcoming."

We are aware of the seriousness of this phenomenon; yet we would like to point out the sociological and psychological reasons that on the one hand explain those shortcomings, and on the other, make their elimination difficult. It is, however, the farthest thing from our mind to excuse the shortcomings or to alleviate their significance with the inviting possibility of frivolous witticism by saying that during an earthquake it is not customary to debate the finer points of etiquette. We know that this matter of etiquette, the outward appearance of Hungarian Jewry, is most illustrative and conspicuous in these days. Thus from the point of view of formulating public opinion it exposes them far too much to enmity.

Yet it must also be said—we repeat, it is not in our defense but rather in an effort to seek an objective explanation—that in no group of people, no matter how closely knit by common beliefs, interests, or sufferings, do all members personify its virtues and sins in a uniform manner. There are worthless or vulgar individuals and strata in organizations of the highest caliber, in institutions and associations, in religious congregations, nations, and academies, unable to rise to the heights of their laws, professions, and roles, or meet the moral demands of their positions. Such individuals may also be found among the Jews of Hungary.

In the decades prior to the current tribulations the Jewish community was held together only by a common faith. Like society in general, it was divided by enmities and differences. How could a uniform Jewish behavior, manner, and outlook have evolved when Jews themselves were dissimilar in degree of wealth and education, as well as in inherent qualities such as temperament and taste, or even rural and urban influences? True, in view of the past two decades, in which they were exposed to ever-increasing and oppressive political, cultural, and economic restrictions and branded as a community of individuals possessing common traits and qualities, the Hungarian Jews ought to have developed a uniform and conscious form of Jewish behavior that would have been correct from the practical point of view. Also, it would not have added needless fuel to anti-Jewish sentiments. Such a uniform behavior is in the offing, yet one must clearly realize that to restrain the unbridled emotions of irresponsible, lazy, ill-mannered, and tasteless individuals, or those who are so stupid and unsuspecting that they do not realize their dangerous predicament, is by no means an easy task.

We will do everything possible to restrain them and will not shift any sort of responsibility to those who, in the beam of the searchlight that has been aimed at the Jews in a sharp and one-sided manner, take notice of the uncouth behavior of a relatively small minority more readily than the demeanor of the majority, who bear their fate with such discipline and good taste—one might even say discretion—that they would not offend anyone even if it were a matter of life or death. Yes, my dear sir, we would like you to realize that the bearers of shortcomings do not bear the shortcomings of hundreds of thousands. They are not among those who feel most acutely the weight of these difficult years. Those who have become desperate are not the ones who strayed from the accustomed form, but mainly those who feel even nowadays that they have the right to behave immoderately, as if they were still judged by a different standard.

And another thing, my dear sir. We have tried our best—and we will continue to do so—to mold the behavior of the Hungarian Jews not only by good morality, good taste, and the conventions of the times, but, if all reasoning is to no avail, by the greediest and sanest interests of opportunism as well. However, we must also declare that despite everything, we do not believe that we would do the right thing if with passionate puritanism we cautioned the Jews of Hungary against all that makes life what it is. We could deceive you by pathos and excessive demands. It would be hypocritical if we expected the Jewish masses to give up even that which is not offensive to either good taste, public interest, or individual preference: their cultural needs and—so long as we can provide them—a civilized appearance, a modest social life, children's toys, or even recuperative vacations in the mountains or by the lakeside for those who are ill or fatigued. We do not believe that it would be proper or realistic to promote asceticism; it is the prerogative of the privileged and those who possess the requisite physical and spiritual heroism, whereas, we repeat, we must consider a many-faceted multitude. Moreover, it is not our intention, not even in these perilous times, to sow in Hungarian Jews the seeds of the belief that to take their share of fresh air, sunshine, and the basic physical and spiritual joys of life would be to commit a sin against God and mankind. Yet we expect them to abide punctiliously by the standards their present condition dictates, as well as the constant, conscious awareness of the danger of intemperance on the part of the few that might mislead even those who mean well.

We, of course, would like to make every Jew sensitive to the virtues of moderation, self-criticism, and responsibility, though we know that we can hardly expect such a thing to take effect overnight. We are asking you to consider the behavior of the majority of the Jews, which is neither showy nor shallowly hedonistic. It is serious: one might even say grim. The reason for this is not some systematic propaganda of etiquette, but rather the good upbringing and culture provided in family and school and finally, but not insignificantly, the historical fate of Hungarian Jewry.

With full awareness of your good intentions, permit us to make the following request of you. Call the attention of your friends and acquaintances to the fact that to mistake the demented behavior of a few degenerate individuals for the behavior of the whole of Hungarian Jewry would be an optical illusion that should, in the interest of verifying reality, be scrutinized for the sake of accurate sociographic orientation, if not for the sake of humanity.

In conclusion, permit us to express our gratitude for the good intentions you have displayed in wanting to be of help to us.

Géza Ribáry

The Most Important
Present Tasks and Duties of
Hungarian Jewry

*As vice-president of the Jewish community of Pest, Géza Ribáry (1889–1942)
had the difficult task of overseeing its manifold functions in the early years
of the Second World War. When the torrent of anti-Jewish laws and regulations was unleashed, Ribáry put his considerable legal experience to good
use by explaining their meaning and implications, and offering advice to his
frightened, less knowledgeable coreligionists. He was a frequent contributor
to Jewish publications and a coauthor of Az ügyvédi rendszer magyarázata
[Explanation of legal procedure] (1938). The following essay is translated
from "A magyar zsidóság legfontosabb mai teendőiről és feladatairól," in
Ararát, ed. Aladár Komlós (Budapest: Országos Izraelita Leányárvaház,
1941), pp. 12–14. By permission of A Magyar Izraeliták Országos Képviselete.*

When a gardener raises a plant with great care he must protect its life and
assure its growth in two ways.

There are necessities of life that must be provided for all plants alike. They
must be protected against the heat of the scorching sun by placing plaited
rush mats over them, against the searing dryness by watering them, against
high winds by erecting a picket fence, and against the midnight frost by
covering them with sheets or placing them in a hothouse.

There are, however, procedures that are applicable only to certain kinds
of plants, or become necessary only in certain places and under certain
conditions. Such is the one involving the subterranean snail, which, with
loving preference, chews on the roots of certain plants only and multiplies in
a certain type of soil only, threatening the plants it prefers with destruction.

When we speak of the future tasks and duties of Hungarian Jewry, they
must likewise be divided into two groups.

Our lives and future are inextricably fused with the destiny of the Magyar
people. It is for that reason that we must participate in the constructive work
of the Magyar people with unabating enthusiasm and unbroken faith in the
reaffirmation of our emancipation, notwithstanding the likelihood that in
certain respects we may not reap the fruits of our labor in the near future.

In addition to our commitments, we must be on guard to defend our right to live and protect our future against anti-Semitism, that dangerously menacing disease.

The defense against anti-Semitism may be undertaken by resorting to two devices. First, we should attempt to persuade those who suffer from this malady that it is permeated with bacteria which threaten to destroy not only the patient in whom a scheming doctor may wish inject such bacteria, but the doctor as well. The effectiveness of a cure for the cause of the disease, economic stagnation, is equal to zero. We should not and must not interest ourselves in serums that cause only harm without the slightest curative effect.

At present I consider this device in the struggle against anti-Semitism altogether ineffective and recommend that its deployment should not be brought up for discussion.

The atmosphere created around us by the ideologies that are saturated with anti-Semitism renders the weapon of persuasion useless. It is for that reason that we must resort to the other weapon in the struggle against anti-Semitism. We must increase our virtues a hundredfold and eliminate our mistakes. With iron will gained by heavy physical work, with spirit made exalted by knowledge and culture, and with a soul made noble by unselfish, helpful service to others we must create an atmosphere around us in which the weapons of anti-Semitism will be rendered ineffective.

I cannot repeat often enough that there are two virtues in particular which we must inculcate on our coreligionists: modesty and steadfastness. Unfortunately we have often witnessed the manifestation of immodesty on the part of our wealthy coreligionists. Spinelessness, however, is an attribute of the shipwrecked in Jewish life. Due to the enduring tradition of generalization, all of us are victimized by the disadvantages that these seemingly conflicting qualities, which evoke both hatred and contempt, have created. Speaking for myself, I believe that our most important tasks are the elimination of mistakes due to immodesty and spinelessness, and the institutionalization of the virtues of modesty and steadfastness. We must strengthen them in all walks of life, in the area of mental and physical work as well as in recreation and social contacts.

The elimination of our seemingly conflicting shortcomings and the intensification of our virtues will undoubtedly provide a middle course on which we shall advance, leaving behind the harmful atmosphere of anti-Semitism, until we regain the position in this land that we had earned by the common destiny we share with the Magyar people, and by our passionate devotion to the Magyar ideal.

Lajos Dénes
Two Letters

One of the most prominent community leaders in interwar Hungary, Lajos Dénes (1879–1942) was an indefatigable protector of needy Jewish women and orphans. As president of the Jewish Women's Club of Pest, he was active in a variety of humanitarian causes. An educator by profession, Dénes enriched the cultural life of Budapest's Jewry with his talent for organization and patronage of artists and writers. He was also the author of a number of works on aesthetics. These two letters are translated from "Két levél," in Ararát, ed. Tibor Kőrösi (Budapest: Pesti Izraelita Nőegylet Leányárvaháza, 1939), pp. 91–95. By permission of A Magyar Izraeliták Országos Képviselete.

1.

Dear Professor:

Recently I've had an argument with a Christian friend about Jews. It occurred to me that it's been exactly twenty-five years since our graduation banquet. I accompanied you home. We walked on Andrássy Avenue and the Kőrút, discussing anti-Semitism.[1] Though I knew your views, I confessed somewhat timidly that I had often been treated offensively by teachers and classmates alike for being a Jew.

"Why do you say for being a Jew?" you interrupted. "If you were treated offensively, it was for being a human being."

Thereupon I cited a case. I remember, sir, that you called my offenders fools and uneducated barbarians and added that only by not being overly sensitive would I be able to retain my dignity as a human being and defiantly disregard such crude remarks. Then you said:

"No one can deny that there are anti-Semites. They've been taught to be that way. They absorbed contempt, even hatred, for Jews at home. Yet they're ashamed to reveal their true feelings in public. They sense that such feelings are incompatible with their dedication to culture. And the more cultured they become the more desperately they conceal, even suppress, their hatred of Jews, a feeling that has become almost instinctive for them. I believe that with continued progress in culture and on an even higher level of objectivity and refinement they will be able to suppress such feelings altogether and will not differentiate among human beings except on the basis of moral, intellectual, and social values and abilities."

Then, sir, I inquired if you thought your optimism realistic. You replied:

"My dear friend! I'm a pedagogue. I would not be fit to be one if I weren't an optimist. Optimism is faith. Faith in a better future and in the betterment of mankind through education. The question is not whether such a view is realistic but whether the line of progress, extended in theory, will lead in that direction. Well, I believe that it will."

That's what you said, sir, twenty-five years ago.

Permit me, now, after twenty-five years, after the line of progress, not in theory but in reality, has led through the various versions of the *numerus clausus* to an anti-Jewish legislation in our country and to the position of Jews in highly cultured Germany, to ask you, sir, again with due respect. Do you still believe that culture will eventually eradicate hatred in man's soul, that man will be judged by his positive human values, not merely by his accidental human shortcomings, religion, and color of skin, that there will be a time when "Do not do unto others" will be obeyed throughout the world even if those "others" happen to be Negroes, Armenians, or, let's say, Jews? Do you still want to teach me that?

Your old, faithful student,
X.Y.

2.

My dear Friend:

I still do, indeed, and I still believe that. Of course, I must amplify the view that I held then, though it has not changed in essence. This is neither a correction—I would not be ashamed if it were—nor a change of conviction, but a fulfillment. It is like a densely foliated and abundantly fruited tree, a fulfillment of what it was twenty-five years ago, not its corrected counterpart.

I would like to amplify two points.

1: I do not wish to cite the oft-mentioned historical observation—though I myself believe it to be true—that there are setbacks in the development of intellectual life. True, it explains a great deal, though perhaps not as much as the fact that we used to err in determining the level of culture attained at a given time. We must not believe that the Goethes, the Humboldts, and the Fichtes of an era and the masses in their respective countries had reached the same level of intellectual sophistication. It takes a long time for the main body of an army to reach a point that the vanguard has already passed. Power, however, is held and exercised by the former, not the latter. Yet how far do the masses lag behind the level of intellectual sophistication of a Goethe, a Humboldt, or a Fichte?

Will they even reach it? My God, at one time even autos-da-fé were a popular pastime. Not anymore. . . .

2. The second with which I must amplify my old views is as follows. Let's assume that all lawyers, the fair-headed, or the thin are persecuted or discriminated against solely on account of their profession or physical characteristics. The most natural thing in the world would be if lawyers threw in their lot with one another and joined forces—fair-headed and thin persons likewise—even though it were determined that it would be a colossal error to put all lawyers, fair-headed or thin persons, in one group in consideration of their human rights. Yet it would be an even greater mistake if they did not join forces and did not defend themselves. This does not contradict what I said twenty-five years ago, that if you were treated offensively, it was as a human being, not as a Jew. Then they would have been ashamed to admit that they persecuted or discriminated against a person because he was a Jew. Whenever they did so, they reasoned that it was on account of human shortcomings, but then they should have applied the same rationale against a Christian too. Nowadays they can legally persecute or discriminate against even the finest person and justify their action simply by saying that he is a Jew. The new techniques of open attack that the anti-Semitic side has adopted forces the Jewish side to devise a new defensive stand. Nowadays it would be downright foolish or criminally self-deceptive to think that we enjoy equal rights with our Christian countrymen. We are exceedingly unlucky, to be sure. No, we must realize that we have been made inferior and we must acknowledge this status as well as its consequences.

Will cultural progress ever rectify this situation?

My dear friend! I believe and declare that only cultural progress can and will rectify this situation. I can almost hear you say, "But where will I be by then?" You may be right. Perhaps we will not be here by then. However, our children will be here.

And he who thinks of them must be an optimist.

With kindest regards,
Your former professor

Ottó Komoly

What May Jews Learn from the Present Crisis?

Though an engineer by training and a fighter by experience and disposition—he was wounded in the First World War and subsequently rose to the rank of captain in the reserves—Ottó Komoly (Kohn, 1892–1945) is best remembered for his fearless humanitarianism and for his devotion to Zionism in a country where the movement had been facing stiff resistance by assimilationist Jews since its inception. He wrote two books dealing with Zionism, A zsidó nép jövője [The future of the Jewish people] (1919) and Cionista életszemlélet [Zionist view of life] (1942), and was elected chairman of the Zionist Federation of Hungary in 1941. As head of a clandestine rescue committee in 1943 and 1944, Komoly succeeded in helping more than a thousand Jews reach safety. He was killed by Arrow Cross militiamen on 1 January 1945. In Israel a moshav (cooperative smallholders' village), Yad Natan, was given Komoly's Hebrew name in memoriam. "What May Jews Learn from the Present Crisis?" is translated from "Mit tanulhat a zsidóság a mai válságból?" in Ararát, ed. Aladár Komlós (Budapest: Országos Izraelita Leányárvaház, 1943), pp. 15–20. By permission of A Magyar Izraeliták Országos Képviselete.

My response to this question, even after lengthy deliberation and rational speculation, will always be the one that came to my mind as a spontaneous reaction: the position of Jews had been uncertain for long centuries since the destruction of the Jewish state. It has been unstable in the decades since the emancipation of European Jewries. Thus it is only natural that the conflagration sweeping across the world, the like of which is unknown in the annals of mankind and the ravages of which afflict peoples much more powerful than ours, is raging more violently and causing relatively greater damage in the communities of the Jews than among the ranks of other peoples. The lesson to be learned from the present crisis can only be one: this uncertain situation must be terminated and Jews must be placed in such circumstances that will allow them to stand firmly on their own feet.

My discourse would become excessively lengthy if I attempted to search our whole history for causes in an effort to identify the historical events, mistakes, arrears, behavioral patterns, or perhaps racial attributes which may have caused the evolution of the Jewish way of life to take a course that was to lead through unending sufferings, first to the Emancipation and then to a conscious effort on the part of a significant portion of Jewry to assimilate to the peoples surrounding them. It may be proved that at the close of the nineteenth century the segment of Jewry that had extricated itself from the great centers of Jewish life in the East and in the old ghettos—some of which may still be found existing in the West, though considerably reduced in size in comparison with the ones in the Middle Ages—had come to believe that its ties with Judaism were only of a religious nature, and that in all other respects it belonged to the people among whom it lived. Jews of this kind were convinced that the seemingly isolated manifestations of distrust and hatred they experienced from time to time were merely atavistic, soon-to-be-disappearing, ephemeral phenomena which ought not to be taken seriously.

Only a few saw clearly that things were not what they appeared to be. They knew that the prevailing conditions, seemingly favorable and tranquil in contrast to times past, were the ones which were transitional and ephemeral and that the glowing embers lying on the bottom of the underestimated problem would, in an opportune moment, set the pyre of the Jewish Question, believed to have been extinguished for the time being, on fire. The occasionally detected, disturbing phenomena and the unorganized manifestations of hatred had led these few to conclude what we today, from hindsight, must inevitably accept as true, namely, that the Emancipation and the attempts at assimilation have not terminated the Jewish Question. It is still waiting to be solved. But now it is up to us and the other peoples of the world, whose help we solicit, to solve it. It has been determined that anti-Semitism is, in effect, caused by the inability of Jews—excepting a negligible number—to assimilate, partly because they prefer to adhere to traditional religious values and forms and partly because their environment is not such as to demand that they assimilate. For these reasons they are invariably viewed as an alien group that keeps its surroundings in a constant state of tension. Like a living organism that tries to remove the alien substance that irritates it, peoples try to be rid of those Jews whom they are unable to assimilate.

This conclusion is just as valid with respect to places where Jews formed closed communities as it is where they seemingly mixed with the people among whom they lived, though their number exceeded the level at which they could be absorbed by the host nation. In addition, the social and economic stratification of Jews stands out in sharp contrast to the organizational structure of societies around them. Jews have in proportionately excessive numbers occupied positions that were, so to speak, in the window of social life, and called upon themselves the attention of other segments of the population to a greater degree than desirable. In an effort to justify their viability and civil equality, the present and preceding generations of Jews stressed—almost flaunted—the virtues that some of their members had in fact acquired.

Such an attitude, however, only evoked negative criticism and a heightened animosity that are directed toward every Jew, whether or not he has indeed risen above his non-Jewish countrymen. Liberated from centuries-long oppression and from the damp walls of ghettos, middle-class Jews thrust themselves all too eagerly upon the opportunities that the period following the Emancipation provided for them. They spent more money than they could afford and lived more ostentatiously than the non-Jews of a comparable social level, thereby making their financial power appear greater than it actually was. Simultaneously, their sense of responsibility to the Jewish community diminished at the same rate with which they became alienated culturally and morally from ghetto life and the spirit of Judaism. This period was, unfortunately, the highwater mark of liberal ideologies, which concealed the frequently unrestrained individualism. Nothing remained, therefore, that would have counterbalanced these eccentric inclinations or caused with its disciplining effect individual Jews and the leaders of the Jewish community to think more realistically and behave more rationally.

I would not want to make the mistake of holding the Jewish community and its leaders exclusively responsible for the present catastrophe, without taking into account every possible mitigating circumstance. There are indeed mistakes that other people, non-Jews, have made, there are the vicissitudes of social and political life, and there is the unfortunate international situation, which all community leaders must take into account if they want to draw lessons from them. Let us, therefore, briefly and without explanation look at the mitigating circumstances as well.

Conditions at the end of the last century and the beginning of the present one were such that they easily misled those who, by failing to see what actually lay at the bottom of things and by being blinded by the love and devotion they felt toward the people among whom they lived, became convinced that they would most decorously fulfill their obligations toward their country by breaking with the traditions of their past and severing all ties with Jews living in other countries. As late as a decade ago even a superficial observer would have disputed the likelihood of what has since actually happened to the Jews. A person is inclined to believe in the permanency of relatively favorable conditions and is reluctant to attribute any importance to portentous phenomena. The leaders of the Jewish community did not, and (guided by their observations then) could not, view as a sin or a fatal mistake the way Jews lived in a liberal society after they had been made citizens of equal standing with non-Jewish citizens.

Though these may be considered as mitigating circumstances, the Jewish leaders, in contrast to those who had correctly recognized the existence of the Jewish Question and the acute danger it presented despite the seemingly tranquil conditions, made the mistake of misjudging the circumstances and thus misguidedly failed to make preparations for the elimination of the mistakes. Those who knew better pointed out the right path that would have led to the solution of the problem, but their number was negligible and their financial resources too limited to implement their ideas before the catastrophe struck. They argued—and nowadays there is no serious-minded Jew who would not acknowledge the veracity of the Zionist rationale—that Jews would be unable to assimilate and would remain aliens wherever they lived as long as they were unable, unlike all other peoples, to have a country of their own in which they were the dominant group, occupying all sectors of social, economic, scientific, artistic, and financial life, thereby proving the falsity of the view according to which Jews live off the work of others.

Furthermore, they would be able to reciprocate the hospitality—that is what many people think the way they are treated at present is called—which they enjoy in the lands of the Diaspora. They became convinced that the experiences of the decades since the start of the modern Zionist movement, as well as the lessons of the more distant past, had proved that only Palestine, the Holy Land, Eretz Yisrael, was that sole point on earth which was able to tie to the soil Jews now living in the unhealthy social environment of the *galut*[1] and forge them into a healthy-living and naturally and constructively thinking community.

That their belief was not a fantasy is proved by those who succeeded in implementing the plan within the framework of the Palestine Mandate and in continuing this work—albeit in modest circumstances—without interruption in the past twenty-and-some-odd years. Had the great masses of Jews and their leaders been sensitive to political realities and responded with the needed financial sacrifice that the Zionist leaders demanded from them, it would have been possible to do many times over what had been accomplished with modest means. In that case, instead of the Palestine which with a Jewish population of 300,000 had stood ready to absorb another 300,000 Jews fleeing from the catastrophe, there would have perhaps been 1.5 million Jews preparing the land for the absorption of another 1.5 million, many of whom—*rebus sic stantibus*—were instead destined to perish miserably. I will leave it to the imagination of every rationally thinking person to speculate how much better off the Jewish people would have been in that case.

The Jews did not take advantage of the opportunity that the Palestine Mandate had offered. They were parsimonious and small-minded. Though people suffer and pay for their mistakes, they also find them to be instructive. We have already had our share of suffering; let us hope that we will still have an opportunity to learn from the lessons. These lessons are as follows:

1. Our style of living and position in society should be such as not to give others the opportunity to see us constantly in *premier plan*. Let us awaken to the consciousness of the unity of our people and the obligations it imposes upon us.

2. In addition to the unfailing fulfillment of our duties to our Hungarian

nation, let us with all of our talents help create the independent national home of the Jewish people in Palestine, where every Jew who cannot or does not wish to assimilate, or is prevented by those among whom he lives from doing so, may find a place. By restoring to the Jewish people the respect of the world and making them the equals of other politically independent nations, the Jewish national home will enable those who chose to stay behind to assimilate, thus terminating that situation in which the Jew is the lightning rod in every storm as well as its most pitiful victim.

László Gömöri

Two Skits

The author of many humorous essays, sketches, and plays that were staged in the cabarets of Budapest, László Gömöri (b. 1908) has been a frequent contributor to Hungarian newspapers and magazines. His acerbic philosophy of life is usually softened by humorous presentation. Some of his writings have also appeared in German, Dutch, Swiss, and American publications. These two skits are translated from "A messzehordó," and "XIV Lajos," in Hinni kell! [One must believe!], ed. László Palásti and László Gömöri (Budapest: László Bánházi, 1939), pp. 39–47. By permission of A Magyar Izraeliták Országos Képviselete.

1
The Long-Distance Gun

Like a graduating senior in love, the powerful director of the munitions factory flashed a smile at Professor Oprix as enchanting as if the old, wrinkled scientist were a pretty girl. It was the long-distance gun, the professor's invention, that inflamed his heart. They sat face to face in the thickly carpeted office. The director was filled with enthusiastic curiosity.

"My chief scientific adviser has already briefed me, but perhaps we should start from the beginning. You are working on a new type of long-distance gun, aren't you? May I inquire as to the actual distance your gun can cover?"

The world-famous professor of explosive chemistry leaned forward in the comfortable leather chair. On his face wrinkles started to dance.

"I don't know for sure, yet. The calculations will determine it accurately. I can certainly guarantee a few thousand kilometers. We'll see . . ."

"And the shell?" asked the director.

Oprix pulled out of his briefcase a sheaf of papers filled with mathematical calculations. He held them in his hand but did not look at them.

"It is 800 meters long and 250 meters wide. It weighs a million tons. According to my calculations three such shells can demolish a middle-sized country. Three," he mused, "perhaps four."

The director flicked a tiny speck off the lapel of his jacket.

"And will all buildings collapse?" he asked gently.

"Every one of them," Oprix nodded. "The mountains will fall down, the waters will flood, and there will be an earthquake."

For a minute there was silence. Each was absorbed in his thoughts. The director visualized a fast-flying volcano, a guided volcano that concealed a huge quantity of dynamite. He was amazed. How fast was the progress of technology!

"Of course," the director noted quietly, "the long-distance gun will create a new situation in warfare. Personal combat will end."

"Yes, yes," the professor agreed, "the army will consist of three men only. A crane operator, a skilled worker, and an apprentice who will oil the motor. The rest is up to the steel and the explosives. The shell will fly over the neutral countries and fall on the land of the enemy. It will cover a thousand kilometers in less than two minutes. If you light a cigarette when the worker ignites the engine, by the time you finished smoking it the war will be over. And mankind will again enter an age of peace. The state of war will last for four to five minutes. A little longer, of course, if the target is eight to ten thousand kilometers away."

The director picked up a red pencil and started playing with it.

"Could your gun cover, say, ten thousand kilometers?"

"Perhaps even more than that," the professor blinked. "I haven't as yet been able to determine the degree at which the type of acid that I mix into the explosive compound will gasify. I'd like to ask you to be patient for a few weeks longer."

"Will three weeks be enough?"

"Why, certainly."

"Well," the director rose, "I shall personally inform the chairman of the board that you will turn over the plans and final calculations three weeks from today."

He pulled out a checkbook. He wanted to offer an advance payment.

"Will a million pengös be sufficient?"

"No, thank you," Oprix protested, "money comes last. I work unselfishly, in the interest of mankind."

The director extended his hand. "So do I. Believe me, all my life I've been guided by public interest. Often I even forget about eating when I am absorbed in studying a new mine or the complicated model of a flame thrower. I am not interested in material success. My only reward is the gentle rejoicing over a work well done."

They were at the door. Oprix stopped and wiped his forehead. "Yes, in every country there are a few superior beings, like us, who are dedicated to the cause of progress. If it were up to the people, they would now be where their ancestors were two thousand years ago. They'd still be throwing spears at one another."

Again, they shook hands cordially. The professor's bent figure disappeared in the winding corridor.

Three weeks later, as they had agreed, the professor called on the director. His back was a little more bent and his wrinkled face looked tireder than before.

"I've finished it," he said as he sank slowly into the armchair.

The director could hardly control his excitement. His eyes were wide open and his hands trembled.

"Well, how far can it carry?"

"A hundred thousand kilometers. That's the maximum distance."

"A hundred—" the director was unable to finish his question. His mouth was agape. He had to start a new sentence.

"Professor," he gasped, "you're the greatest genius ever to walk on the face of the earth."

The professor did not seem to hear the director's praises. He kept staring before him and continued slowly, "The minimum distance—that's sixty thousand kilometers."

The director turned pale. He thought his hearing had suddenly become impaired.

"How? What? How many?" he asked trembling in alarm.

"Sixty thousand kilometers."

"But my good man, the entire globe from the North Pole to the South Pole is less than that. Not even half of that."

The genius lowered his head disconsolately. "I know," he sighed, "the invention isn't perfect."

The director jumped to his feet. He leaped to the professor and shook him by the shoulder.

"We can't use it for anything this way. The shell will explode in space. Please, make it perfect. Reduce its minimum distance."

He took his hand off the professor's shoulder. Oprix stood up and shook his head quietly.

"I've already done what I could. At first, the minimum distance was seventy-five thousand kilometers. I reduced it to sixty thousand. No more. I'm a fool."

He bowed and started leaving the office. He kept blinking, and looked awkward as he tripped twice on his way to the door. The inventor of the long-distance gun was shortsighted. He calculated in hundreds of thousands of kilometers, yet he could not see beyond his nose.

At noon, the chairman of the board dropped in on the director. Immediately he asked about the invention. "Well, what about the long-distance gun?"

The director made a discouraged gesture. "It's no good," he mumbled, "the earth is too small."

2

Louis XIV

Twice I sifted through ancient mythology in vain. I could not find even the trace of it. Of all the gods and demigods whom the Romans and Greeks had invented, they forgot only one, it seems. There is among them no mythical being who always ate yet was never full, and the more he drank the thirstier he was. That vain, eternal man whose bread was glory and whose wine was fame, and who was starving after he ate himself full, and was thirsting while he drank is absent from the legends of the Middle Ages as well as the works of modern poets.

Yet man is like that; he always was and always will be. Of course, there are also exceptions. Take me, for example. When I became a published author for the first time—a four-line poem with my name under it—I was a little drunk with glory and in the exhilaration of fame I imagined that on the streetcars and in the public squares people were reciting my poem to one another.

They did no such thing. How could that be, what was the reason? I used to ponder. The rhymes were brilliant, the ending sparkled, and the weekly in which it had seen the light of day was published in a run of four hundred copies. All right, people did not recite it to one another, I tried to calm myself, but they should at least have talked about it:

"Have you read it?"

"How can you even ask?"

"Well, what do you say to it?"

"Colossal."

"It goes from hand to hand in our house."

"Likewise in our office."

"I'm not surprised."

People talked about other things altogether. I wrote another poem for the next edition. It had eight lines. Subsequent editions contained some of my humoresques, satirical pieces, jokes, and skits. In a year my name was familiar to the editor.

Well, yes, that's the way it was, fifteen years ago, at the start of my career. Today I can say without immodesty or vainglory, relying on purely objective phenomena— I don't want this to sound as if I were bragging, but it was only yesterday that a very good friend of mine, an intern in a mental hospital, looked me up.

"Imagine," he said in considerable excitement, "they brought a man to my ward who is obsessed with the idea that he is a humorist. As a matter of fact, his obsession is that he is—you."

I always knew that the whole country was reading my unpretentious skits and that my modest name was quite familiar in highly cultured circles throughout Europe. This frantic success, however, caught even me by surprise. Madmen have various obsessions; this one thinks that he is Louis XIV, another that he is Julius Caesar, or Napoleon, or perhaps Voltaire, or even Batu Khan.[1] It was my turn now.

"Did he actually mention me by name?" I inquired coyly.

"Sure. Of course. He keeps introducing himself and he always says your name. And he adds haughtily: 'humorist.' "

I had arrived at last. Without a doubt I was a known author. Slowly the outlines of a skit were forming in my mind. On a visit to a mental hospital, a cabinet minister walks from patient to patient while listening to a professor explaining to him what each patient's obsession is.

"This is Buddha . . ."

"This is Svatopluk . . ."[2]

"What about that one?" asks the cabinet minister, pointing to a third patient.

The chief physician leans toward the minister and whispers my name into his ear.

"A great humorist," the minister nods. "I'm familiar with his works. A brilliant mind."

Inside, however, he is envious of me. He tries to remain unfazed.

"Isn't there one here," he asks casually, "who— ha-ha-ha —has the obsession that he's I?"

The chief physician apologizes, flinging out his arms, "No, Your Excellency, no one here is like that."

My physician friend had only dropped in on me for a few minutes. As he was leaving he turned back and said, "If you're curious about him, come out. I'll be glad to show him to you."—"O yes, one of these days, maybe. I'm really interested in this thing. From a scientific point of view, of course. By the way, tell me, do you cure these madmen of their obsessions in a short time?"

"Not at all. It takes many, many years."

"That's all right. There's no hurry."

I started whistling as soon as he was gone. That was really something, a serious matter, not like the one with the four-line poem fifteen years before. It might very well be that in that moment in the mental hospital three people were playing cards: Moses, Svatopluk, and I.

Next day I rushed out to the mental hospital. My physician friend took me to the garden, where in an arbor four people were playing rummy. One of them was my man. Pretending to be aloof, though my heart was pounding, I inquired about the obsessions of the other three. My friend discreetly pointed from one to the other.

"This fellow's obsession is that he's a train conductor, the other thinks that he owns a tobacco shop, and that one acts as if he were a bank official."

I gasped, with my eyes popping out.

"Napoleon, Louis XIV, Svatopluk—?" I muttered in embarrassment.

The chief physician of the hospital was approaching us.

"My journalist friend," the intern introduced me to the chief physician. He joined us for a walk in the garden. Meanwhile, I was becoming livid with anger. Nowhere a Buddha, a Philip IX, an Ivan the Terrible. Only a head-waiter, a ticket collector, and a pipeman—obsessions like that.

"What about an emperor?" I asked the chief physician, aghast.

"We've got one. He thinks that he's Napoleon, but he's been with us since the good old days. Nowadays," he waved in resignation, "we've got only small-timers: a bookkeeper, a fireman, and a humorist. Yessir, the world has changed a great deal. People no longer yearn for gold mines and diamond fields. A modest income is the ne plus ultra of their dreams, and small, fixed jobs are their obsessions now. Louis XIV, Napoleon, and Moses have ceased to be the subjects of obsessions. No one wants to be Louis XIV nowadays."

"The great dreams are party leadership and political prophecy," the intern observed.

Like a drowning man, I was groping for the last straw.

"Have you got party leaders and prophets?" I asked eagerly.

"Those don't get sent here anymore," the chief physician shook his head. "The man with an obsession that he is a prophet will be made into one by the mob."

We came to a wiry, balding man. He was crouched on the ground, pouring sand into bags of various sizes.

"May I help you?" he asked in an inspired voice. "Would you like anything else?"

He was selling ten dekas of salt, a half kilo of lentils, and a quarter kilo of flour. His face was shining in otherworldly happiness.

"To be the master of the world is not an unreachable obsession," the chief physician went on. "To be a grocer, that's another matter altogether."

The Crisis of Jewish Life[1]

Translated from "A zsidóság életproblémája," in Ararát, *ed. Aladár Komlós
(Budapest: Országos Izraelita Leányárvaház, 1943), pp. 11–15. By permission of A Magyar Izraeliták Országos Képviselete.*

In the present situation Hungarian Jewry is faced with two problems: existence and nonexistence. There have been many crises in the four-thousand-year-long history of the Jewish people, but such convergence of all the problems created by the implicit and explicit meanings of life, amounting to an absolute choice between survival and extinction, is a hitherto unknown phenomenon. The question today is twofold: What will the Jewish people mean to the peoples of the world in the future and what do they mean to themselves now? It has become our obligation to address ourselves directly to this question. And as we search amid doubts and misgivings, examining both our approaching fate and our accusing and defensive conscience for answers, it is becoming apparent that either one solution must be found or there will be none at all.

It is now certain that the Jewish people have reached a line of epochal division in the first quarter of the twentieth century. The naïve faith in progress and the illusory sense of security that prevailed in the late nineteenth and early twentieth centuries have collapsed. Were only the Jewish people affected by this momentous change? The historic tremor that had shattered both the fervent Weltanschauung of the Jewish people in the previous century and the optimism that their assimilation into the bourgeoisie had nurtured was also the one that rocked to its foundation the social order of the whole of mankind, the guiding principle of which had been the gain derived from liberty, progress, and individual initiative. The fate of the Jewish people has always been paradigmatic, concomitant with the fate of mankind. Recent events have provided a horrible testimony to this fact. Though the realization of this truth is a fundamental one, it does not absolve the Jewish people from examining themselves and drawing the consequences from this new turn in their history.

Many farsighted Jews are examining their consciences nowadays. Most of them manage to react with remarkable facility. The first conclusion: the

Jewish way of life of the immediate past, the assimilated way of life, has failed. In order to survive, the Jewish people must find another alternative. In the language of practical politics the demand is made, "We must end the coexistence of Jews and the European peoples."

Undoubtedly this observation is based on true knowledge. After all, the gloomy pictures of recent history loom before us, and we feel the spiritual crisis amid these astonishing setbacks that make us come face to face with our own past. We feel the travesty of the deceptive solutions of the Age of Emancipation, and the troublesome spiritual transformation which it produced. We feel the mutually complementary features of resentment and self-depreciation that the Jewish character absorbed under the weight of partial emancipation and imperfect assimilation and which in the non-Jewish environment were believed to be "Jewish flaws." Unfortunately this mentality not only persisted unaffected, notwithstanding the pronounced antiassimilationist tendencies, but most often it overcompensated. Thus the conflicts in the inner world of Jews remain as unresolved as the problems of their environment.

The real Jewish Question may be formulated briefly as follows: How will Jews benefit by remaining a separate group in society? They must not be satisfied with the answer that they want to survive because they exist and that they want to exist in order to survive. This purely biological—or political, as politics is the biology of society—program may not be applicable to Jews. They had, as the people of an independent nation, flunked the test of such a program once, and it was in their prostration that they acquired that peculiar way of life by which they became inextricably fused with the lives of other peoples. The Jewish State fell, as did Moab, Edom, Assyria, and the Hittite empire. According to the law of politics a great force overwhelms a lesser one, and it is the fate of the latter to give way to the former. Peoples are survived only by their cultural, not political, contributions. No one knows of Moab and Edom nowadays, but the ruins and writings of Athens still bear witness to its glory.

The Jewish people revealed strength of character and the will to live by their success in remaining an identifiable group, following their political and military failures, and by perpetuating themselves through participation in the great and universal human creative processes. And whereas the ruins and writings of Athens are confined to the ethereal life of intellectual exclusivism, the Jews succeeded in achieving a historic paradox: they became their own monuments and cultural accomplishments, and transformed that which had survived the political destruction—religion—into the very essence of their existence. Yet it was precisely due to this paradox that the problem of the Jewish people has become critical on two counts. First, they reached an age in which religion was no longer accepted as setting the unchallenged standards of life. Second, due to the peculiar exclusivism of their own development, their religion became more and more rigid, fixed, and conservative—conservation being its chief function—and thus drew away from the vibrant and absolute inspiration that had made Judaism an essentially creative force.

This is the reason why all present attempts to change Jewish life avoid the religious motive. The desire is to create a religionless Jewry, yet to keep identifying that people as Jews. What purpose will such an undertaking serve? Mankind has always needed the Jewish people so that it would have the group in which the Word of God was born. Does mankind need another kind of Jewish people that no longer spread the Word of God, that merely live because they have no other purpose in life but to share in the self-perpetuating process of biological existence?

There are those who will reject the premise of such a question because they believe that the restoration of the Jewish nation and its political independence will automatically resolve this problem, and that following the founding of the state the destiny of the Jewish people will be no more questionable than that of the Germans or the French. The question, however, is far too complicated to lend itself to such a simplistic solution. As no one is thinking nowadays of restoring Moab and Edom—the same would be true of the Germans and the French, had they lost the attributes of national existence hundreds or thousands of years ago—the mere fact that the Jewish people constituted a nation at one time does not justify the restoration of their national exclusivism. More than that is needed. The survival of the Jewish people is justified solely by the service they have rendered to mankind. They may take the risk and suffering that are the integral elements of continuity only if they are willing to go on performing such services as before, perhaps even more zealously in the future.

Mere existence, however, will not suffice. Though there might be such turns of fortune in the near future as will necessitate major geographic dislocations for the Jewish people, it would be a serious mistake to regard these movements as constituting the solution. Dislocation may be a necessity, but not the goal. For no place on earth, however advantageous geographically, can provide the prerequisites of Jewish national existence for the endangered segments of Jewry, or even for a significant portion of them. Palestine might become the national home for a fragment of the Jewish people, yet not even that fragment will be assured of safety from external and internal dangers. As regards the Jews who will settle in Palestine, the constant pressure of power politics to which they had to adapt themselves throughout the history of the Diaspora will make them acquire the peculiar characteristics of the argumentative Eastern behavior that the British, in describing the virtually institutionalized friction between Mohammedans and Hindus in India, call "communalism."

What is the solution then? Let us draw the consequences from the disappointments and mistakes of the past, but let us do it consistently and with conviction. Let us not condemn to death, either spiritually or morally, the

Jewish communities whose very existence is already menaced due to the pressure of external forces. It would be difficult to discuss this question further at this time. The expulsions of Jews in the ancient world and in the not-too-distant past took place under circumstances that were unlike the ones which prevail at present. Every habitable part of the earth is filled to capacity and every migratory movement is destined to stumble over barriers that are not only political and legal in nature, but also psychological. For this reason, let us not expect a great deal from superficial, geographic solutions.

We must think of providing, if possible, healthy living conditions for those Jews who in the course of the next two decades will be affected by the technical aspects of geographical dislocation. The twofold question, What will Jews want to be? and, How do they want to make themselves useful? however, remains unanswered. Only an inner revival will create the precon-ditions for the proper solution of our existence. Only if we discover once more that we have a mission in the world, a religious ideal, which is the spreading of the Word of God, will our position be firm and will mankind acknowledge our contributions. Obviously, not every Jew can be a prophet, or even a deeply devout soul. Yet the solution of the Jewish Question will not be solved unless the prophetic spirit is reawakened and accepted by the whole of the Jewish people. Let no one say that this solution is too ethereal. It is our only chance to be a part of the community of peoples. The Jewish people have sacrificed enough; the sacrifice we must make now will be for mankind, in the name of the Almighty.

Hugó Csergő

Like Fish in the Water

Versatility and professional excellence were the most easily discernible features of the life of Hugó Csergő (Honig, 1877–1944). After completing his legal studies he became a journalist. In 1907 Csergő received the coveted Francis Joseph Prize in recognition of his literary activities. From 1914 to 1921 he headed the Department of Social Welfare of Budapest, which he had founded. His experiences and observations form the backdrop of an impassioned indictment of the social injustices in Hungary's class-conscious society, Budapesti nyomor vöröskönyve *[The red book of misery in Budapest] (1919). Csergő was also the author of many poems, short stories, and plays, some of which were staged in Budapest.*

The illusion of law, order, and economic stability, foundations on which the Hungarian Jews of the interwar period erected the structure of their social and cultural life, and the belated realization of the vulnerability of such convictions form the backdrop of the following selection. It was translated from "Mint hal a vízben," in Magyar zsidók könyve *[Hungarian Jews' book], ed. Jenő Nádor (Budapest: OMIKE Sajtócsoport, 1943), pp. 73–76. By permission of A Magyar Izraeliták Országos Képviselete.*

"He lives like fish in the water." How do fish live in the water, anyhow?

Recently we received a carp as a gift. When I went into the bathroom in the morning, our carp, fat and dignified, was swimming in our tub from one end to the other and back. What a carefree, harmoniously built creature of the universe, I thought. It was like a gentleman of means in the good old days, living a life without worries—like fish in the water.

"Just you wait! You'll soon stop acting so self-confident, dignified, haughtily phlegmatic!"

Let's play a little game. I grabbed the chain of the stopper and yanked it out of the hole. Immediately the water started gurgling down the drain, steadily and unobstructedly. The water level kept decreasing millimeter by millimeter, almost imperceptibly. For a while our portly carp paid no attention to this disconcerting development and continued swimming up and down in the tub in its accustomed, dignified manner.

It took that stupid, fat, self-confident creature five minutes to realize that something catastrophic was happening. Under, above, and around it the water was growing lower and lower, and its fins were already sweeping the smooth bottom of the tub. Suddenly sensing danger, such panic overtook it that I could not help myself and burst out laughing. Splashing and jumping, it ploughed the steadily diminishing water. It swam faster and faster, in an aimless zigzag pattern, as if it had in a flash realized its fate, yet was trying to stave off the approaching danger with a sudden surge of desperate might and will to live. Its struggle lasted for seconds only. Then, almost instinctively, our not-so-stupid and portly carp turned up at the end of the tub by the plug-hole, near which, at a distance of a few centimeters, the stopper had been dangling limply at the end of the chain.

I was mystified by the intuition which that stupid fish was able to muster up for such a unique display of logic. However, the fact remained that it had done so. The purposeless flapping of fins and tail changed to a conscious, planned activity around the stopper. It kept maneuvering until it succeeded in slapping the stopper into the plug-hole. And as it sensed—I am certain that it did—that it had stopped the draining of the water, it placed its entire body over the lifesaving stopper, protecting the precious remnant of its sustenance. Though its gills were still rising and its mouth gasping for the bubbling water, its eyes seemed to reflect returning confidence as it was sprawled over the stopper.

"Look at that ingenious, sly little devil!" I thought. "You won't outsmart me, your fate!"

I yanked—it was a strong yank at that—on the chain, pulling the stopper out of the plug-hole. I cast it over the edge of the tub. It would certainly be out of the carp's reach. The slow draining of the remaining water presented a new challenge in its life-and-death struggle.

However, our portly and smart carp—I had to admit that it was definitely smart—did not leave it at that, and refused to give up. As soon as it discovered the source of danger—I am convinced that by feeling the direction in which the water had been flowing it came to the logical conclusion—the carp almost stuffed all its big stomach, which reminded me of the ones the canons were sporting, into the plug-hole, hoping to place itself as an obstacle in the path of the steadily decreasing water.

It put up a heroic struggle. Its gills were flapping violently, eyes popping out in despair, and mouth gulping down the bubbly water which by then stood only about four or five centimeters deep on the bottom of the tub. As the water kept flowing down the drain, lowering the level in the tub, that poor, fat, stupid carp—yes, stupid, if it had thought that it could alter fate—was visibly losing strength. Suddenly it turned on its side, freeing the hole through which the remaining water was slipping away. The carp looked as if it had lost the fight. The wretched creature lay defeated on the bottom of the tub; eyes lackluster, mouth agape and gasping, and body completely dried out.

"Well, what do you say to that, you helpless plaything of my whims? Alive as long as I will it! Carefree, calmly swimming beneficiary of my mercy! If I choose to withhold it you are dead. If I renew it you'll come to life again, living like a gentleman of leisure in the good old days, well heeled for the rest of his life."

With a flick of my hand I replaced the stopper and turned on the faucet. The life-giving water burst out in a thick spout, leaving a fine, powderlike veil of mist in its wake.

Within seconds our carp was gulping down its only source of sustenance. Within two minutes it was lifted by the steadily rising water level, within five minutes its gills became fully operational, and within ten minutes it was swimming, flapping its fins and tail and occasionally colliding with the stream of water, its back breaking it into millions of glittering drops. As the water filled the tub to the top, our carp became its old self again: a fat, self-confident, dignified, and carefree creature, promenading from one end of the tub to the other and back, and behaving as if its life had never been in danger—like fish in the water.

Like fish, we float about in the tub of life, as long as there is water in it. And like a big child, fate plays games with us. Sometimes it fills the tub of our lives with water and sometimes it pulls out the stopper, letting the water escape. As long as the tub is full we enjoy ourselves immensely, like fish in the water, foolishly and arrogantly, realizing the finiteness of things in life only when suddenly under, over, and around us the water starts diminishing. Then we flap and jump about—oh, what a comical sight we are!—fighting in a life-and-death struggle with instincts sharpened for survival.

As if it were up to us, as if we could prevent that big child, fate, from playing its cruel game.

It is no use. If that big child, fate, wills it, life is ours and we may live like fish in the water. If it wills it otherwise, our flapping, turning, and jumping will be to no avail and despite all of our ingenuity and craftiness we will, like fish, turn upside down on the bottom of the waterless tub of life.

Sors bona, nihil aliud. . . . Good fortune, nothing else. . . .

Ákos Molnár

The Great Invisible

The poems and short stories of Ákos Molnár (1893–1945) were often compared with those of the great French writer Guy de Maupassant, the difference being in Maupassant's profound sensuality, which Molnár's work
lacked. Some of his critics accused him of being "cruel and coldly ironic,"
qualities they attributed to him because of the passionless accounts of his
experiences in the First World War—he was severely wounded and lost an
arm—and because of the way he demonstrated concern for his coreligionists
in the rising tide of anti-Semitism. Molnár's strong sense of humor, vivid
imagination, and mastery of the Hungarian language helped him become one
of the most widely read Hungarian-Jewish writers. Of his novels and short
stories, Tizenkét lépés [Twelve steps] (1933) and the pessimistic "Új albérlő"
[New tenant] are the ones most frequently cited. He was also a regular
contributor to Jewish publications in the 1930s and early 1940s. As a dis-
abled war veteran, Molnár was for some time exempted from the anti-Jewish
laws. Shortly before the liberation of Budapest by the Soviet armies, both he
and his wife were brutally murdered by Arrow Cross militiamen.

In the following selection, written in the aftermath of the introduction of
the First and Second Jewish Laws (1938 and 1939), by which the government
drastically reduced the number of Jews in the professions and retroactively
nullified the conversion of Jews to Christianity as of 1919, Molnár bitterly
allegorizes the anti-Jewish regulations that became a distinct feature of the
Hungarian solution of the Jewish Question. "The Great Invisible" is translated from "A nagy láthatatlan," in Ararát, ed. Aladár Komlós (Budapest:
Országos Izraelita Leányárvaház, 1940), pp. 154–58. By permission of A
Magyar Izraeliták Országos Képviselete.

I am a widely experienced, five-year-old dachshund. Until now I was
convinced that man was the perfect being, who gives orders to everybody,
but takes orders from no one. I attributed to him even those mysteries of the
manifestation of life which a dog might never explain, barring, of course, the
unlikely possibility of a genius of the canine race yet to be born. Those
mysteries are as follows: that he will go without eating from morning till
evening, although he could eat; that he will not enter every door, although
he possesses the wonderful ability to enter and exit through doors; and that

he will pass by fireplugs with indifference, although they are full of the most exciting news and information. I accepted those mysteries because a deity is perfect only if it is surrounded by secrets. That way it is possible to worship it truly. But is man really a deity? A horrible night had to come before I realized that even he was ruled by invisible, odorless, mysterious, and cruel entities.

On a humid, foggy evening, I was wandering about in the garden. I was bored. Of the many different kinds of fragrance that moved in my direction there was not one worth investigating. Suddenly I discovered a freshly dug hole at the bottom of the fence. I sneaked through it without hesitating. I was perfectly aware of the fact that what I had done was forbidden. I have neglected to mention a peculiarity of my masters and the more strongly smelling and less elegantly dressed submasters, namely, that no matter how devoid they are of even the faintest sign of envy toward me, they cannot bear to see me on the other side of the fence. Their reason for it is beyond my comprehension.

I was ecstatic as I ran out of the all-too-well-known garden into the much more entertaining world beyond the fence. I was frolicking and jumping up and down, excited by a thousand different kinds of smells. I enjoyed the peculiarly alternating light and shade, for it is light under the streetlamps, dark beyond them.

As my immoderation gradually subsided, I calmly continued jogging along the road. All of a sudden—I must have been quite a distance from our house—and so unexpectedly that it was impossible to think of preventive measures, something rolled past above my head with a terrifying rumble. I screamed in terror and felt a maddening pain in my leg. I lay bleeding and tormented in the mud in the middle of the road. My attacker was already far away and my tear-filled eyes could not even make out its lights. Loudly complaining, I struggled to get on my feet. I could not do it. I fell back into the pool of my blood and screamed, calling my masters as loudly as I could. It was to no avail. Strangers gathered around me and comforted me, I must say, with such compassion that the respectful love and devout enchantment I had felt toward people grew even greater in me. The bystanders lamented and patted me as I was moaning and complaining in pain, and, I must admit, in growing impatience. For compassion is a nice thing, but I wanted to see some action. It appeared, however, that I judged our noble masters prematurely, for as I was thinking such ungrateful thoughts about them a policeman was already telephoning the proper authorities.

I learned the contents of his conversation from what he said to the bystanders when he arrived, gasping for breath. "I called the Office of the Poundmaster for the dogcatcher's truck . . ."

"In other words," I thought in bitter disappointment, "dogs who are the victims of accidents are taken there, and not to their masters." Besides, words such as *poundmaster* and *dogcatcher* awakened something of a dim, unpleasant memory in me. It seemed as if some of my colleagues had already mentioned those places as being the worst fate that can befall a dog. It is possible, however, that my colleagues were misinformed, because the bystanders and the policeman meant well by me.

"Well, what about it?" The bystanders pressed the policeman for an answer.

"They said," the good-natured policeman responded with indignation, "that their truck is being repaired but they'll come for the dog tomorrow at noon."

Despite my utter despondency, I was pleased by the general indignation that followed the policeman's words.

"That dog can't just lie there until noon tomorrow!"

"That's right, that's right. It can't lie there . . ." I yelped and moaned dolefully.

"Isn't there some regulation or ordinance covering a thing like this?"

It was the first time that I heard the names of those two frightening deities. I did not know then that it was those two invisible, unsniffable entities who ruled over man. A big argument developed, but I could no longer listen to it, as I was on the verge of fainting. The word *revolver* struck my ears and the policeman's deep voice responded. He said something to the effect that according to a regulation only the poundmaster was authorized, that he himself could not do it.

"Do what?" I wondered. The poundmaster, however, did not come. Meanwhile, some of the bystanders left and new ones came who approached me with the same affection as the others. They patted me and I returned the kindness with the dutiful wagging of my tail. Yet nothing happened. They placed delicacies in front of me—broiled sausages, my favorite, among other things. I used to be ready for all kinds of senseless ventures. Now I could not eat a bite. An unfamiliar male voice complained indignantly that he had called the vet, but that he would not come to a stray dog either.

"I'm not a stray dog," I moaned. "I have a visible means of support."

My protest remained a voice crying in the wilderness. I knew that everyone felt for me, yet no one helped. The kind policeman lifted me up—the move was accompanied by such pain that I almost committed that most shameful sacrilege of biting my benefactor—carried me a few feet away, and placed a blanket around me. It came in the nick of time because it was d— because it was very cold and my teeth chattered. I was moaning and whining. I could not lick my wound, because it hurt even more when my tongue touched it. No one of the original group of bystanders remained around me. The policeman's replacement came. He was a new man. He also patted and comforted me, but could not do anything either. The regulations did not permit him.

Gradually I resigned myself to my fate and became convinced that I was going to perish there. Tears filled my eyes at the thought that I would not be able to bid my beloved masters farewell. Although I was dazed and exhausted, I was still whining almost mechanically when a couple walked toward me. Again the accustomed patting, display of pity, etc. I did not even look at them. It is strange, however, that in the life of dogs everything turns out contrary to expectation. The couple engaged the policeman in a lengthy conversation and finally the man handed him some money. The policeman whistled to a taxi, gave the money to the driver, and ordered him to take me to the police station. I breathed a sigh of relief. I was saved.

I will not forget that ride as long as I live. That cab shook like h— it shook terribly. I begged the driver in a heartrending voice to stop the car because I could hardly stand the pain, but the only thing that I accomplished by it was that the good man occasionally patted me and said, "It's all right, little doggie, we'll be right there . . ."

At the police station—the morning was already breaking over the city—the driver was given a letter and told to go to the School of Veterinary Medicine. I was subjected to further shaking and suffering. The driver kept patting me on the way there, and I cannot stress enough what a blessed, kind creature that man was. That is, what a blessed, kind creature he could have been had he not been ruled by regulations. So what happened?

The driver carefully lifted me along with my blanket and woke the porter by knocking on the door. That one did not even want to come out, at which point the driver started reading him the letter, "It is respectfully requested that the canine which had been injured by a vehicle be given first-aid treatment and kept there until the arrival of its owner or the poundmaster. Respectfully . . . Precinct No. . . . Sergeant."

I was panting with joy. I thought that my tribulations were finally over. However, my happiness was premature. The porter did not even want to hear about me. "There is no regulation or ordinance that says this hospital has to give first-aid treatment to dogs. The physician on duty cannot be disturbed with such stupidities. You must pay the fee of a night visit and expenses for ten days in advance. Then we'll keep the dog. That is Paragraph 8 of the Regulation. Stray dogs belong under the poundmaster's jurisdiction. And that's that!"

As the driver held me in his arms, we were like beggars standing in front of the door.

"Take me to Regulation," I begged him. "If he sees me like this, in a pool of blood, he'll take pity on me."

"Damn those regulations!" cursed the driver, scratching his head. "What am I going to do with you, you poor creature?"

"Take me with you until my master comes," I sighed.

"I can't even take you with me," the driver said as he held my trembling face in his warm hands. "I don't have room for you."

I wagged my tail silently, hoping that it would be of help. I was seized by an ominous feeling. Everyone loves and respects me. Everyone knows very well that it is impossible to live without dogs. Yet nobody dared challenge the Regulation. I thought with awed respect of the Regulation that could not care less what happened to injured dogs.

Finally, in spite of the Regulation, things turned out well. They always do. But until then how much terrifying fear, despair, and suffering! The driver simply left me in front of the porter's door. Trembling, shivering with cold, and with an anxiously pounding heart, I lay there until the porter found me later that morning. And marvel of marvels! He who had pushed me away so rudely a short time before looked around, obviously to see if the Regulation was watching, and took me into his room. He nursed me, because love can overcome the Regulation. On the third day, my master came for me.

Thus I solved one of the mysteries. I found out the hard way why I was not allowed outside the garden by myself. From then on the door could stay wide open; I did not dare stick even my nose past it. So it was that my deity became a mystery poorer in my eyes. And as far as the Regulation is concerned—well, let's not discuss it. I am much too tactful to make man feel that forces more powerful than him rule him, too.

Part Two
In Memoriam

Sándor Scheiber

The Very Good: A Eulogy[1]

Maintaining the high standard of scholarship which such internationally acclaimed predecessors as the orientalists Ignác Goldziher (1850–1921) and Ármin Vámbéry (1832–1913) had set, Sándor Scheiber (b. 1913) is the most prolific and best known of Hungarian-Jewish scholars. He is an authority on Jewish history and folklore, director of the National Rabbinical Institute, and editor of the Magyar-zsidó oklevéltár *[Hungarian-Jewish Archives] and the* Évkönyv *[Yearbook] of the National Representation of Hungarian Jews. In addition to the numerous articles and reviews that appeared in Hungarian and foreign scholarly journals since 1933, Scheiber is the author of such works as* Magyarországi zsidó feliratok a III. századból 1686-ig *[Hebrew inscriptions in Hungary from the third century to 1686] (1960), and* Héber kódexmaradványok magyarországi kötéstáblákban *[Remnants of Hebrew codices in cover plates in Hungary] (1969). "The Very Good" is translated from "A nagyon jó: Emlékbeszéd" (Budapest: n.p., 1947). By permission of A Magyar Izraeliták Országos Képviselete.*

A few hours more and we shall be covered with the shadow of the day about which we may echo the words of the biblical Job, "Let it not rejoice among the days of the year."[2]

The horrible memory of New Year's Eve of 1944, when nearly forgotten folk customs such as feigning murder or dressing up as animals were rekindled in beasts who played politics, looms before us. These executioners, however, acted out their roles in real life. They abandoned their humanity and turned into beasts. They wallowed in murder, the death rattle of thousands of innocent people, the blood of our martyred brothers, the agony of parents, and the screams of children. They took satanic delight in watching the writhing victims of their mass murder, every one of whom was carrying a world into his death. Perhaps they hoped to ease their guilty consciences—they had in their madness and treachery sacrificed the nation and the capital—in the middle of the siege of Budapest, amid bombs exploding and airplanes strafing the streets, by sending additional thousands of people to their death. They claimed that it was on account of these people— children, the elderly, the sick, girls, and women—that the city was falling. Standing on heaps of bodies and intoxicated by the smell of blood, hyenas bade the old year farewell and greeted the dawn of the new year.

Jews, with the Old Testament, describe differently the first bringing of matters to an end: the completion of the work of creation. It is celebrated as the victory of kindness. "And God saw every thing that He had made, and, behold, it was very good."[3]

These are only words of satisfaction, nothing more.

In the ancient Jewish method of interpreting scripture, the *midrash*, only three things are believed to be truly good.

1

According to some rabbis, man could be truly good. Those of us who on this day of mourning look back at the passing shadow of our brothers who perished on the Danube embankment, in hospitals, ghetto basements, and protected houses would like to caress them once more with the following, perhaps belated words: "*Tov meod*—everything about you is good, nothing is bad." After all, no one is as good to us in life as our fathers and mothers, who devoted their lives to us and struggled for us; our brothers, with whom we shared the memories of our youth; our wives, companions in both happiness and misfortune; and our children, the extension of our beings, the fulfillment of our lives.

In an African tale, it was foretold that the crown prince of the Vagadu empire would not be able to sound his harp unless he took it into his battles and the blood of his loved ones was spilled on it. "The wood must absorb the blood," blood from their blood, gasps from their gasps. I have been allowed to act as the spokesman for your pain and mourning perhaps because on my pen, too, was spilled the blood of that dearest woman, whose name did not become famous and whose image is not perpetuated by a marble statue. Only in our hearts will her memory live forever. She was my mother, who, like your mothers, had never hurt anyone and was kind even to strangers. Yet on this day two years ago a deadly bullet ended her life, a fate she shared with common criminals. How could that bullet, which had pierced her dear heart, have known that it had been beating only for others? How could that bullet have known that hardly a few hours passed since the frail woman had seen the coffin of our father, the pious rabbi, and returned to stay with her children at a place that was thought to be safe? How could the bullet have known that the blood of the mother would spill on the hand of the son? Even in death she feared for him.

Tov meod. For us, kindness has disappeared with her from the face of the earth.

2

Then, in the depth of our sorrow, when both tears and blood gathered in my eyes I felt—you felt the same way, my brothers, didn't you?—that Rabbi Meir was right: only death can be truly good. Believe me, the reason that we did not die of our terrible sorrow but escaped with our lives is that all of us were Death's betrothed. We knew that we would be separated from our loved ones for a short time only. It was simply a matter of who would follow whom in a few hours or days.

Who rejoice unto exultation,
And are glad, when they can find the grave?[4]

There we shall see them again and forget our horrible experiences; the light of kindness and truth shall again shine upon us.

We have seen blood, misery, tears, pain, destruction, murder, famine, humiliation, oppression, and unfathomably great suffering. Have we not seen enough?

". . . it is better for me to die than to live."[5]

Yes: we must live as long as we may,
Yes: that is the rule.
But how shall we live our life
If it causes us pain?[6]

3

It did not happen that way. We were liberated. Surrounded by joyously exulting and dancing people, embracing one another, we started out with uncertain steps. Feeling our way amid burning rubble and charred ruins, and stumbling over heaps of corpses, we searched. Not for our homes, for they were lost forever. We did not seek revenge, we did not ask for compensation. Our souls did not thirst for such ends. We searched for the surviving members of our immediate families, so that we might tell them what the fate of our other loved ones had been on that bloody day. We groped along in the dark of the morgues, looking for the bodies of our parents and relatives amid thousands of frozen corpses. Yet even as we staggered and searched someone was very good to us. It was the Almighty, who embraced us silently and unexpectedly. In our parents' stead he took our hands, stroked our faces, and wiped away our tears. He healed the gaping wounds of our souls, covered us with the veil of time dipped in the elixir of oblivion, guided our steps, and returned us to our places among the living. He laid responsibilities and work on us and assigned to us a new purpose in life. He gave us no rest and did not let us languish lest we have time to think, to meditate, to remember. He taught us to live again.

Yes, we must live as long as we may. We shall live with our maimed bodies and bleeding hearts, never too far from the graves. This life is unlike the life we lived before. It is devoid of warmth, cordiality, direction, or inspiration. We are still searching for our fathers, in whose presence we were always children, and for our mothers, whose blessed hands held together our families, which fell apart when they were no longer with us. We are still searching for the calming presence of our husbands, for the omnipresent thoughtfulness of our wives, and for the bubbling laughter of our children.

We conceive of humanity as composed of two parts: the living and the dead. Nowadays the dead seem to outnumber the living. To some extent we live in a world of dreams and memories.

> I live among those who lived in other times:
> Whatever life withholds, death provides.[7]

There will perhaps be a time when these memories come to life again, and the images of our past take shape and lead us in our paths.

Only a few hours remain before tens of thousands of joyously exultant people will start celebrating. They will bid the old year farewell and greet the new year. May they amid all the merriment be reminded that there are people who will never again laugh on this day, who will never forget its horrible images, and whose constant and haunting companion until their dying hour will be the sound of the harp that is stained with the blood of their loved ones. Leaning over it we listen to the mournful tune. It all comes back to us: the last sigh, the last good-bye, the last kiss, the last prayer. This is our inalienable, sacred legacy. In the depth of swirling, surging, and reeling memories we search for our martyrs so that we may join them in this hour of remembrance.

AMEN.

Samu Szemere

The New Duties
of the Hungarian-Jewish
Literary Society[1]

When Samu Szemere died in 1978 at the age of ninety-seven, Hungarian Jewry lost one of its most erudite scholars. He was a lifelong student and admirer of Italian, German, and Jewish philosophers and writers, particularly Giordano Bruno, Hegel, and Spinoza, about whom he wrote and whose works he translated into Hungarian. Kunst und Humanität: Eine Studie über Thomas Manns ästhetische Ansichten *(1966) is perhaps his best-known work. Szemere also distinguished himself in the service of the Jewish community of Budapest as director of the Jewish Teachers' College and an editor of* Évkönyv, *the Yearbook of the Hungarian-Jewish Literary Society. The following address is translated from "Az Izraelita Magyar Irodalmi Társulat új feladatai," in* Évkönyv, *ed. Samu Szemere (Budapest: Az Izraelita Magyar Irodalmi Társulat, 1948), pp. 9–16. By permission of A Magyar Izraeliták Országos Képviselete.*

HONORED ASSEMBLY,

As a special sign of his infinite mercy the Almighty allowed us to gather in this place again and continue, or rather renew, the work of the Hungarian-Jewish Literary Society that was interrupted almost five years ago. It has become a painful custom in these days to transform the initial meeting of every Jewish assembly into a solemn memorial. For there is no Jewish community that has not lost some of its members. In our Society, too, gaping, empty spaces bear witness to the great Jewish tragedy. Let us remember the martyrs among our members and coworkers who have fallen victim to the horrible catastrophe. The ornaments of the Hungarian rabbinate have perished: Immánuel Lőw, rabbi of Szeged and honorary member, who was called "the most learned rabbi in the world," Béla Bernstein, rabbi of . . .[2]

The soul of the remnant of Hungarian Jewry is still writhing from the pain that the events of the past catastrophe have branded into it. I have not forgotten and cannot forget the mental and physical suffering and humiliation. Neither have the springs of tears dried up—perhaps they never will—that the loss of our loved ones had caused to gush forth. Ever since the earth started trembling under their feet, a feeling of uncertainty about their very existence has overtaken the children of this wounded generation. It will still be a long time before they regain their mental equilibrium, the more so as a feeling of loose-footedness keeps growing ever stronger because they stand dumbfounded before the catastrophe that befell them and the whole of European Jewry.

We have become accustomed to seek the meaning in history, so that we may be able to observe the interdependence of events as the fulfillment of significant goals and teachings. Thus we accept the bad, if we bring ourselves to see it, as the necessary precondition of good, and acquiesce in the belief that every phase in sociopolitical development and in the growth of morality in society is born amid the sufferings of labor pains. But what meaning should we attribute to the bestial rage that sent hundreds of thousands—millions—of innocent people to their deaths? How should we comprehend the reason for children who had hardly tasted the sweetness of life, vigorous men and women, and the tired elderly falling victim to starvation and freezing or the other diabolical inventions of inhumanity? What higher morality or philosophically justifiable ideal could have been fulfilled by such uncontrollably raging hatred and uninhibited murderous instinct as we have witnessed? The will to live is an eternal law of nature, yet in this instance millions and millions of lives were brutally extinguished. By what rationale may such an act be explained as constituting an integral element in the divine plan without making it look like an act of blasphemy? How many promising starts remain unfinished! How may great talents could not develop or perhaps even be born! What is the meaning of all this? The answer to it lies beyond human comprehension. This most meaningless and overwhelming historical experience of ours and its fundamentally brutal reality render even more painful the wound that the tragedies of individuals and communities inflicted on our souls.

Not even the sympathy of the non-Jewish society—that sympathy is manifested in very small doses only—has had a soothing effect on the pains of the Jews. We should not, however, belittle this gesture of conscience toward us; rather we should accept such a display of compassion as a gratifying manifestation of solidarity among human beings. It is, after all, the acknowledgment of the fact that the past catastrophe which struck the Jews stands, in terms of both dimension and brutality, unparalleled in the annals of world history. We have, however, but small cause to accept the compassion of non-Jews. Sad as it may be, we must point out that the waves of anti-Jewish feeling are soaring again. Its motives are quite familiar to us. But I am not referring to neo-anti-Semitism. The problem is much more elementary. A large segment of non-Jewish society is still unwilling to take notice of what happened to the Jewish people. Even men of great culture, whose good faith we have no reason to doubt, listen without the slightest shadow of amazement and distrust to the many accounts of the death camps, the marches in freezing weather, and the large number of Jewish victims. The minds, accustomed to deal with the probable, are unable to absorb the heinous crimes, the enormity of which goes far beyond human imagination, that were committed against the Jewish people.

There is a great need here for resolute and informative work. There are, of course, less than well-meaning people, who do not want to see the extraordinary in the catastrophe of the Jews, simply inscribe their sufferings and losses on the balance sheet of the war, and insist that non-Jews too have suffered and lost a great deal. These "equalizers" do not want to notice the glaring fact that there is an unequalizable difference between those who suffer or perish with weapons in hand and with untarnished human dignity and those who fall prey to murderous instincts, deprived of all means of defense, cast out of a society of equal rights and privileges, branded and humiliated, and left to the mercy of others. It is very difficult, if not impossible, to change the minds of people who do not feel this difference. The bases of our viewpoint and theirs bear no resemblance to each other. They cannot perceive—it is our most wholeheartedly felt conviction—that the gravest crime man can commit against his fellow men is the mockery of human dignity. This crime has been committed against the Jewish people in proportions hitherto unseen.

How did the Jewish people behave in this tragic situation? It may be stated within the bounds of objectivity that during the period when they were deprived of their civil rights the Jews bore their humiliation with dignity. They neither accused nor clamored, but endured with silence. Large numbers of them were deprived of the right to work and earn wages, in an effort to demoralize them and drive them to committing crimes. It did not work. The crime statistics did not change on account of the Jews. They displayed no less self-control in face of the postliberation period, when the full panorama of the brutal nakedness of their losses in both life and property was revealed to them. Not even that prompted them to swear vengeance. No Jew, having escaped from the hell of deportation or returned after years spent in labor service camps, is known to have vengefully attacked his torturers, the despoilers of his home, and the murderers of his defenseless relatives. Retribution belongs to the executors of criminal justice. Objectivity, not self-praise, leads us to declare that the behavior of the Jews was an example of patience and self-control that bordered on heroism.

It is, however, understandable that while Jews lost faith in many traditional ideals they were unable, in the early stages of recovery, to substitute new ones for them. Moreover, it was only natural that they, whose lives had been disturbed so brutally, would regard the rebuilding of their livelihood as their most urgent priority. Thus the foremost task of those who are entrusted with guiding the course of Jewish culture is the raising and strengthening of souls. The objective of this effort is threefold. It will help those who despite their great losses still regard their inexplicably saved lives as worth living, those who carry a spiritual vacuum within themselves to turn toward new ideals, and those preoccupied with the struggle for material gains to retain their sensitivity toward spiritual values so that they may always feel that only through striving for spiritual values can the true meaning of life be realized.

The Hungarian-Jewish Literary Society must also participate in this universally instructive work. There are, however, some concrete tasks which only the Society is qualified to do and obliged to accept, such as the collection of documents relating to the history of Hungarian Jewry since the First World War. We are aware that a similar effort in this direction has been initiated elsewhere and that numerous useful data for future historical writing have already been collected. This fact, of course, does not render unnecessary the work of our Society to the same end. Such an undertaking must be conducted in accordance with the prevailing techniques of scholarly research, encompassing all aspects of Jewish life, and it must provide a comprehensive historical perspective. It is imperative that we start this work without delay—witnesses to the events of this period are still with us and the memories are fresh—for by documents we mean not only public records, laws, and regulations, but also the testimonies of eyewitnesses, which for the historian constitute no less important sources of information, as they often illuminate the spirit of an age more deeply than do official documents. A more distant task—it may be undertaken only after the collection of documents has been completed—is the graphic description of the history of this period. Today we can only hope that at an appropriate future time a scholar of broad vision and masterful expression will come and commit to writing this most tragic chapter in Jewish history, not only with complete objectivity, neither exaggerating nor belittling any of its aspects, but also with heartfelt compassion for the fate of the Jewish people.

Another task of our Society springs from the reality of the rebirth of the Jewish State. If there is one historical event that amid our mourning and the present convulsions of the world fills us with inspiration, it is the fact that the Jewish hopes, dreams, and prayers of the past two thousand years are about to come true. We are watching in amazement a historical miracle, a visual yet mysterious interplay of historical forces. Our happiness, of course, is not undisturbed. Bloody battles are being fought in Eretz Yisrael[4] and we do not know when that fervently desired tranquil state of affairs that is the sole guarantee for peaceful development will come. We are, however, convinced that it will come. Our objective, therefore, is twofold: to watch closely every manifestation of life in Eretz Yisrael, the creative forces in particular, and to establish the closest possible ties with her culture. This task has never been alien to us. It has always been our pleasure to feature articles relating to the Holy Land and to the new Hebrew culture in our yearbook, and the studies analyzing the events of the previous year have consistently reported the work of rebuilding Jewish life in Palestine and any event that had a bearing on Eretz Yisrael. We must cultivate this relationship in a more comprehensive and intensive manner in the future, systematically planning the exchange of cultural values and achievements.

Moreover, we must turn our attention toward the question that relates to the new translation of the Pentateuch. The last translation that our Society had prepared, the so-called Herz Bible, is out of print already. We feel that there is a need for a new translation of the Bible, including not only the Pentateuch but also the Prophets and the Writings, which will be made available to a wide readership at a relatively low price. The Bible Committee, in cooperation with scholars whose help we may count on, has already drawn up the appropriate plans, and their realization now depends solely on the acquisition of the necessary funds.

Last but not least, we must make certain that the work on the Hungarian-Jewish Archives is continued. We had regarded it completed with the publication of the fourth volume of the Archives. However, new material has come to light from hitherto unexplored collections. The published volume is expected to contain twelve to fourteen folio pages, and it is now up to the Society to make it available for scholarly preparation. We believe moreover that systematic research might reveal additional, as yet unknown sources.

These are, I believe, the long-range goals of the Hungarian-Jewish Literary Society. I must, however, not leave unmentioned two urgent projects that are closely related to the present. We are approaching two jubilees. The first is the semicentennial of the founding of our Society. It should have been celebrated in 1944, and we had made some plans to that effect. What we missed then—it was not on our account—has not lost its timeliness. The other is the 1948 Centennial. We, too, must participate in the celebration. I merely wanted to call attention to these tasks. The Literary and Lecture Committee will make the discussion of their implementation its first priority.

Honored Assembly: the remnant of the Hungarian-Jewish community has given ample evidence of its vigor and will to live by recovering at a rapid pace from its affliction, leading a full life, and adapting itself to the work of rebuilding our country. Within its domain it has succeeded in reactivating its synagogues, schools, and social institutions. The large number of cultural events and meetings of other sorts in the capital and in the countryside attest to the agility of the intellectual life of the Jewish community. The rebirth of our Society has rekindled the light on the top of an old watchtower in our cultural heritage. We hope that it will cast its light in an ever-widening circle, so that it might attract more and more of our coreligionists to the Society. We believe that the work of the Society that is about to commence will not be unworthy of the achievements of the past. In order that we may continue the work of our predecessors and succeed in accomplishing our new goals I call upon all of our members and the whole of Hungarian Jewry to support us in our endeavors.

Pál Kardos

Revisitation

Pál Kardos (1900–71) was a leading literary scholar. He was best known for his voluminous biographical studies of famous Hungarian writers and poets (Nagy Lajos élete és művei *[The life and works of Lajos Nagy]* 1958; Babits Mihály, 1972). *Kardos was also the author of a number of monographs and studies on Jewish subjects* (Adalékok a hajdúböszörményi zsidóság történetéhez *[Addenda to the history of Hajdúböszörmény Jewry]*, 1949; "Marxizmus és a zsidóság" *[Marxism and Jewry]*, in Évkönyv, 1948). *"Revisitation" is translated from* "Viszontlátás," *in* Évkönyv, *ed.* Sándor Scheiber *(Budapest: A Magyar Izraeliták Országos Képviselete, 1970), pp. 250–53. By permission of A Magyar Izraeliták Országos Képviselete.*

The morning had hardly broken on 15 May 1944 when I was already awake. I had to be up so that I could catch the early morning train for Hajdúnánás.[1] After all, I was carrying in my pocket a draft notice marked SAS [Sürgős, Azonnal Siess], "Urgent, Hurry Immediately" that instructed me to report on that day to the Royal Hungarian Military Recruiting Center for labor service. I tried to get dressed quietly so that I would not arouse from their restless, nervous sleep the families lying around me. Yes, families. For the apartment in which I spent my last night as a civilian used to belong to my parents, but did so no longer. For some days previously it had belonged to the ghetto, and was full of relatives and friends who had been forced to leave their apartments in other parts of the city. I was about to step through the door when my parents awakened after all. My father only stared silently, but my mother sat up in bed. Seeing my shaved head, the heavy knapsack on my shoulder, and the shapeless boots on my feet she cried out: "That I have to see you this way!" She would never see me again in any way. My wife, who had gotten up when I did, accompanied me to the small station at Hatvany Street. Leaning out of the window of the slowly departing train I could still catch a glimpse of her. She stood with her customary straight bearing, head held high, and a firm look about her. On her smart dress even the yellow star, which had been forced on us as a sign of shame, seemed to shine encouragingly. That is how I saw her for the last time. Since then I have not seen any of my family, including my son, my only child, who was still sound asleep when I left.

I had to wait for more than twenty years before I could see them again. This year, in 1964, it became possible for me to cross the border to Austria. The last time I had been there was in 1937; I had been vacationing with my family at a small spa in Lower Austria. It was in the direction of this beautiful place, where mountains and valleys, forests and meadows followed one another, that we were now driving. There were four of us. My second wife, who had returned me to life and sustained me in it after the terrible blow, also accompanied me on this trip. We were sitting in my nephew's car. He was a well-known physician in Szeged.[2] He too was searching for his loved ones and was accompanied by his wife.

When on the last morning of August we managed to extricate ourselves from the Viennese traffic and reached the huge and wide highway, we felt that we were in the midst of the whirlpool of a great international life. We were engulfed in a swarm of cars that bore the license plates of every country in the world. They were overtaking or yielding to one another, rumbling along at a high speed. The wide valleys, the distant mountain tops, and the nearby towers were bathed in the golden rays of the late summer sun. They would bounce off the ripples of streams and brooks and cast blinding sparks on the windshields of oncoming cars. So that's how the gold of foreign tourist traffic was flooding this pleasant little country, I mused.

Soon my nephew turned the steering wheel of the small Trabant[3] in a westerly direction. The engine groaned as we approached the mountain. We drove along winding roads, past foaming streams nestled among cliffs, and through ever-narrowing mountain passes. Our hearts started sinking as the scenery became more beautiful and picturesque. The words withered on our lips and we stole glimpses at each other. We were nearing our destination.

No, it was not the small village where I had spent that happy and beautiful summer. On one of the signposts we noticed an old, familiar name: Wiener-bruck. Our destination, however, took us in a different direction. We were driving toward Göstling, an even smaller village lying in the valley of the unpredictably winding Ybbs River. Göstling an der Ybbs! Yours became the name of hope, redemption, and salvation when in the summer of 1944 a postcard from the *Lager* in your outskirts, addressed to me, arrived in our labor camp in the plain of Bükkszállás near Zombor.[4] A postcard with the handwriting of my father, my son, and my wife! From concentration camp to labor camp, from inmates to inmate, but still from the living to the living.

Göstling an der Ybbs! You became for me the name of death, destruction, and despair when I learned from those who returned in the summer of 1945—later it was also confirmed by official records—that at dawn on 13 April 1945, a few hours before the arrival of Soviet troops, an SS unit massacred all inmates of the *Lager:* women, children, and the elderly.

I looked around. Nothing unusual. Perhaps under different circumstances I would even have said that it was heart-rendingly beautiful. How truly meaningful the oft-used phrase had become in that instance! The village was nestled in a narrow valley surrounded by pine-covered mountains. As we stepped out of the car the icily fresh, cool air engulfed us. An old stone church with a narrow door and a high steeple stood in the middle of the village. We noticed a couple of two-story houses, a *Gasthaus*, a beerhall, and the municipal building. Friendly frame houses with gable roofs. In front of them signs with the inviting message, Rooms for rent. It was a typical Alpine village, whose economy depended partly on its forest and meadow and partly on vacationers.

We, however, were looking for a cemetery. Though we soon found it, following a kindly worded direction, even minutes seemed painfully long. It was a tiny cemetery, hardly larger than a good-sized lot. Looking more like a garden, it was covered with the lush, blooming flowers of the late summer. The low-lying wooden graveposts and stone crosses were almost hidden amid the magnificent crowns of dahlias and chrysanthemums. Only a slender, black, clustered column stood out to the right. On it was the gilded hexagram of King David.

That was it.

Under the star were Hebrew letters and below them an inscription in German listing the names of the eighty Hungarian-Jewish martyrs whose earthly remains had been laid to rest there. Actually it was what remained of the remains, because, as I learned from contemporary records, the people had been locked in their barracks and burned alive. Were they really martyrs? No, only victims. Martyrs were always asked if they preferred to abandon their faith or to perish. In this instance there was no choice.

The names were listed on two sides of the column. My eyes slid down to the letter K. Dr. A. Kardos, that was my father; K. Kardos, that was Klári, my wife; and F. Kardos, that was Ferike, my son. My mother was not among them. She had been taken to the hospital in November 1944 and poisoned after being declared incurable. There were many familiar names inscribed on the other side of the column, as well; names of friends and relatives. My nephew, too, found the names of his mother and younger sister: C. Winter and S. Winter. Then there was G. Weisz, the name of his and my son's grandmother.

No, it was not supposed to hurt anymore. Twenty years had gone by. No, I could not allow vengeance to fill my heart; rather, I owed gratitude to the Jewish community of Vienna that had raised the memorial, the kind old woman who looked after the flowers on the grave, and the good-natured teacher who reminisced about the inmates of the camp. She said that relations with them were good, perhaps even friendly. I could have asked her a few more questions and my son's figure might have emerged from one of her answers. I could not, however, bring myself to ask those questions. My voice cracked.

What did I finally bring away from the cemetery in Göstling? Only what I had taken there. The conviction that we must fight: for a future that will know neither bloodshed nor race hatred. We must fight for the children of others. For peace.

Dezső Kellér

Inventory: From My Diary

For nearly a decade following the end of the Second World War, Dezső Kellér (b. 1910) was one of the most popular emcees in Budapest. The author of many humorous sketches, Kellér has written a number of books on his experiences in the world of laughter: Kis ország vagyunk *[We're a small country] (1964),* Pest az Pest *[Pest is Pest] (1967),* Kortársak és sorstársak *[Contemporaries and companions in distress] (1971), and* Leltár: Naplómból *[Inventory: from my diary] (1976). The following excerpts are translated from "Leltár: Naplómból," in* Évkönyv, *ed. Sándor Scheiber (Budapest: A Magyar Izraeliták Országos Képviselete, 1975/76), pp. 228–30. By permission of A Magyar Izraeliták Országos Képviselete.*

1

I got to know Miksa Wolff in the 1930s when, as one of the interested authors, I traveled to Szeged to attend the rehearsals of *Magic Ship*. I noticed that he always hung around the theater and was in thick with the actors. I naturally concluded that he was one of the gang. I didn't take him for an actor—his small English moustache seemed to confirm my diagnosis—but rather for a conductor, a manager, or something like that. Then I learned that he was a landowner who was crazy about the theater and would do anything to rub shoulders with actors. In those days a story involving him got around. Now that I'm taking inventory of things, that story begs to be released from my diary.

A new Catholic church was being built near Szeged, financed by public donations. Miksa Wolff contributed a respectable sum to help defray costs. Following the consecration ceremony, a delegation visited the landowner and its leader thanked him, in the name of the congregation, for his generosity.

"And we owe special thanks," the leader of the delegation said in conclusion, "in that Your Excellency, despite being a Calvinist, has been so helpful in the building of a Catholic church."

"I beg your pardon," said Miksa Wolff smiling, in an attempt to correct the misunderstanding, "I'm a Jew, not a Calvinist."

"We know that," nodded the leader, "but we didn't want to offend you by coming right out with it."

2

Dezső Sebestyén, nicknamed Dódi, was an inexhaustible anecdotist and the owner of a thousand phonograph records. He told me the following story many times.

In 1942 he was drafted into the labor service. He was instructed to present himself at an army post at seven in the morning. Though he arrived a half-hour early, there was already a long line of people waiting. He stopped at the edge of the sidewalk and started looking the people over in the hope of seeing somebody he knew. He had hardly reached the middle of the line when suddenly a sergeant appeared at his side.

"What are you doing here with your mouth open, damn you?" he shouted. "Why aren't you standing in line?"

Then followed a kick with the tip of a boot that was so hard that our friend knocked over six other men as he fell.

"Believe it or not," Sebestyén concluded, "in that moment I lost all interest in labor service camps."

3

If I ever get out of this alive . . . In July 1944 the 103rd Railroading Labor Service Company was assigned to repairing the tracks in the vicinity of Mátészalka.[1] Despite little knowhow and experience, I too took part in these operations. I swore a sacred oath that if I ever got out of this alive I would, after the end of the war, immediately make a public statement requesting that nobody travel on the section where I had ballasted the tracks. It never actually came to that, because the tracks received a direct hit during an air attack and were repaired by expert hands afterward.

If I ever get out of this alive . . . the expression became a constant refrain whenever our thoughts wandered into the uncertain future. Everybody colored his illusions to suit his fancy. Pipe dreams of all sorts, ranging from potato noodles to trips around the world, ascended from the depths of our souls. The sincerest person who revealed himself to me was a fellow inmate named Wagner. In civilian life he had been a goldsmith. Perhaps he only wanted me to know what a modest and good-hearted man he really was, when, in an emotion-filled moment, he pulled his wife's photograph out of his wallet and held it up for me to see.

"Believe me, I don't care about anything . . . if only I and my wife would stay alive."

I could almost picture the Wagners as they sat at the bottom of a crater surrounded by a barren, dreary wilderness that was devoid of living things. Mr. and Mrs. Wagner! How happily they would live ever after!

Sándor Schwartz

I Was a Forward on the
Soccer Team of Auschwitz

The source of the following selection is an anthology that was prepared under the supervision of the Committee of the Persecutees of Nazism and published in 1975 in commemoration of the thirtieth anniversary of the Soviet troops' liberation of Hungary from Nazi and Arrow Cross control. The articles, short stories, and poems were written by both prominent and less well-known Hungarians, Jewish and non-Jewish, and are based on experiences in Hungary as well as in the most infamous concentration and extermination camps in Germany and Poland from the time of the German occupation (19 March 1944) through the bloody aftermath of the Arrow Cross coup (15 October 1944). Reminiscences of the martyrs of Hungarian culture and sports, and excerpts of descriptions of the trials and executions of war criminals round off this important work. The brief narrative of an otherwise unknown survivor, Sándor Schwartz, sheds light on a sordid spectacle of extermination-camp life that is no less shocking than the better-known inmates' orchestras, choirs, or theatrical groups. Schwartz's account is translated from "Csatár voltam az auschwitzi futballcsapatban" in Mementó: Magyarország, 1944 *[Memento: Hungary, 1944] (Budapest: Kossuth, 1975), pp. 150–52. By permission of A Magyar Izraeliták Országos Képviselete.*

On 29 June 1944, a hot summer day, we were driven from the brick factory in Debrecen[1] to the train. I was the eighty-fifth to enter a freight car. A Hungarian gendarme and an SS soldier bolted the sliding door, and I wound up by a window with iron bars across it. The train rumbled for three days. On the first of July we reached Auschwitz.

It was dawn. Even from behind the iron bars of the window I could see the barracks. SS soldiers ripped open the doors and motioned to the ghosts in striped clothing. The old inmates rushed into our freight car, pushed everyone out, and tore the packages out of our hands. Then we were led before an elegantly dressed SS officer. Only later did we learn that he was Dr. Mengele.[2] My head was shaved and the hair was removed from my entire body. The petroleum bath came next.

Later two SS officers stepped into the room. "Is there by any chance a professional soccer player among you?" asked one of them. Five of us put up our hands. I had never been a professional soccer player, but I used to play in the county league. I had confidence in myself. The SS officer pawed me; he made me feel like a horse. A blond, thin-haired Polish *Kapo* and a young Hungarian stood beside him.[3] The Hungarian, I learned later in the day, had come from Balmazújváros.[4] His name was Rezső Steinberger. (He is now the director of the Milan Football Club.) "We'll soon see if you know how to play soccer," said the SS officer, and motioned us behind the barracks. A ball was brought out and we had to play. First, two of my companions were tried out. They were kicking the ball quite awkwardly; their dribbling was no better. I could see from the faces of the SS officers that my two companions had not undergone the test well.

Then it was my turn. Though my wooden shoes bothered me, I tried to move briskly. First I had to head the ball back to them and then trap it. It went well. I was assigned to the Birkenau team. Its only other Jewish player was a certain Weigner from Kispest.[5] The remaining nine members of the team were from the gypsies' barracks.

All this happened on a Saturday. Our first match was on the following Sunday. We had been warned sternly that the team had to win. I remained alone with Steinberger, who cautioned me against getting injured. Anyone who was hurt would wind up in the gas chamber, he said. In the morning we were taken to a barracks, where we put on uniforms. It was there that I got to know Weigner and the gypsies. They gave us jerseys made of black silk. The playing field was covered with wild grass. It was behind the gas chambers and the crematorium. I was made right fullback; the goalie and the midfielders were gypsies.

Smoke kept coming out of the chimney of the crematorium throughout the entire match. They were burning my friends from Debrecen. I could not help thinking that if I was injured they would simply throw me off the field straight into the crematorium. In the second minute a high ball flew toward me and I managed to volley it forward, avoiding an onrushing winger. The SS officer applauded. I had made an auspicious start. In the tenth minute we got a goal. I felt that we were playing for our lives. We managed to score the equalizer in the forty-fourth minute. During half time we were given lemons, and the SS officer demanded victory. In the eighteenth minute of the second half I broke loose, but was tripped. We were given a free kick. I drove the ball into our opponents' goal from eighteen meters out. We embraced one another. The SS officer jumped into the air joyously. Two minutes later a penalty kick was awarded against us. It was converted. The score was 2–2.

Nothing went right for our forwards. Suddenly I noticed that the SS officer had pulled his revolver out of the holster and was pointing it toward us, indicating that he would shoot us if we did not win. Our right winger must have also caught a glimpse of the revolver because he redoubled his efforts. He dribbled by two defenders to score the winning goal. Our lives were spared. We received a premium: a huge pot of potato soup.

The soccer team was quartered in a separate barracks. I became a protected person. We were not made to work on account of the daily training sessions. The black jersey was protection against everything. New groups were led by the training camp on their way to be gassed. By the time the training session was over, there was nothing left of them but smoke.

It was a regular training session, with running and ball-handling exercises. We played our second match on Thursday. We did not know in advance who our opponents would be. None of them was Hungarian; all of them were prisoners, however. They must have been there longer than we because they were thinner. Our side won 5–1. We were already leading 4 to nil when pandemonium broke loose. We had scored the last goal from a penalty kick, and the three SS officers who had accompanied our opponents were drunk. They ran into the field and started pushing the referee, kicking him. When he began to bleed they chased him off the field. One of the linesmen was made referee. I could see that he was trembling as he stepped on the field. We won the match by a score of 5–1. After that we even got meat. We played one more match and won that too.

Following the fourth match all of us were ordered confined to our barracks. It was forbidden to step outside. The rumor spread that there would be executions. They liquidated the gypsies' barracks; all of the gypsy players wound up in the crematorium. With that our team was dissolved, and I became a factory worker.

In a few months we had to play again. By then, however, I was twenty pounds lighter. I was selected for an international team. The team we were to play was made up of well-fed Germans who had been assigned to various positions in the concentration camp. The team of the "skinnies" was playing the team of the "fatties."

I played center forward but I could hardly run. I was merely dawdling on the field. I knew that we were not allowed to win, so I would have kicked the ball past the goalpost from even the most advantageous position to keep that SS sergeant, who stood by the goal and threw temper tantrums whenever his team was under pressure, from starting trouble with me.

I spent more time lying on the field than standing. We were beaten by a score of 8 to nil. The officers of the concentration camp celebrated their victory.

That was my last match. I kept working and living in constant fear of the gas chamber. At the end of January 1945 the victorious Soviet army reached the camp. I was saved.

László Gerend
Expelled from Our Town

Contributions like the following are characteristic of the commendable effort that has made the Hungarian-Jewish Évkönyv *an indispensable source for the study of the Holocaust and a permanent literary memorial to it. Operating under the assumption that every survivor willing to relive, record, and share painful experiences is an important source of information, Sándor Scheiber, editor of the* Évkönyv, *has been instrumental in preserving accounts of experiences that otherwise would have gone unnoticed or remained familial, oral history. László Gerend (b. 1900) was trained as a physician and conditioned to treat human tragedy with dispassionate efficiency. The account of his experiences, however, is filled with bitter emotions as he describes the mechanical uniformity of deportation procedures and the predictability of fate. In addition to the startling details of personal tribulations, Gerend provides a fine psychological study of zealously cultivated communal faith in the success of assimilation, an illusion that, in the final analysis, was the real tragedy of Hungary's Jewry. "Expelled from Our Town" is translated from "Kiűzettünk városunkból," in* Évkönyv, *ed. Sándor Scheiber (Budapest: A Magyar Izraeliták Országos Képviselete, 1977–78), pp. 159–82. By permission of A Magyar Izraeliták Országos Képviselete.*

At dawn the gendarmes kicked in the door. "Get out, Jews!" they kept shouting. "Get out!" They attacked the ghetto, rousing the wearers of the yellow star from their dark sleep. We had known since the night before that our life in the ghetto would come to an end. The next stop in our journey to the netherworld was the brick factory.

I jumped out of bed. It was getting light. I washed myself a little and dressed hurriedly. My wife and daughter were getting dressed, too. We ate hastily and ran to the courtyard, leaving behind everything we had. Between my wife and me stood our daughter, clutching my hand, the hand of her strong father. The young child seemed to be firmly convinced that her father, big and powerful, would protect her against all dangers. But the vultures were already circling over our heads, depriving the fathers of their magical power. There we stood, feeble and paralyzed, surrendering ourselves and our families to their beaks and claws.

On 19 March 1944 Hitler had ordered his armies to occupy Hungary. Suddenly stormy clouds covered the already menacing sky of the Jews. Our hearts were filled with foreboding. Following the end of the First World War, the Peace Treaty of Trianon awarded Ruthenia and Upper Northern Hungary to the newly established Czechoslovak Republic. In 1938 Ruthenia was returned to the mother country, whose anti-Jewish laws were extended over Ruthenia as well. The revocation of handicraft licenses and the suspension of civil rights had only a slight effect on our town, Munkács.[1] According to the census taken during the Czechoslovakian occupation, the majority of the Jews of Munkács declared themselves to be Hungarian. Indeed, it was on the recommendation of Aladár Vozáry, the commissioner and member of Parliament for our town, that after 1938 the government cited us for our patriotism. The German occupation put an end to our relatively tranquil life. In a matter of weeks the Nazi laws destroyed the work of hundreds of years. We knew that we faced a deadly enemy and feared for our families. Hitler, the Führer of the Nazi Reich, wanted in his hatred to annihilate all Jews. Everyone knew that.

The local authorities hastily enforced the anti-Jewish laws of the Nazis. In the early days of April an order was issued: we were to sew the yellow star on our garments so that we could be identified on sight. Those on whom the yellow stigma of hatred was pinned ceased to be human beings. The law painted all Jews yellow and cast them out of society, though their roots had been firmly planted in the soil of their country for centuries and they had contributed with hard work to the building of their nation. The poison of hatred, however, withered away those thick roots in a matter of days. The powerful oaks fell to the ground. Then the rootless trees were stacked in wagons, separating valuable timber from firewood. The second order, issued at the end of April, expelled us from our homes. We were moved into a closed ghetto. We had lost our homes, jobs, and valuables. Everything. Waiting eagerly for us to leave, the hungry predators quickly looted our abandoned homes. We were moved into No. 2 Rákóczi Street, an apartment building that was part of the ghetto. It belonged to Sajovics, the owner of the brick factory. Each family was assigned a room, and all of us shared the kitchen and the bathroom.

The third order, issued on May 15, forced us even out of the ghetto. We were told to go to the courtyard. We owned only the ground on which we were standing. Gendarmes with fixed bayonets lined us up in rows. The mark of our destiny, the yellow star, was proof that no stranger had mingled with us. The silence was deathly; the children instinctively kept their mouths tightly shut. The star-marked herd stood ready for the road. A soldier kept straightening the lines with the butt of his rifle. No one cried out. Everyone knew the unspoken order: "Bear up and obey! Do not incite those in authority against yourself. They are only too eager to exercise their power and show their superiority over the oppressed." There were indeed many rookie policemen who ran about eagerly, hoping to prove themselves before their officers.

I stood at the end of the line, clutching my briefcase. It contained my carefully arranged papers, the documents of a citizen. Documents verifying my identity, occupation, place and time of birth, and family—when and where my father and mother were born. We had left behind everything we possessed, but without documents a person was not a human being. I kept clutching the briefcase with its precious contents, the proofs of my being. I trembled when a gendarme shouted at me, "Throw that briefcase away! You cannot take anything along!" My fingers loosened their grip without hesitation, and my briefcase, filled with the terribly precious documents, fell to the ground. An ominous inner voice whispered. "Don't feel sorry for it. You won't need it." The state reclaimed the documents that I had gathered in a lifetime, acting through a gendarme to deprive me of my civil rights. The yellow star remained my only document, testifying to my guilt among the guilty. The state had ceased to protect me; the protection of aliens was not its duty. Suddenly my heart was filled with painful helplessness. I could not protect those who looked to me for protection either! Though I had no documents to prove the identity of those who belonged to my family, I could still grasp my daughter's warm hand. Her grip tightened as if she were saying, "Don't let go of my hand, Daddy. Hold it tight; I won't be scared."

"Start marching," came the order. The homeless people of the ghetto houses walked across the gardens and through the rear exit to Dankó Street. It was also one of the streets of the ghetto. Its dwellers were devoutly religious Jews. They, too, had been ordered to leave their homes. Men with their heads bowed, women and children, infants in their mothers' embrace, the elderly and the sick—a people branded. The houses of the ghetto stood empty. It was in the early morning hours that we, the expelled offspring of many generations of forefathers, slowly set out in the direction of Munkács. We walked along Beregszászi Street on the way to the brick factory, our new home. We were paying for our grave sins. We were Jews, God's chosen people. Chosen for humanity, progress, and suffering.

Except for the marchers and their armed escorts, the street was empty. Yet behind the dark, closed windows, curious eyes were watching. What could have flashed through their minds as they discovered, one by one, childhood playmates, schoolmates, friends, doctors, lawyers, storekeepers, tradesmen, good neighbors, and former comrades-at-arms? As long as the laws did not distinguish between Jews and Christians, and as long as the hate-mongering agitators, who had come for that purpose, did not start intriguing, the population of the town, people of varied religious and national origins, lived peacefully and respected one another. Nearly half of the thirty thousand people were Jewish. The Nazi hatred struck like lightning, burning the ties of friendship. The ragged army of the expelled moved slowly under a relentless barrage of blows administered by policemen who had been brought there. Wielding clubs, they kept urging the tired group to quicken the pace. At last we reached the Sajovics Brick Factory, located at the end of the street, near the train station. The owner of the factory and his family were also among us.

The sentry met us at the gate, and we marched into the sprawling factory. It would be the temporary home for thousands of people. With its barren, muddy grounds, the factory held out little encouragement for us. Our new quarters were the dark tunnels of the kiln, a covered desiccator, boarded warehouses, and sheds without walls, the tops of which were supported by beams. My entire family was there: my wife, daughter, mother, two older brothers with their wives, my mother-in-law, and my wife's sister. We made our home in one of the airless, winding tunnels of the kiln. The women made up the beds. The space allocated to our family provided each of us with a sleeping area seventy centimeters wide. The mattresses were stuffed with a mixture of straw, hay, and tree leaves. Blankets came from the homes of those who had already been deported.

We kept sinking deeper and deeper, from the ghetto apartment, equipped with every modern convenience, to the dreary brick factory. Our supplies were provided by the Jewish Council, which still operated in the town. It was through the Council that the Nazi headquarters communicated its orders to us. We had to turn in not only money and jewelry but also porcelain dishes and silverware. In the brick factory the inmates were fed quite well. Cooks prepared our food in huge kettles on a caboose, and a baker in town supplied the bread. We ate from mess tins; our only utensil was a spoon. The most degrading place in the brick factory was the latrine. Yet at least one basic rule of civility was retained: the men's section was separated from the women's. The latrine was an enclosed, stinking pit with a single board serving as the seat. It was a mockery and an abuse of humanity. Perhaps we were no longer human beings except in basic necessities, for the merciless order of nature made no exceptions: all of us went to the latrine. When it rained, the path leading to it became miserably slippery and muddy. Yet no one complained. Man is strong: he can endure many things.

The first day had passed. At bedtime I noted that instead of the boots that I had placed by my bed for such eventuality, I had put on my regular shoes in the confusion of our departure from the ghetto. They were light walking shoes, unsuitable for long marches. Well, it was too late to do anything about them. The boots—not to mention the other things we left behind—would make someone happy. I lay on my bed, dazed. My wife and my daughter were next to me. I kept thinking, did man, culture, civilization amount to so little that they could be swept away by the wind? Did the hand that struck with the stamp of punishment brand us forever? The history of our people, filled with suffering, pain, and blood, was merely something to read on the pages of the past. What we were going through would be history in the future. My thoughts were disorganized; it was all very confusing.

I spun the reel of my life with dreamlike speed. Images kept popping out of the past. I started humming the little song that we used to sing to the accompaniment of our teacher, Mr. Tulcsik, who played the violin. I was then a first grader in the Fő Street Elementary School. In those days elementary schools were called grade schools. In the first and second grades, classes lasted from eight to ten in the morning and from two to four in the afternoon. In the winter it was already growing dark a little after three. It was usually at that time that Mr. Tulcsik, our teacher, took the violin out of its case, placed it under his chin, and gave us a nod, indicating that he was ready to provide the musical accompaniment to the song we were about to sing in our thin voices:

It's already evening, late evening,
Only the shepherd's fire flickers, oh, but far away.

Far away, far away,
On the plains of the Alföld.

The village is quiet,
Not even a bat is in flight.

It's already evening, late evening,
Only the shepherd's fire flickers, oh, but far away.

Crouched on the small school bench and looking around in anguish, I noticed the shepherd's fire in the darkness of the classroom. My six-year-old heart was filled with terror as I kept staring at the distant shepherd's fire that flickered in the mysterious night. In the deep silence not even a bat was in flight. I kept repeating, in the dark desiccator, "It's already evening, late evening, only the shepherd's fire flickers, oh, but far away."

On occasions, the teacher's daughter, Piroska, substituted for him. I was very fond of her. She was kind and light-hearted. She often took me to their ivy-covered house, where there were always cookies waiting for me. I was a young, rosy-cheeked boy then, and Aunt Piroska talked to me as lovingly as if I were her child.

In the winter we used to have big fights, throwing snowballs at one another, on the wide street in front of the school. There were no automobiles in our town then; not even wagons interrupted our fierce battles. Afterward I would go home with my cheeks flushed, and could hardly wait to sink my teeth into a big slice of soft, homemade bread on which either chicken fat, butter, or plum lekvar had been spread. My grandmother used to make lekvar from pitted Beszterce plums in the vineyard under the open sky. Early in the fall we picked the soft, ripe, sweet blue plums and pitted them. Then we dumped them in a large brass kettle that we carried, hanging from a rod, on our shoulders. We set fire to a bunch of dry vine shoots under the kettle. The scented, crackling flames would slowly melt the plums into heavy syrup. It took constant stirring, from morning to evening, to make lekvar. It was long after it had got dark and the embers of the vine shoots had turned to ashes that dull, puffing steam bubbles started breaking through the hardened crust of the lekvar. Finally the thick black lekvar was scooped into pretty, painted earthenware pots, covered with pieces of homespun linen, and stored in the cool pantry. Not a single pot ever got mouldy.

It was May. Almond, apricot, plum, and cherry blossoms had already withered, but the apple and pear trees were still in full bloom. Their white and pink crowns were waiting to be pollinated so that their fruits would start ripening. Perhaps my little daughter was dreaming of a life filled with beauty and happiness. She was breathing softly as she lay next to me in the hay. Annika was thirteen. May was the most beautiful month of the spring, the early spring of her budding life. The mind of a child could not comprehend the cruel force that had grabbed her from the clean bed and cast her into the brick factory. She seemed to sense that something terrifying was happening around her. Her tightly shut lips and fluttering eyes betrayed her fear. My child was scared and suffering. What could I do? What could I say? Words would not change the cruel reality, the brick-dust covered clay ground of hell, the brick factory, and the latrine. At bedtime she snuggled up to me. I stroked her silky brown hair and took her protectively into my arms. "It's already evening. Late evening."

The blooming trees had disappeared by the time we woke up in the morning. At one time—oh, how long ago that was!—I used to lie on my back, watching the clouds swim by in the blue of the sky. The white clouds spread tranquility and joyous peace. I was filled with the many beautiful things nature provided. Now I lay the same way, on my back, in the brick factory that was our prison. In flophouses, destitute but free men lie by choice in the dreary environment. Fate, however, had pounded us into this stable. We were worth even less than the vagrants in a flophouse. We were destitute, but without a will of our own. What next?

The Jews of the countryside had already been deported somewhere. To the Hortobágy,[2] some people said. It was a vast expanse, big enough to accommodate all the Jews in the country. Only for the duration of the war perhaps? Apparently the Nazis had ordered it. What would we do in the Hortobágy? Work, some people said. Work what? Nobody knew. The important thing was that we were still good for work. Then they obviously needed us—needed our work, rather. In agriculture or military production? We could hold our own in both. We had always been hard-working citizens, honest people, and good taxpayers. We had lived for our families. We had to daydream and to praise ourselves; we were frightened and wanted to believe in the future even if it sounded like a fairy tale. We had to believe in and hope for something. We could not just lie indifferently on our cots like dumb animals that did not sense their doom until they were already in the slaughterhouse.

Perhaps the Hortobágy camp did not even exist, and the authorities merely spread false news about it in order to calm the people. Yet that news traveled fast, instilling hope and tranquility in grim-looking fathers and anguished mothers. We clutched at every straw in our desperate hope for a good future for our children. We wanted to believe that our children, who could not have sinned yet, would be spared. We were prepared to withstand humiliation of all sorts and to do the most debasing work so that the lives of our children would be spared. That is why we, fathers and mothers, put our heads together, trying to determine what to do. Even the skeptics were willing to give credence to the news. Perhaps it was true after all? It might not even be all that bad in the Hortobágy. I kept quiet, and did not reveal what I had learned about the deportation of the Jews from the countryside.

We had known about it even before we were taken from our homes. Then it was rumored that only Jews living in rural areas would be deported. By early May they had indeed been taken to the brick factory by train or wagon. On the instructions of the Jewish Council, Jewish doctors were on duty in case the inmates needed medical aid. I too volunteered for duty. We took turns visiting the brick factory. The sentry stopped us at the gate, and we showed them our identification papers. In the office it was recorded that we had come with permission; we had to present ourselves again on the way out. One of the offices became a makeshift convalescent room. The embarkation of the rural Jews soon began. On one occasion I made a routine inspection of the long line of railroad cars. Those who were left behind temporarily were taking tearful leave of their relatives and friends. As I walked along the railroad cars I kept inquiring of those inside if they needed anything. I followed the winding tracks and reached the engine at last. I struck up a conversation with the conductor and asked him where he was taking the train. "Only as far as the Slovakian border," he replied. "We'll hand it over to the Germans there." That is how I discovered the mysterious destination of the train. I recalled that in 1942 I had heard someone mention a certain Auschwitz where the Germans were rounding up Jews. That was all he knew. The name stuck in my mind; it had a threatening ring to it. We had heard of the fate of the Polish and Slovakian Jews as well as those from other countries. All that, however, happened far from us and we did not want to think about it. We tried instead to dispel the depressing thoughts. "Such things could never happen to us," we used to say.

I took leave of the conductor and started walking back. As I left the turn I could see the whole train. Much to my surprise, the people had disappeared from the platform. I had a bad feeling as I walked on. Suddenly I noticed a group of officers standing at a distance of about fifteen meters. Someone in a freight car called out for water. I replied that I would bring some. "What are you yapping for, there?" one of the officers yelled at me. I walked to him hurriedly. Though my armband, bearing the Red Cross, was self-explanatory, I identified myself as a doctor and reported that someone had asked for water. "Let them hang themselves!" shouted one of the officers, slapping his boot with a riding stick. It was only then that I recognized him. He was Márton Zöldi, the infamous gendarmerie captain. "Beat it! Now!" he yelled at me. He did not have to say it twice. I hurried away to get out of the sight of that awful man. I remembered that when we were still at home we heard that Zöldi had gone in person with a group of gendarmes to Commissioner Vozáry's home and had his Jewish mother-in-law, Mme Albert Gergely, dragged away. Only Jews with Christian spouses were exempted. In 1945, what Zöldi had wished for those in the freight car came true—for him. As a war criminal, he was sentenced to death by a Yugoslav court and hanged.

Having completed my rounds I returned to my home. I did not want to create panic, so I did not tell even my wife what I had heard from the train conductor. I thought of leaving town, but I let myself to be calmed by the rumor—I learned later that it had been spread intentionally to mislead us—that only the rural Jews would be deported. We believed everything we wanted to believe. Every piece of good news was received with jubilation. We heard of those who had gone to Budapest with false papers. Though security was tight on both trains and stations, some Jews managed to evade detection. It was easy to melt anonymously into the teeming crowds of the capital. It was possible to disappear from the town, but not from the brick factory. Schlüssel, the furrier, hid out with his family in the basement of their house. A devoted employee provided their daily food. They managed to live through the occupation that way. László Jávor, the owner of the bookstore, found refuge in the attic of his housekeeper's home. Mihály Steinbach, a young merchant, survived the Nazi terror with the help of a Christian friend.

After the deportation of the rural Jews, those from the town took their place. Our fate would be played out on a train too. Escape, however, did not seem impossible. I thought about it constantly. Each day, large covered trucks carried bread to the inmates of the brick factory. The owner of the bakery was a good friend and unhesitatingly agreed, at my request, to smuggle me, my wife, and my daughter out of the brick factory. We would be picked up at an inconspicuous place and driven out of our cage, hiding under a canvas. We would get hold of false papers and travel to Budapest. The plan sounded practicable. While discussing it I told my wife what I had heard from the train conductor. The Hortobágy camp was a lie. The train passed through Slovakia, and then where? Should only the three of us try to escape? What about the rest of the family? The baker would take only three people on his truck. We deliberated, racking our brains, but could not go through with the plan. I decided to go directly to First Lieutenant Kiss, the commandant of the camp, and ask him what the authorities held in store for us. Our decision to escape would depend on his answer. I had known him since my physician-on-duty days and thought of him as a well-meaning fellow. One day he drove me to my office in town so that I could extract his orderly's aching tooth. The huge policeman slowly lowered himself into the dentist's chair. "You'll make sure that it doesn't hurt, won't you?" he said ominously as his hand slid toward his revolver. I understood him only too well. I would pay with my life if I caused him pain. Such a gentle, sensitive executioner! He could not even stand pain. I thought of a wise saying, according to which everybody possesses sufficient willpower to bear another person's pain.

I visited the commandant in his office. He greeted me in a friendly manner. I started out by saying that some disquieting rumors about our fate had gotten around. People talked of Hortobágy, but I knew that there was no truth to it. I had found out, I went on, that the trains were directed eastward, toward the Slovakian border. I implored him to tell me what our fate would be, where they would take us. I feared for my family; I feared very much.

We would indeed not be taken to the Hortobágy, he replied, but to a place where our work was needed. The young people would work and their labor would exempt the elderly. I believed that he was telling me the truth. He wanted to give me hope, not to mislead me. We had no cause for fear. No one's life was in danger. The Hungarians had concluded a pact with the Germans and we would substitute for the workers who had gone to war. I thanked him for his seemingly believable explanation. I was calm and filled with hope as I told my wife of my conversation with the officer. We would not have to escape from the camp and leave the elderly behind. Who would work in their place if we left? My four young brothers-in-law were in labor service companies. There were no young men in the brick factory. Instead of doing military service they had been taken to labor service camps. Most of them perished during the war, the victims of disease and brutality.

We would stay, my wife and I decided. We felt good knowing that we had done the right thing. As the head of the family, I was the one who had to work. My work would protect my family. We would stay together, sharing our fate in common. There was happiness in our voices as we told the rest of the family what the lieutenant had said. They were listening to the good news with expressions of joy on their faces. My two brothers were still in good shape. They were strong, able-bodied men who would give a good account of themselves, exempting their wives from work. They had no children.

My mother vowed that she would work too. She would show them how to cook really tasty meals. Her strudels had no equal; she could roll the dough so thin that it looked like an exquisite veil as it lay on the tablecloth. Few people could duplicate that, she would boast. Of course, she added, a person had to use good Hungarian flour, otherwise the dough would tear easily. The poor creature brightened, just thinking that she might again be of use to us. She had worked all her life and brought up seven children. She had a knack for dividing the money my father made as a civil servant so that there would be enough for every day of the month. She had been widowed after being married for fifty years, and lived with her children. Aside from my father's death, the other great tragedy in her life was the loss of one of her children. After graduating from medical school, my brother Ferenc started his internship in Prague. In 1938 the Nazis occupied Czechoslovakia. In 1942 Czech patriots killed Heydrich, the Gauleiter of Czechoslovakia.[3] The Nazis went on a rampage and arrested many people. My brother was taken away from his apartment. We learned of his fate only after the mailman delivered a letter bearing the swastika to my mother. The Nazi headquarters in Prague had ordered my mother to provide information without delay as to the whereabouts of her late son's valuables.

My mother did not cry. She only stared at the letter with dry, impassive eyes. As if she did not comprehend what she had been told; as if she presumed that no one born of a mother could be so evil as to inform her of the death of her beloved little Feri in such manner. It would be her fate to survive the Nazi madness and learn that it had destroyed three more of her sons. In the brick factory she still had the will to live, at least for the sake of her children.

Conditions in the brick factory started deteriorating rapidly. It was not long before the news came that we would be transported to our new place of work. After the usual rumors and excited guessing we learned of our future from a reliable source. That night we slept peacefully on our makeshift beds. In the morning we were in high spirits. We washed in bowls; we had managed to bring warm water for the women to their washroom, a section separated from the sleeping area by an outstretched blanket. Then breakfast: tea, coffee with milk, bread, and butter. The Jewish Council had provided us with food in sufficient quantity.

The first group was scheduled to leave on May 19. The air was filled with tension. Many inmates had volunteered for the ride to Hortobágy in the hope of getting out of the brick factory as soon as possible. We had been ordered to select from among us clerks who would make an accurate and detailed list of the deportees. Everyone was ordered to give his name, time and place of birth, and occupation. It looked as if they were really taking us to work. Why else would they have to have all that information? There was even a little shoving to get in line. The first transport consisted of about fifteen hundred people. Embarkation started early in the morning.

Suddenly First Lieutenant Kiss called out to Dr. P.Z. and his wife. Under the Czechoslovakian occupation, Dr. P.Z. had been the president of the Sport Club of Munkács, but took an active part in the Hungarian Sport Club as well. "On your knees!" the lieutenant shouted. Dr. P.Z. and his wife sank to their knees side by side. "You call yourselves Hungarians, you dirty Jews?" he roared, and motioned to a huge, bearded policeman—the one who was so afraid of pain—who started slapping their faces. "Harder!" the bespectacled officer commanded his man. His glasses glittered in the sunshine as the policeman's blows fell with even greater force. "You call yourselves Hungarians, you dirty Jews?" the officer kept asking, as if possessed. The two kneeling on the ground bore up under the heavy beating with heads held high and without shedding a single tear. They neither moaned nor pleaded for mercy. That is how they displayed their superiority over their torturers, whose enjoyment they would only have increased by crying. We respected them greatly for their heroic behavior. The Sport Club had been founded by those who loved sport. None of its members was asked about his religion. That question had never come up. We knew one another and everyone was respected according to his performance.

Though a Jew, Dr. P.Z. had been the leader of the Hungarian Sport Club in Czechoslovakia. That was the sin for which he had to atone. Following the punishment both he and his wife were thrown into a freight car. Dr. P.Z. was assigned to the *Sonderkommando* of the Auschwitz-Birkenau concentration camp. Such an assignment was tantamount to a death sentence. The members of the *Sonderkommando* were on duty at the crematorium. It was they who placed into the crematorium the bodies of those who had been killed in the gas chamber. Before that, however, they were instructed to knock the gold caps off the victims' teeth and remove their jewelry and rings. It often happened that they had to place the body of a close relative or a friend into the crematorium. The length of their service was unpredictable, though it rarely lasted longer than three months. The members of the *Sonderkommando* were usually executed so that no witnesses to the obscene spectacle would live to tell about it.

Those who were left out of the first transport were quieter than usual. They waited with mounting impatience to get on the next train, away from the prison of the brick factory, away from filth and shame. They had no idea what they were facing, yet they wanted to get away from the brick factory. Perhaps it was true what was said about the Hortobágy, after all.

I must also relate the torture of László Gerő, the former owner of the Gold Star Hotel and Café in Munkács. I want to put it down on paper, so that every detail of this evil act will be a matter of record. My popular young friend with the pleasant smile was taken into the guardroom for questioning. His interrogators wanted to know where he had hidden his money and jewelry, or to whom he had given them. They interrogated him for hours. Then he was placed on a stretcher and carried to the doctor's room. I was allowed to visit him. He lay on the stretcher in silence, his face puffy, his eyes bloodshot. He had been severely beaten; no portion of his body, not even one the size of a hand, remained untouched. His torturers had worked him over most efficiently. "They beat me," he moaned, "they beat me hard. They were after my money." He could not swallow even a drop of tea. I gave him a morphine injection; he fell asleep peacefully. When the train was ready to leave he was placed in a freight car. He went to Auschwitz on a stretcher.

The brick factory was evacuated gradually. Even those Jews who had been granted certificates of exemption were put aboard. For a while, Jewish veterans of the First World War who had been decorated with gold medals were accorded preferential treatment.[4] They did not have to leave their homes and were spared the humiliation of the ghetto and the brick factory. The exempted Jews would never be deported. Heroism would receive its just reward. Hateful men, however, tore the gold medals off their bearers' chests. They were dragged directly from their homes to the trains. Only the head of the Jewish Council and his family received special passes from the Nazi headquarters and were allowed to leave town.

By May 24 the brick factory stood empty. We boarded the train by climbing up a ladder. There were only a few of us in the freight car, so there was plenty of room to lie down. There were eleven of us on one side, about the same number of our friends on the other. Our supplies consisted of bread, butter, salami, and a large jug of water. A bucket had been provided for our bodily needs. By comparison, the latrine was more comfortable. If we had been reticent before, we were tongue-tied now as we took our places on the floor of the freight car. At dusk the sliding door was shut. We listened anxiously for any sound on the outside. We grew impatient while waiting for the train to start moving. Our destination had to be better than the prisonlike freight car. Suddenly a shot rang out, a single shot. Our hearts beat in our throats, and there was a deathly silence. Then voices chanting *El mole rachamim*, the Hebrew song of mourning, were heard in a nearby freight car. Someone had shot at the train. The bullet passed through the wooden wall of the freight car and killed Mme Gellér, née Irma Schulz, a former teacher at the Jewish high school. "O merciful God," the doleful voices kept chanting. The assailant felt no compassion toward the deportees; since the freight cars carried a multitude of people, he did not even have to aim. The bullet killed the young teacher. It was the coup de grâce of our lives until then. The train started moving amid the cries of mourning. It must have looked like a funeral cortège as it slowly rolled into the next station. I could see the sign from the tiny window of the freight car. We were in Munkács. The train was shunted to a siding for a while, but then it picked up speed, taking us away from the town where we were born, had played, and had worked. Only the graves of our fathers remained as reminders that Jews too had once lived in that town.

I loved my town, where I had a happy childhood. The long, straight Sugár Street ran from the train station to the center of the town. On both sides of the street long lines of lindens and sycamore trees accompanied the visitor who got in the one-horse hackney coach that was parked in front of the station. The driver holding the reins was a Jew. He did not drive on Saturday. In compliance with a commandment of his religion, he rested on the seventh day. He would hire a young man if it was his turn to be on duty in front of the station. Reaching the center of the town, Fő Street widened into a square that, in turn, halved the street. Surrounded by an iron rail, the flowers of a well-maintained little park provided a refreshing sight. Huge lindens lined the edge of the wide sidewalks. That was the strollers' street. The soldiers' walk was on one side of the street, the gentlemen's promenade on the other. In the evening, as well as on Saturday and Sunday morning, a multitude of strollers filled the street. On Saturday, drawn shutters testified to the holiday, for the people of Munkács had two holidays every week: Saturday and Sunday. Most of the merchants were Jews. By selling their merchandise at a very low profit the Jewish merchants had made Munkács the least expensive town in the country. Most of the craftsmen were also Jews. The products made in their small shops were sold all over the country. But even among the carriers there were Jews who made a modest living by pushing their carts laden with merchandise.

Spread out over the mountain slopes, vineyards and orchards flooded the marketplace with their delicious fruits. In the outskirts of the town hard-working Bulgarian farmers grew vegetables. On Monday (or "Mundy," as the Munkácsians pronounced it) and Friday the Hungarian, Ruthenian, and Swabian farms delivered geese, eggs, milk, butter, cottage cheese, and other foods in enormous quantities. In June, village girls sold little dark-red wild strawberries that had been picked in the forest and stored in glazed pots. We called the large garden-grown strawberries *szamóca*. They were also sold by street vendors and their smell filled the inside of the houses. Mushrooms were picked in beech and oak forests. They were strung like a garland and dried hard, either by the sun or by the low heat of the oven. Freshly picked wild raspberries were sold by the container. We never bought raspberry juice in the store, but made it at home. My mother would usually buy a five-kilo sugarloaf, because it was cheaper than granulated sugar. The sugarloaf, I remembered, was wrapped in heavy black paper, though I had not seen one since my childhood. By the end of the summer the fruit of the thorn-covered mulberry bushes had ripened sweet. We made delicious preserves from it at home. The wagon drivers delivered firewood cut from elms and oaks to the houses. We cooked with wood, not coal.

My thoughts kept returning to the past as my mobile prison took me somewhere unknown. A thousand years ago Árpád, the conquering Magyar chieftain, took a rest here after his troops had crossed the Straits of Verecke and swooped down from the mountains.[5] Running in its rock-bottomed bed, the crystal-clear waters of the Latorca River provided a refreshing drink for man and animal alike. Situated in the eastern tip of the Alföld, Munkács was built on the left bank of the river.[6] From the east, low-lying semicircular mountains protected it against the strong winds of the winter. To the south, a domelike, lonely mountain rose out of the plains; on its top was the ancient castle of the Rákóczis.[7] Ilona Zrínyi, mother of Ferenc Rákóczi II, the leader of the *kurucok*, defended the castle, fortified with sturdy ramparts, against the besieging Austrians for three years.[8] The armies of General Caraffa failed to break the spirit of the heroic woman.[9] Only after Dániel Absolon, her secretary, had conspired with the captain of the castle to betray her did the Austrians succeed in taking the castle in 1668. In 1944 the Germans occupied the whole of Hungary without encountering resistance. We did not have the likes of Ilona Zrínyi.

A long time ago, looking out of the window of a passenger train, I bade farewell to the castle, knowing that I would see it again. On the way home, just as we had started preparing to get off the train, its sturdy high wall came into view. Before the First World War it stood empty, gates wide open. As a young student I used to take the half-hour walk with a group of friends to Várpalánka, the village that lay in a semicircle around the castle. Deep moats surrounded the castle. Access to the huge gate that opened out of the wall could be gained only by walking across a wide wooden bridge. In the middle of the cobblestoned courtyard a covered well, three meters in diameter, had provided water for the heroes of the distant past. Slaves turned the huge wheel that made the heavy chain roll on a thick crossbeam. A strong screen covered the mouth of the well, so there was no danger in our leaning over it. We would yell into it and try to estimate the depth of the well by the velocity of the echo, or throw pebbles into it and count the number of minutes that passed before the splashing of the water was heard. We wandered over the massive ramparts made of huge blocks of natural stone that easily withstood the impact of the heavy cannon balls that Caraffa's artillery had hurled against them. Looking down from their top we could see the bright silvery course of the winding Latorca River. Not too far beyond it the tower of the Szekler-style town hall could be seen rising high above the straight, tree-lined streets.

Meanwhile, the train kept running on its rattling wheels. Would we see the castle again? In the freight car the light of a small lamp dispersed the darkness. I watched the faces of my loved ones with anxiety as they lay on the floor. I still believed that we were being taken somewhere to work. Before that, however, we had to endure humiliation. A bucket instead of a latrine and an outstretched blanket instead of a fence. Whoever happened to stand by the window threw out the stinking contents of the bucket. We were no longer civilized human beings, only miserable, though still hopeful, worms. That is how we lived, humiliated but not ashamed. *Naturalia non sunt turpia*. That which is natural is not ugly.

The train picked up speed as if it wanted to be rid of its load. The wheels kept clattering incessantly, racing across the points of the stations at Batyu and Csap.[10] Where now? Not southward, to the Alföld, that much we knew already. Looking out the window of the freight car we could see the names of the stations. The train headed north. It was late in the evening when we rolled into Kassa.[11] The door slid open. There were gendarmes standing along the train with bayonets fastened on their rifles. We were forbidden to get off. Then an order was issued that required us to turn in all of our valuables. The baskets held by the gendarmes were filled with money, watches, diamonds, signet rings, and wedding rings. We were warned that if anyone withheld anything valuable everyone in the freight car would be shot. Each new order heightened our fears. We gave up everything we had and received only water in return.

In the morning we went on. Bypassing Eperjes, the train took us across Slovakia, which the Germans had occupied.[12] It rumbled through the Jablunkovsky Pass and we were on Polish territory. An ominous feeling overtook us. Perhaps it was an animallike instinct that made us feel that something terrible was awaiting us. Those assigned for work were not transported as we were. Our only hope was the promise of work that the commandant of the brick factory had made to us. The young would work so that the old might be exempted. He may only have wanted to calm us. Perhaps even he did not know what awaited the passengers of the Jews' train. Yet even as we were, lying close to one another in the darkness of the freight car, we did not discuss our fears. Each of us kept our thoughts to ourselves so that our loved ones would not become frightened. We kept sinking lower and lower into the depths of humiliation. First the ghetto apartment with all the conveniences, then the brick factory, and finally the freight car with its stinking bucket. These were the well-thought-out and prepared steps of our descent into hell.

On 26 May 1944 the train rolled into the portico of hell, Birkenau. It was the antechamber of Auschwitz, a name that was to become the perpetual reminder of murderous human brutality. The cemetery of six million nameless graves. Osviecin, as it is called in Polish, is found near Kraków on the map.

The train stood still in the station. Annika, my daughter, was beside me as I looked intently into the darkness. Flames shooting high from distant chimneys painted the horizon bright red. The sight of the ghastly light filled me with terror. "What's that horrible fire?" my daughter asked in anguish. I don't remember what I replied. I embraced her, trying to calm her trembling body and soul. I sensed what kind of chimney would emit such flames. But what was it that had frightened my daughter? In their infinite barbarism, the Nazis wanted to obliterate even the traces of their victims. Nothing but dust and ash were allowed to remain. Dust and ash. Time would slowly heal the painful wound, but I could never forget my daughter's question. It remains branded on my soul forever. There should be a permanent memento inscribed in the sky over Auschwitz, the sixth commandment of Moses: Thou shalt not kill. As I embraced my child and wife I could almost hear the old school song: "It's already evening, late evening, only the shepherd's fire flickers, oh, but far away."

It was already morning when we heard the sound of approaching steps. The door of the freight car was pulled open and men wearing striped clothes instructed us to get off. They spoke in an urgent but not unfriendly manner. We stayed close together. The two-day journey had left even the young faces pale. Gradually everyone got off the train. Those wearing the striped clothes, called "Canadians" in the jargon of the camp, were selected from among Polish and Slovakian Jews who had been deported earlier. They quickly ordered the men to stand apart from the women and advised the younger women that it would be to their advantage to put makeup on their faces. We could not, then, have comprehended the reason for this. Except for a quick kiss we had no time to bid farewell to one another before we were separated. The children clutched their mothers' hands.

An SS sergeant announced that all doctors and dentists should present themselves to him. A good sign, I thought. They needed doctors; therefore we would be assigned to medical duty. We hurried to him. He asked us if we had any drugs with us. We emptied our pockets in front of him. "*Gut, gut,*" he said. Encouraged by his response we told him eagerly of the drugs that we had left in the freight car. I ran back to fetch them. The SS sergeant praised us for our efforts. His behavior made me bold; I asked him if we would be allowed to stay with our families. "*Natürlich,*" came the good-natured reply. We would join them after we had taken a bath. I rushed back to tell everyone the good news. Among the slowly walking women I found my wife, daughter, mother, mother-in-law, and sister-in-law. "Don't be afraid!" I shouted joyfully. "The sergeant has just told me that after the bath we'll be together again." I went on speaking rapidly. "Don't be afraid!" Then they were gone. I started looking for my two brothers and father-in-law. We discussed the sergeant's words with obvious relief. My brother Sándor thought that if doctors were needed so were pharmacists. Naturally, everyone would do what he could do best, Oszkár, my other brother, reasoned. He was a general practitioner. My father-in-law, Ernő Weinberger of Kajdáno, the sturdy former president of the Chevra Kaddisha in Munkács, wondered what use he would be to the Nazis.[13] Despite his seventy years, he was a man of erect bearing. "Don't worry, I'll work," I told him encouragingly. "The main thing is that we stay together."

The women had already disappeared from sight when we were ordered to move forward. Soon our column was divided. As we reached the front of the line an SS officer, standing facing us, motioned my father-in-law to the left and the three of us to the right. I noticed that all of the elderly and the physically infirm had been directed to the left and all of the able-bodied to the right. I could still see that the prisoners who had stood on the left were boarding a truck. The officer directing us was the infamous Dr. Mengele. He was assisted by a few SS men, who made sure that none of the elderly turned to the right. The selection went quickly. Dr. Mengele had already sent millions to the gas chambers; he had great experience in deciding who was to die. I was so tense that I could not think straight; I did not comprehend the meaning of the procedure. Perhaps the elderly would be spared from walking. They would probably have to cover a greater distance. I still desperately wanted to believe the SS sergeant's words about the family staying together after the bath. I kept telling myself, "We'll meet soon. We'll be together again."

The sign above the gate in the iron fence read, *"Arbeit macht frei."* Work sets man free, indeed! Led by the inmates in striped clothing, we walked through the gate. The wire screen that was stretched out between tall concrete poles told us that we were in prison. A sign with a death's-head on it warned that the iron fence was charged with high voltage. We moved into the bathing compound, took off our clothes, and threw them in a pile. We were allowed to keep our shoes, however, probably because the stock of wooden-soled boots was low. I used my shoes as a hiding place for the valuables of a civilized man: a bar of soap, a toothbrush, a pocket knife, three handkerchiefs, and the Medical Association card. After all, I would have to prove that I was a physician. Aside from the hidden treasures I had nothing to remind me of my past. Nimble-fingered barbers shaved everyone's head. The hair was piled up high. Clutching my shoes, I stepped into the shower room. We had been given soap and towels. Showering proved an invigorating experience after the filth of the brick factory and the freight car. The warm water coming from the shower head suddenly turned cold. Then it was shut off altogether. Next group! They let us shower, so the information that we would work must have been correct. The commandant of the brick factory had not lied after all. I picked up my shoes, which I had carefully placed in a dry spot, and walked into an adjacent room, where each of us received an undershirt, a striped suit, and a round, striped, visorless cap. We began trading with each other until everyone's clothes were the right size. I stuck my rescued treasures into my pocket, and gave a handkerchief to each of my brothers. After we had gotten dressed we took a good look at one another. Who was this? Who was that? We were an indistinguishable, phalanxlike mass.

A prisoner who had been there for some time—he was called a *Kapo*—lined us up. Then we marched into a long building that had a low ceiling. It was divided by a wooden bench that measured half a meter in both width and height. There was a row of triple-decked bunks on either side. The two-meter-wide bunk was called a *Koja*. A distance of one meter separated the bunks from one another. As we filed into the building our leader ordered us to lie down, ten men to a bunk. We lay so tight that if one of us wanted to turn the whole row had to follow suit. The seventy-centimeter-wide berth in the brick factory suddenly seemed luxurious. The *Kapo* had been ordered to place a thousand men in the barracks, and it was not even empty when we arrived.

We soon learned that orders had to be obeyed; the *Kapo* proved to be a quick-handed fellow. A warning was usually accentuated by a slap with his hand or a blow with his stick. We also realized that in the barracks we were involved in a life-and-death struggle. We underwent a total transformation. Pieces of linen inscribed with numbers were sewn on our jackets. Thus we lost our names, too. The numbers became our names. To this day I don't know why they didn't tattoo us. According to standard procedure, workers had their lower arm tattooed with the same number that they wore on their chests. In the afternoon we were served dinner: a slice of bread and a little lekvar. On that day our starvation began. It was to last for eleven months.

The next day we noticed a group of women—they had arrived in camp the same day we did—standing across the path that separated the two rows of buildings. They looked back at us carefully. We hoped to discover the familiar faces of relatives and friends. The women's heads were shaven and they wore ill-fitting summer dresses that distorted their figures. Their heads were bare. Here and there an arm would go up in the air in an uncertain sign of recognition, only to be lowered in disappointment. No, that was not the one after all. We had all been made to look alike. We could not recognize one another in our new appearance, heads shaven and wearing prison stripes. We stood along the two sides of the path. Though we were separated by a distance of only ten meters we looked like strangers to one another.

At last I discovered Klári, my sister-in-law. The dress she was wearing made her look like a scarecrow. "Klári!" I shouted, and waved to her. At first there was a blank expression on her face. Then she recognized me. She was the only one of the family that I could see. "Where are the others?" "I don't know," she answered in a subdued voice. "They aren't with us." "They must have been taken somewhere else," I persisted. Klári did not reply, only her eyes grew brighter. We had to return to our barracks. We waved good-bye to each other. The next time I would see her again was after our liberation.

After we had returned to the barracks I approached our leader, the *Block-ältester*, and inquired if he knew of the whereabouts of our families. We had been told that families would be allowed to stay together, I persisted. I awaited his reply with fear. He looked directly at me and blurted out with cruel honesty, "You idiot! Where do you think they are? In the air! Everyone's in the air!" He shouted these last words. I felt panic as I listened to him, but I did not understand what he was trying to tell me. I suppose I did not want to understand. All I could do was repeat in a despairing voice that it could not be true. The *Blockältester*, himself a Jew who had been deported from Poland a few years before, took pity on me. "My family went up in the air through the chimney, too," he consoled me in a quiet voice. "It's going to happen to all of us." He put his hand on my shoulder, then turned away. I understood. We shared the same fate, the same pain. He did not want to hurt me with harsh words; he only wanted to exorcise his own deep-rooted pain. No one had heard him. I climbed up to my bunk and lay next to my brothers. We did not talk of our families; we could not bear touching our fresh wounds. Evil, a new-honed knife, had stabbed us. We would only have lied if we had encouraged one another; yet by remaining silent we let grief gnaw at our hearts. The brutal honesty of the *Blockältester*'s words was a death-blow, the harsh tone of his voice dispelling all my hopes. We lay on our bunks in self-torturing silence.

On the fourth day—it was the end of May—we were put into freight cars again. It was rumored that we would be transferred to the concentration camp at Warsaw. After four days of physical and mental suffering we were only too glad to leave Auschwitz. Thousands of years before, unending sacrifices were made in honor of Moloch, the deity represented by a statue with the head of an ox. In that iron statue there was room for one sacrifice only. The Moloch of the twentieth century wore a swastika on his forehead and consumed his victims by the trainload, victims that the gas had choked and the crematoria burned to ashes so that not even a trace of them would remain. Millions were turned into ashes on the sacrificial pyre.

An old soldier guarded us in the freight car. He kept watching us as we sat in our striped clothing. His probing eyes seemed to want to know why we were there. At last he could no longer conceal his curiosity. "Why are you here? What are you guilty of?" he asked. "We are Jews," we replied. "*Schon gut*. That's fine," he said in a friendly manner, "but what have you done?" "Nothing. We're Jews. That's our crime." The expression on his face showed that he did not believe us. He had been transferred to Auschwitz from somewhere in Germany and assigned to the trains. He did not seem to comprehend the meaning of Auschwitz. It seemed plausible that he had not been allowed entry into the area surrounded by the iron fence and guarded by watchtowers. According to Nazi propaganda only criminals were deported. The official communiqués were silent about the fate of those who had been deported to Auschwitz from Polish, Czechoslovakian, Hungarian, and other occupied territories. Our guard asked us no more questions. What was the use? All confirmed criminals lied and denied their guilt. Despite his sixty years and the old rifle that he was holding, he was even perhaps afraid of being among so many criminals whose souls—although criminals were not supposed to have them—were burdened by those horrible crimes. Such thoughts must have been circulating in the brain of our seemingly good-natured guard. In his tattered uniform he looked more like a civilian than a brave soldier. At last the door was locked and the train rumbled out of the station. We were on our way to Warsaw.

István Tamás

Irma and Irén

István Tamás (b. 1932) is atypical of the new generation of Hungarian writers in his treatment of the Jewish Question. He courageously approaches the Jews' fate out of personal initiative, not out of the institutionalized antifascist stance that is commonly found in socialist societies. His writings reveal a considerable sensitivity, surpassing that of the official recognition of the Holocaust's effect on its survivors. Though Tamás is only half Jewish, his consequently limited and peripheral perspective is shared by many sympathetic outsiders, who recognize that the bearers of the long tradition of discrimination and persecution are unique in possessing those feelings which only personal experience can generate. Nevertheless, he manages to convey to his readers enough compassion for and understanding of the shattered world of the remnants of Hungarian Jewry to give rise to the hope that the true dimensions of the Holocaust are being sensed, at long last, by those who will be shaping Hungary's literary taste and public opinion in the future. "Irma and Irén" is translated from "Irma és Irén," in István Tamás, Tizenhárom hónap [Thirteen months] (Budapest: Szépirodalmi Könyvkiadó, 1977), pp. 179–84. By permission of A Magyar Izraeliták Országos Képviselete.

The phonograph is playing the ancient Hebrew mourning song. I don't understand a single word of the sobbing man's; I only sense his unfathomably deep sorrow. I had bought the record in Prague a long time ago. I liked the seven-armed candelabrum, the menorah, on its cover. I played it a few times; it always made me sad. Now that Irma and Irén are gone, the strange words (though I still don't understand them) and the rabbi's—or is he a cantor?—faltering voice have taken on a new meaning. He is imploring, threatening, and arguing. He cries out in anguish, then calms himself; he is accusing, besieging, and adoring the Almighty. He takes Him to task. Suddenly his own boldness frightens him and he throws himself to the ground exhausted, rending his clothes. Then he starts it all over again, crying out and calming himself. And when he says, *"lechai—budachai"*—I'm sure I wrote it incorrectly, but that's what it sounds like—he seems to be shouting all the way to heaven. "What more do you want from us, God of Israel, you horrifying and merciful, malevolent and beloved, sanguine . . ."

I will tell the story of Irma and Irén as best as I can. They were young women who lived in Tapolca[1] in the 1930s. Both were in their late twenties and married, and both had children. They knew each other well—Tapolca is a small town—and would meet, as was the custom, at parties, in the syna-gogue, on the street, and in the marketplace. The years passed. One day Irma and Irén's husbands were called up for labor service in the Ukraine. There they perished. Soon thereafter Irma, Irén, and their children—they were about ten years old then—were taken to Auschwitz, Dachau, or Mauthausen. I don't know where, exactly. There was an ample selection of such destinations. The children were cremated, but the mothers survived. Though they found no joy in living after that, they obeyed life's command to live. They persevered as best as they could, on foot, on train, leaning on bladeless shovel handles, and taking help from well-meaning civilians and soldiers who were horrified at the sight of the returnees. At last Irma and Irén returned to their homes in Tapolca. Where else would they have gone, then?

As I was saying, neither woman had much desire to go on living, but they knew full well—their parents had given them a good upbringing—that not to live, even when there was no cause to live, was immoral. It isn't clear which of the two, Irma or Irén (I can't say for sure because I didn't know them then, although it was probably Irma, who was more practical then Irén), suggested in 1946 or 1947 that instead of each living on her own, the two of them should live together. So one moved in with the other. Then one of them married a good man; the other also got married, so I heard, but the man, though she never spoke of him, was no good and she divorced him in a few days or weeks. Yet even while they were married the two women spent much time together, as they truly enjoyed only each other's company.

I didn't know Uncle Pista, the good man whom one of the women had married. I was told that he owned a horse, liked to play cards on Sunday afternoons, and was fond of good pastry. He too had lost his family. When he died in the mid 1960s, Irma and Irén were again left alone. They sold the house and moved into a two-and-a-half-room apartment.

They weren't in want of anything. Irén had a job, and Irma owned a vineyard near the Balaton.[2] They made their wills, each leaving everything she had to the other.

It was then that I got to know them.

The two women radiated gaiety and sadness. Once on Christmas eve, at the start of our acquaintance, I visited them. They served hot chocolate, walnuts, fruits, and mashed sweet chestnuts. Tibi, the manager of the local supermarket, was virtually bathing in whipped cream and kept moaning about how much weight he was putting on. Irma and Irén's quiet, self-effacing demeanor rubbed off on all of us. As I was driving home in the gently falling snow I thought of the Christmases of my own happy childhood, of Irma and Irén's children, the two Jewish children who were burned virtually before their mothers' eyes, and of the Christmas of all the dead people who need not have died. The windshield wipers were pushing the snow away with rhythmic monotony as I drove on the snow-covered shore of the Balaton, with my daughter sitting by my side. My daughter, alive and healthy. They had not burned her.

It was a beautiful but sad journey. Was it in 1965 or 1966? I don't remember which.

Irma and Irén were left alone, looking at each other amid the piles of chestnut-soiled plates.

I don't think they ever cried. They were not the kind of people who would have tormented each other with grief. They probably cleaned off the table quietly, exchanged a few words about us, although none of us, not Tibi, not Jóska—Jóska Szigethy, their doctor, and the kind and intelligent Ella, his wife, two infinitely understanding and utterly devoted friends—or the mashed and sweetened chestnuts could have been of great interest to them. Then they went to sleep.

That's how Irma and Irén spent many a Christmas eve.

They were together, yet each was alone.

Alone under the thick eiderdown quilt with their little cremated sons or daughters—and I don't even know for sure if there were also girls among the children, for Irma usually spoke of boys—Irén would sometimes cry out in her sleep. One sunny day in September all of us drove to Badacsony.[3] Irén sat next to me, Irma on the back seat. We laughed all the way to Badacsony. From there we continued on foot. They knew every path. Irma had lived there for a long time; her husband was an engineer with the local quarry. We must have made a strange sight: two elegant, elderly ladies on the arms of a youngish man. Suddenly tears swelled in the eyes of the women. It was September, as I mentioned already, and a young boy—he looked about ten—with a schoolbag in his hand ran past us. He stopped at a short distance from us and started to whirl, flailing his arms, yet clutching the bag. He was rejoicing at the bag, the school, the world, and life. In the narrow path his playfully flailing arms occasionally brushed the vines, causing them to bend and drop a few leaves. As the boy whirled, Irma and Irén stood motionless on the dirt road. The waning rays of the autumn sun caressed their silvery hair, and their glasses were soon covered with a delicate veil of mist. Yet they remained silent. They had learned that in difficult moments it was better not to say anything.

Though we talked about many things afterward, we knew that the happy afternoon had vanished. The playful little boy had turned it into a joyless, black-rimmed afternoon, filled with the deathly memories of cremated little boys.

Still, there were many other happy afternoons and evenings to come.

In the early winter sunset, as the waning light of day slowly disappeared into the corners of the rooms, the two women sat in quiet solitude, surrounded by the darkened contours of their furniture. Their parents (local merchants, the owners of vaulted, cool wine cellars, who did business with hard-bargaining, bearded old wine brokers from Vienna and London, and who died as respected Hungarian citizens) had bought it in the last century. On a huge serving table two candlesticks stood amid old silver plates. Despite her agnosticism in all other respects—at least that's what she used to say—Irma lit the candles on Friday evening as she had been taught by her parents. And though she was a highly sensitive and educated person, one used to making up her own mind, she always performed that ritual.

"I don't think there's a God," she said as she stepped to the candlesticks, holding a match. Then she thrust her index finger under the quiet Jóska's nose. "Some doctor you are! You can't even make my rheumatic finger well!" she burst out indignantly, and without waiting for a response, she lit the candles.

"Your finger? I can't cure that," said Jóska gently and for the hundred thousandth time. "I'm only a doctor, not a magician. Besides, is that your biggest problem?"

"It is!"

Before we departed Irén fixed the collars on our coats, our hats and caps. "It's windy outside, children."

Of the two she was to die first. She suffered a stroke, and lingered for six months, paralyzed, silent, and bewildered. Her eyes lit up when visitors arrived, and though they lost their glitter at the sight of the unpleasant ones, she radiated joy in greeting those she loved. She was buried beside her husband.

Left alone, Irma grew even sadder, cleverer, and bleaker than she had been before. She knew that no earthly power could crack the shell of her loneliness. She usually spent the afternoon among friends. Then she was lively and talkative; her good ideas and strong character attracted everyone. The following conversation she once had with a foolish woman was typical of her.

"How do you spend your evenings, Irma?"

"I watch the wall."

"Not TV?"

"No."

"Why don't you watch TV, Irma?"

"Because I'm addicted to the wall."

"You're a strange woman, Irma."

"Yes, I've become strange."

On a gloomy and chilly afternoon last fall she became ill. Jóska rushed to her side, carrying an electrocardiograph.

"Heart attack?" asked Irma.

"You should go to the hospital."

"Forget it. Let me die."

"You're talking nonsense. We'll go at once. You'll get well again, but I can't tell you anything for sure yet. The condition may even clear up by tonight."

In the hospital she asked for a tranquilizer. She fell asleep, but awoke in a little while. "Don't think that what you gave me helped," she said tartly to the anxiously waiting Jóska. In a few minutes she dozed off and died in her sleep. She was seventy years old.

She was buried on a chilly, foggy afternoon. Four old men carried the simple black coffin to her parents' grave. A young rabbi spoke with fervor, but because of his youth he sounded inexperienced in matters of life and death, and when he reached the sentence about the saintly woman who was lying in front of us I expected Irma to cry out from her coffin, "Balderdash, my son! You stop that talk at once!"

She did not cry out, however. She was pleased that she had died.

As we walked through the seldom-visited old Jewish cemetery we were at a loss as to whether we should remove our hats and caps. There was no one, for she had no relatives, to whom we could express our condolences. So each of us went on our way.

Ernő Szép

Three Fellow Men

Like a wise child lost in the puzzling world of dispassionate adults, Ernő Szép (1884–1953) was an awestruck and wide-eyed observer of life's unpredictable twists. Though he was born in the quiet, uneventful monotony of a small town—Huszt—Szép's intellectual and emotional world was that of Budapest's bustling and deceptively carefree middle-class society. The gem-like poems and finely woven novels written in an almost precariously fragile style reflect his love of the city. He is best remembered by the novel Lila akác *[Purple acacia] (1919). Szép also wrote many subtly humorous short stories and one-act comedies, some of which have appeared in German and English translations as well. Not until the faint yet already ominous outlines of the Holocaust became visible to the Jews of Hungary did the dark side of life cloud his innocence and sunny disposition. Blind hate and man's unfathomable inhumanity are masterfully etched in his most realistic novel,* Emberszag *[Human smell] (1945), written in the immediate aftermath of the Second World War about the tribulations of Budapest's Jewry. "Three Fellow Men" was translated from "Három felebarát," in* Évkönyv, *ed. Samu Szemere (Budapest: Az Izraelita Magyar Irodalmi Társulat, 1948), pp. 124–26. By permission of* A Magyar Izraeliták Országos Képviselete.*

Every time we talk about the persecution of Jews in the recent past, someone inevitably makes a comment to the effect that there were good Christians, too.

Indeed there were, though the number of those who saved the lives of Jews by hiding them, or held the valuables of their Jewish friends for safekeeping—and returned them afterward—was lamentably small. But we can also call those Christians good who not only behaved humanely and refrained from parroting anti-Jewish phrases, but gave practical expression to their compassion and sympathy toward us as well.

The First

She was the wife of a high-ranking army officer, a milady. She was beautiful and always dressed elegantly. Her hats were from Margit Roth's shop, the most fashionable hat salon in Budapest. On a fine day in 1939 she went shopping—she told me this story later, herself—at Margit Roth's. She entered the store, tried on a few hats as usual, lit a cigarette, and asked the owner to come over to the small table with the lace tablecloth and vase on it where she had been sitting.

"Sit down for a while, my dear Margit; I'd like to talk something over with you. You may not have heard yet—I don't think it has been made public—that they are going to take stores away from their Jewish owners. Yes, my dear Margit, you can imagine how unhappy I am to be the bearer of such bad news. When, you ask? Well, my sweet, it's a matter of a couple of months. They've just started working on the pertinent motion in the Ministry of the Interior. What a pity, my dear Margit, that you're Jewish, too, or of Jewish origin, anyway. Your conversion will be of no help to you, of course.

"Anyhow, my dear, this beautiful store will be taken away from you. And because that's the way things are going and though I'm thoroughly ashamed of them, I immediately thought—you know, my dear Margit, that I've always been a good friend of yours, don't you?—that I would claim your salon. I've already discussed the matter fully with my husband and explained to him that we no longer live in a world ruled by conventions, where a woman of my social standing isn't allowed to do anything. You know, of course, that Countess Julia Apponyi herself is running her own salon. We have four children and my husband unfortunately lost his share of the inheritance at cards, back in the days of his captaincy, so this store will be a divine gift for me. I really hope that things will go just as well as when the sign had the name Margit Roth on it. Where should women in society—they're also my best friends, you know—go shopping, if not to my salon? But you know, my sweet, I must also be careful that the salon doesn't become run-down and that I don't make a spectacle out of myself. Otherwise, God forbid, all of my customers will leave me.

"And now, my dear Margit, I'd like to discuss another small matter with you. Would you spend a little time showing me around? I'll be here every day, let's say, from ten to eleven-thirty. I believe that's when you're the least busy. I'd like you to initiate me into the secrets of the hat business and teach me the art of selling. After all, as surely as I'm standing here the store will be mine. My husband has already taken the appropriate steps in that direction, and you too will be happy spending a little time with me, knowing that I, rather than a stranger, will be your heir.

"I'll never forget you for this, my beloved Margit. We understand each other, my pet, don't we? Then I believe I'll start tomorrow. As early as nine-thirty? Of course I can. How sweet of you! My goodness, I must run. I've got an appointment at the hairdresser's. Kiss, kiss, my dear! Till tomorrow, then. Ta-ta!"

The Second

He had a high position in the government. We had served in the same regiment. I ran into him on Vörösmarty Square[1] in forty-four. I was wearing the yellow star on my chest by then. We came from opposite directions, straight toward each other. It was impossible for either of us not to greet the other, although my poor friend must have felt terribly uncomfortable about it. Well, so long as it was unavoidable His Excellency stopped graciously. There was an almost I-am-astonished kind of look in his eyes. "You, too?" he asked. "You, too?" "Of course I'm a Jew. Didn't you know?" "No, old boy, I hadn't the slightest idea. Well, well, who would've thought? But that they would order you to wear that yellow star— that's really too much— that you'd have to walk here in Pest, branded— I'm really very sorry for you, my dear Ernő. The least they could've done was to transport all Jews to Turkestan"—he really said Turkestan—"so that gentlemen like yourself would not have to show themselves in public in such a humiliating manner. Please, don't be surprised, but it's rumored that the Jews will be taken from here to Germany, and only God knows what awaits them there. The Hungarian government could have seen to it before the war that the Jews were resettled in Turkestan, where there was ample space for them. For even though a person might not be a member of the Magyar tribes he could still be honest and respectable. He should not be insulted endlessly, let alone exposed to the barbarism of the Germans. I must tell you, old boy, that I don't regard what's been happening to you as a correct or gentlemanly action, especially in view of the fact that the Hungarian government had ample time and opportunity to resettle the Jews in Turkestan."

The Third

He was a simple peasant, puffing on his pipe quietly and leaning against the doorpost of his house. His wife stood next to him. Both were watching that doleful group of Jews that passed through the village in the autumn of 1944. They dragged themselves along, carrying their heavy sacks, amid the prodding shouts of Szálasi's warriors.[2]

The old peasant's heart was filled with pity as he watched the sorrowful pilgrims. Pushing the pipe from left to right in his mouth, he blurted out quietly, "Poor, dirty Jews!"

László Bárdos

The Csángó Soldier

Combining acute observations of human nature with skillfully drawn images of the labor service, László Bárdos offers a penetrating look at the agony of thousands of Jewish men doing hard labor under the watchful eyes and cocked rifles of Hungarian soldiers. Bárdos, a writer who had experienced this most insidious institution in wartime Hungary at first hand, points out an important, verifiable fact that is usually overshadowed by the well-known and well-documented brutality of Hungarian army officers, noncommissioned officers, and Arrow Cross militiamen: in the prevailing atmosphere of murderous inhumanity, where the lives of the labor servicemen literally depended on the whims of the guards, there were flashes of humanitarianism. Many survivors of labor service companies owe their lives not only to the often irresistibly advancing Soviet troops but also to quick-thinking and brave Hungarian soldiers who, out of compassion or for self-serving reasons, defied the orders of their superiors by protecting the men left in their charge and eventually leading them to safety. "The Csángó[1] Soldier" is translated from "A Csángó katona," in Új Élet naptár [New Life calendar] (Budapest: A Magyar Izraeliták Országos Képviselete, 1959), pp. 66–75. By permission of A Magyar Izraeliták Országos Képviselete.

Captain Keve of the Engineer Corps observed the strict code of elegance even in the world of snow-capped mountains.

"You're mistaken if you think that you've come up here for a vacation." In a vainglorious and impudent tone he admonished the inmates of the labor service camp, who hardly had time to catch their breath following the five-hour-long hike.

Standing on a mound amid slender pines he scrutinized the area around us. The sun looked like a red-hot disc as it prepared to set on the other side of the mountain, where the Romanian troops had been holding out.

"You're going to work hard here," the captain raised his voice and adjusted his black monocle. "And how! I know that all of you are pulling for our enemies. That's why you couldn't be soldiers. So instead of giving blood you'll give sweat. But we'll watch out for your health, you can be sure of that. The air is good, isn't it?"

He waited impatiently for our reply. He tried to inspire us by pointing out the natural beauty of the region. Though we stood there as strangers, unsure of ourselves and filled with uneasy anticipation, we had to admit that with respect to the air, the southern slopes of the Carpathian mountains did indeed seem to be staring at us encouragingly.

"I don't hear your answer!" the voice thundered from behind the black monocle. "I want to hear it! The air is good, isn't it?" he repeated the question. "Maybe I'm lying," he added provokingly.

The noncommissioned officers went to work and started prodding those standing closest to them.

"Answer him! Don't make him mad."

"Yes, sir! The air is good!" the whole company shouted in unison.

"That's better. You should be grateful that you ended up here. And because you'll be working hard at building fortifications for our victory you'll enjoy this good air even at night. That'll be your reward. With my permission."

We looked around. Not a house, a stable, or a pigsty. There was nothing with a roof on it. At a distance a lonely *estenna* stood. Smoke was coming through its door. Obviously someone was inside.

The *estenna* is the home of the mountain shepherd who moves out with his animals to the pasture on the slopes in the spring and will not return to his village until it is time for the first frost to cover the land. He never stays for the fast-moving cold in which birds freeze to death in flight. The *estenna* protects him against the chilly air of summer nights, and on its open hearth a pot of goulash made of the meat of a broken-legged sheep will cook to perfection. Yet both man and animal will take to flight before the approaching winter. Not even those who were born in that region can stand that cold mountain air.

We, of course, learned about this only when the icy teeth of November bit us. For the time being, however, it was still summer and the chilly air felt good after the sweaty march. Below us the clouds were floating by, and below the clouds a small village nestled at the foot of the Carpathians. From time to time the steeple of the church became visible, as if it had poked through the sky. The gentle breeze was chasing the page of a newspaper up the slope. It occasionally caught on a juniper tree or a Christmas tree so tiny that it could have been planted in a pot, then flew on playfully. It must have been wrapped around the lunch of one of the noncommissioned officers.

No one asked, yet we knew instinctively that the whole company was thinking the same thing. Where would we stay? Captain Keve must have heard the silent question, because he soon dispelled the air of uncertainty.

"I can see in your eyes that you're looking for your quarters. You'll have them, don't worry. You'll make them yourselves, from leaves. Corporal Réti!"

"Sir!" A young soldier, wearing the uniform of the alpine riflemen, stepped forward. He was not one of the soldiers who had guarded us since we left home. A Csángó youth, the epitome of soldierly discipline as he stood in attention, he was a child of the countryside. He knew every path by heart, even those that led beyond the border. Three or four kilometers from us, Romanian sentries were scanning the terrain.

"Corporal! Show these men how to make a leaf tent and where they should set up camp. You can use pine branches for featherbedding. Causing damage to the trunk of pines is forbidden. That's all!"

The corporal saluted smartly and made an about-face. He set out to find the place that Captain Keve had designated for us. There were traces of wheels showing the path that was used by humans and animals alike.

"What does he think my mother was? A chamois?" joked Sergeant Sztacho. He sported an Adolph Menjou–like moustache that seemed to suggest that he would have felt a great deal better sitting in a café on one of the main thoroughfares of Pest, and that he wished the whole war, Captain Keve, and the snow-capped mountains of Gyimes were in hell, singly and all together.

At one of the steep climbs near the ridge, a peasant wagon pulled by two oxen came into view. It carried two long wooden boxes on which two emaciated, bearded men sat. From under their disheveled, hairy exterior two palm-sized, parchmentlike patches of yellowish dry skin and two pairs of feverish eyes flashed from time to time. They were inmates of a labor service camp, accompanying their comrades on the last journey. Bathed in the red light of the sunset, the funeral wagon looked as if it had emerged from the ball of fire that was just disappearing from the horizon. It passed by the newly arrived company of inmates. The two men on the wagon kept staring into the air and remained seated on their horrifying cargo. They did not have the slightest intention of striking a soldierly pose.

"What are you carrying?"

"Dead men."

"What did they die of?"

"Spotted fever."

"Where are you from?"

"We're from the North. Kassa."[2]

Corporal Réti listened for a while but then snorted. "Let's get on! Get on, did you hear me? It's forbidden to talk to men from other companies."

The men thought apprehensively of the future and of the steadily decreasing supply of provisions brought from home. In most knapsacks only cans kept in reserve for bad days were left. We could not have known then that they would not last long. They were confiscated, because the inmates of labor service camps were permitted to eat only the rations issued by the authorities, and no more than the officially prescribed portion: for breakfast, black coffee and for lunch, soup, in which a few potatoes and one or two slices of turnip were floating. Those who received a bite of stringy meat were considered extremely lucky. The dinner menu featured *dörgemüze:* dried vegetables full of weevils. It was as a side dish to such concoctions that the good captain, with his diabolical grin, offered the mouthwatering, fresh, mountain air. And it was after eating such food that we had to do hard labor. Thus the only laborers who did not break down in a matter of days were those who either loafed or pretended to work, and who put up with getting kicked, doing pushups or frogleaps, or being punished by solitary confinement at night.

The people of the neighboring villages had already been told that it was forbidden to give food to the inmates of the camp, with or without being paid for it. Those who disobeyed and were caught risked being taken before a military court. Of course, an order like that was rarely disobeyed. At times, however, a Csángó would defy the order and charge at least a shirt for a half kilo of sheep cheese. The inmates who dared to approach the village at night risked all kinds of danger. Those who got caught were tied to a tree with their toes just off the ground. The scene of such punishment was usually the roadside, so that the people could see it and be frightened. Peasants driving wagons cracked their whips over the horses as they passed by the men dangling unconscious, and hurriedly made the sign of the cross. An old woman who happened to walk by shook her fist at the soldiers. "Why are you hurting them? Christ died for them, too."

A cursing, sadistic sentry chased her away.

What could have hardened these soldiers so much that they were devoid of even a spark of humaneness? Many were perhaps still under childhood influences. "The Jew will take you away," was a popular saying with which to scare children. The world of their imagination may have perpetuated the Jew as a peddler with an unkempt beard and a half-full sack on his shoulder, who appeared in the narrow courtyard of an apartment building and shouted in flawed, drawling Hungarian, "What's for sale?"

Others were aroused by the newspapers. They believed in the printed word, and it was a miracle that they did not walk the streets crazed and with knife in hand. There were still others whom misplaced class hatred had rendered anti-Semitic. After all, in many instances "anti-Semitism is the socialism of fools."

"Do you know where you are now?" Private First Class Bene turned to us. "Under the frog's ass."

Bene used to be an office-worker in a beer factory. He walked among tubs filled with malt, preparing statistical reports. His director probably hardly ever looked at him and did not even know his name. Perhaps he did not even know that he existed. That director was now in his platoon, and Bene could torture him to his heart's content. He did not have to fear the consequences of such action. The company commander himself often ordered that the inmates be given a good thrashing.

"I don't hear the swishing of the sticks," he would shout, enraged. "I don't hear bones breaking."

Such outbursts usually took place after it was discovered, in the course of a surprise inspection, that the platoon had managed to spend a whole afternoon without doing an ounce of work. Yet Private First Class Bene did not take advantage of his authority in his dealings with the director. Though he let him know that the director was at his mercy, he tried to ingratiate himself with his former boss by doing him small favors. Under the pretext of conducting physical exercises he spent Sunday afternoons among a group of inmates he had personally selected, and who in more peaceful times were "somebodies." He relished the time he spent in the company of "gentlemen," yet in order to disguise it he would often and without the slightest provocation speak with them rudely, or order them to lie down in big puddles or run up steep slopes.

Eight weeks had passed since Corporal Réti pointed out the place where the new leaf tents that were to serve as human habitation should be erected on the top of the Carpathians. In the first week of September the snow started falling, though it melted within a few days. By then we could hardly be distinguished from the inmates from Kassa who had driven that wagon with the two wooden boxes. We were hungry and exhausted; our clothes were no better than rags. We tried guessing when our time would be up, or at least when we would be ordered to leave the snow-capped mountains, where the top of our tents were soaked through, where at night we tried to huddle as close to one another as possible in order to keep warm, and where the cold and the howling of wolves kept us from falling asleep. Our dead grew in number, though not fast enough to earn the officers' respect. The most despicable of them was the doctor, First Lieutenant Mike. He acknowledged no sickness. No one reported to him sick, for fear of torture. He excused only the dying from duty. Some of the guards could no longer stand watching the beating that was administered under such circumstances, and frequently they would hide those who lay in the delirium of 103- and 104-degree fever. At home they might have been willing to be a party to such beatings, but most of them wanted to leave the mountain top.

Even Corporal Réti made us do those punishing exercises less frequently. He no longer watched hawkishly as the inmates pushed wheelbarrows, stamped the ground, dug trenches, or repaired the breastwork of the wolf trap that kept the rampart from caving in under the weight of the snow.

Once in a while a Csángó peasant turned up on the mountain top. He would have some business there; perhaps he had left something, a pail for milking the sheep or a pair of scissors for shearing them. There were times when the inmates were mending his fence as he arrived.

"Easy does it. Don't do more than what's needed," he said gently to the inmates, realizing that they too were human beings.

The doctor, however, did not see it that way. He kicked even the dead, rolling them over with the tip of his boot.

"Take that louse away!"

Soon Corporal Réti developed a toothache and the chilly winds made it even worse. One evening, after we had returned to our tent, he called for me in an ominous tone.

"What do you think, can the Jewish doctor pull a tooth? Ask him, because I'm not allowed to have him do it."

"If he's got foreceps, he can do it," I replied.

I wondered why he had not gone to First Lieutenant Mike. I could not help asking him.

"That one? I'm not going to put myself in the hands of that executioner. I'd sooner knock my tooth out with a stone."

Corporal Réti had changed, slowly yet noticeably. His transformation turned out to be to our advantage. It was as if his anger had evaporated. If he shouted once in a while it was more out of habit than conviction.

He had been sympathetic with me since we first met.

"Tell me, old man," he asked me a few days after our arrival, "what do you do in real life? Is it true that you're some kind of a pen-pusher?"

My stubby, graying beard must have made him feel entitled to call me an old man. But that I should describe myself as a pen-pusher? I could not be counted among them. I objected hesitantly.

His curiosity was aroused. "Tell me," he persisted, "do you make up stories, too?"

"Sometimes I wrote made-up stories, too, but most of them were not tales. I wrote about poor people who had to be protected from the rich."

"Hmmm." That's all he said. He was absorbed in carving a piece of wood. That evening, after we had returned to the camp, he did not make us do extra work.

That happened in the summer. It was the beginning of winter when Corporal Réti again displayed signs of intense thinking. The slope was slippery and he could not go down to fetch the bark of birch trees that he used for carving. Having nothing with which to occupy himself, he kept watching us.

On that day he did not even try to conceal the fact that he was not interested in what we were doing. An experienced inmate would soon sense when it was possible not to work. Gradually all work stopped. The soldier said nothing. He did not bawl anyone out, though he saw that no one was working and heard us chattering. The lanky Adler scraped a few potatoes into the ashes that remained from the fire he had made by using boards from the fence. He had acquired the potatoes during one of his nightly raids. The corporal did not seem to want to take notice of the unforgivable sin of baking potatoes, either.

"Old man," he said to me casually as I passed by him, pushing a wheelbarrow, "could you explain to me what the difference is between the Christian religion and the Jewish religion?"

"The Old Testament is the basis of Christ's teaching," I replied. "The earliest Christian preachers and apostles were mostly of Jewish origin."

He said nothing. He remained sitting at one place for a long time, resting his elbows on his knees and his head on the palm of his hand. At five o'clock it was already evening. It got dark quickly and rained often, a steadily pouring autumn rain that soaked through body and soul. The leaf tents were drenched. We moved into one of the sheepcotes and filled in its cracks with mud. The man in authority silently acknowledged the fact of our transfer.

Corporal Réti's domain was an abandoned *estenna* in whose open hearth an inviting fire, built from dry pine branches, burned in the evening. We gathered the branches in the daytime, voluntarily, without the corporal's order. The burning pine branches provided both light and heat.

The Csángó soldier liked to sprawl on a basswood bed, the lone piece of furniture in the *estenna*, and stare at the outline of shadows on the ceiling. His pillow was his hands, which he clasped under his head. At first only one or two inmates dared sneak into the mountain hut. Though their eyes were smarting from the smoke, the *estenna*, with its friendly heat, was an enchanted castle in the land of dreams. The soldier on the bed did not move; he lay silent, without a tunic, his collar unbuttoned. He had invited none of us, yet he sent no one out.

The silence inside the *estenna* was greater than on the mountain. The first visitors were followed by others, tiptoeing quietly. Only the crackling of the fire and the dry branches was heard. It was getting very warm. Prehistoric man must have sat by the fire in that manner after he had struck the first spark.

"Old man," the soldier called out when he noticed me crouching among his visitors, "do you know a good story?"

From then on he would go to sleep with someone sitting on the basswood bed and telling him a story. He clutched his hands under his head, stretched out his legs, and closed his eyes. The stories lulled him to sleep. And Pali Kelemen, who had a good voice, made a valuable contribution with his singing. The corporal was also fond of songs, the songs of Alföld[3] that were unknown in this part of the country. Apparently, news of the whole affair got around because one evening someone suddenly tore the door open. Mike, the medical officer, stood on the threshold.

"What's this? A synagogue?" he screamed in a rage. "On the double, Corporal! The rest, get out!"

The *estenna* emptied in a fraction of a second.

"What did I tell you? What?" Mike hissed angrily. "Did you forget already?"

"Sir! I didn't, but . . ."

"What but? No buts! Don't you understand that all these people are enemies of the fatherland? And you're keeping this scum warm here!"

Corporal Réti stood at tight, silent attention. The officer leaned toward him.

"Listen to me! As of today I'll give you forty pengős for every corpse. That's my money, from my own pocket."

Those inmates who had been keeping their ears pressed against the thin-timbered walls of the *estenna* started running in panic lest they be found near the officer. Mike unbuttoned his coat, pulled a notebook out of the outer pocket of his uniform, and took a fifty-pengö bill out of it.

"That's the down payment. Take it." The corporal, however, did not move. "What's with you? Are you playing hard to get?"

The doctor was annoyed. The down payment, it was learned later, came from the money he had been getting for being an enlisted Gestapo agent.

"Please, don't be angry at me," the Csángó boy said with his head lowered, "but I can't take that money, because I won't be able to earn it."

"In other words, you've sold yourself, haven't you?" the doctor cried out in consternation. "Are you getting more from them?"

Corporal Réti did not reply. He stood at stiff attention, his bootless feet touching each other at the heels and his hands pressed to his thighs. He struck a rather comical pose, wearing only his trousers. He had, as always, taken his tunic off before lying down on the basswood bed. Yet even as he was, without boots, he stood head and shoulders above the officer. Mike raised himself on his toes and smashed his fist into the soldier's face.

"The *estenna* is not a house of prayer," he shouted. "Remember that well! Tomorrow you'll present yourself to Captain Keve."

He slammed the door and stepped out into the darkness. He looked around warily by the light of a flashlight. Before he set out he turned the flashlight right and left to make sure that no one was lurking nearby. He could see nothing suspicious in the dense night.

It was not long before the inmates started sneaking back quietly, filling up the *estenna* again. Corporal Réti was lying on the bed, turned toward the wall as was his custom when he was sleeping. Not even the sound of breathing could be heard; only the fire crackled as the flames consumed the broken branches. The Csángó soldier lay motionless. He only pretended to be asleep. He did not want the inmates to see the mark that the officer's fist had left on his face.

The lanky Adler resumed the storytelling. He recalled a beautiful story, one that he had heard as a very young child. Then Pali Kelemen sang in a quiet voice. The others also joined in, humming the melody without the words.

The faint of heart started crying. Everyone was thinking of the same thing: home, where their people waited for their return. Still the corporal did not move. Seeing that it was getting late, the inmates started sneaking out of the *estenna*. Just as the last five of them were about to leave the corporal raised himself on his elbow. He told them to stay, bring their blankets, and sleep in the *estenna*. There was enough room for five more. In the soothing, warm air the five lucky men felt as if they had gone to heaven. In their excitement they could not fall asleep at once, as they usually did wherever and whenever they were permitted to rest. They did not dare move for fear of disturbing their host's sleep. But he could not fall asleep, either. His thoughts kept

him awake. The fire was getting smaller and smaller. Because the thin
branches left no embers, the fire rapidly diminished. The smoke started
irritating the nose, but the men did not seem to mind it.

"Adler! Are you here?"

"Yes, sir, Corporal."

"Tell, me, Adler, who did you hear that story from?"

"From my mother."

"I learned a few from mine, too," Réti sighed. "But not many. The poor
soul died young . . ."

No one spoke after that. In a little while the soldier's deep, even breathing
could be heard. The others fell asleep too, breathing peacefully. The great
silence that was descending on the peaks of the snow-capped Carpathians
appeared to have a sound of its own. Everyone understood it: the shepherds,
the children gathering branches, and the sheep locked in the cote. Even the
wolves howled in awe of it. It was the silence of a contented heart which was
so tranquil that it almost stood still.

Sándor Sásdi

Letter from My Mother

A survivor of Dachau, Sándor Sásdi (b. 1899) is a well-known Hungarian writer. His literary career, spanning more than half a century, is high-lighted by novels such as Egy nyár regénye *[The novel of a summer] (1934);* Fehér kenyér *[White bread] (1946);* Bosszú *[Vengeance] (1969);* Hanna nagy útja *[Hanna's big journey] (1974), and numerous short stories. He is a frequent contributor to Hungarian and Jewish literary publications and a leading memorializer of the experiences of Hungarian Jews in the Holocaust. The following story is translated from* "Levél anyámtól," *in* Új Élet naptár *[New Life calendar] (Budapest: A Magyar Izraeliták Országos Képviselete, 1959), pp. 63–64. By permission of A Magyar Izraeliták Országos Képvise-lete.*

". . . Nor does it matter that you couldn't buy yourself a new winter coat. That old, dark gray one—do you remember?—I sewed on the two buttons at the bottom and stitched the frayed hem of one of its sleeves with silk thread. You weren't quite satisfied with it then, but you have to admit that no one could iron the collar of your shirts as smoothly as I could. 'My mother,' you used to say, and you put your hand on mine, 'My mother knows how to do it.'

It shouldn't distress you, but you spoke sharply to me once or twice. I knew that you'd immediately be sorry for it, and it is also true that I, too, made mistakes once in a while. Yes, I always liked to fuss over your clothes and underwear, especially when you were far away from home. When I mended your things I would forget about the distance. Even nowadays I often sit down with things that need mending, but what comes into my hand most frequently is that little shirt with the ruffled collar. It was your grand-mother who pinked its hem and embroidered a four-leaf clover on the front. Then she made your apron with the large pocket and those ash-gray pants, the first pants you ever got. Uncle Gyula sent them from Pozsony.[1] They were made of a fine woolly fabric, and no matter how we praised them you could not be made to wear them. They're scratchy, you said, and kept asking tearfully for your skirt.

I can still hear that childish whimpering of yours, even though I know that you've become a grown man and gotten married, and that you cough in the morning, find climbing stairs difficult, often feel dizzy, and have trouble with your heart. I beg you to take twenty drops of Myofort daily—you see, I even remember the name of the drug you take.

I am perhaps not so far from you, because I can see the scars of the ugly wounds on your body that you got from that stick-wielding *Todtist* whom you called the Jackal, and the other scars caused by the butt of a rifle or the boot of Oberscharführer Hubert.[2] I often see your tears, my son, and I don't want you to cry on our account. The three of us are well, as are the many others whom you liked so much and with whom we talk about you.

.   I must confess I am still secretly waiting for you to come—I don't talk about this to anybody—as I used to do on Saturday evenings. The train might not even have left for Pécs yet when I was already finished placing the plates and the silverware on the table.[3] I would run to the oven many times to make sure that the food was warm enough for you; I opened your bed and fluffed up the large pillow and the small one too.

Even now I often say quietly to myself, 'My son is coming,' and God will nod. His eyes are as blue as your grandfather's. Once, when the bravest of us asked, he said, 'I did not will this terrible thing; man did it to his fellow man.' I blamed him only once. I still had trust in him as we were pressed into the freight car. My swollen legs hurt, and we were thirsty and hungry. Still I consoled your brother, 'God will help us.' I believed he would, even as they were pushing us around and cursing us. I could hardly walk by then and I was ashamed of my nakedness, but we were promised a bath and I even saw the sign: *'Waschraum.'* They lied to us. Thousands shouted, 'Gas!' or perhaps something else. I could only think of you and blame God. I blamed him though I heard him say, 'Man did it to his fellow man.'

We'll talk about many other things, as we used to after you'd arrived on the Saturday evening train. How we could talk! So much happened in a week that we could have talked till morning and still not finished it.

It is—this I must tell you now—always morning here. The golden sunrise casts a yellow light, like the light of the candles in the thatch-roofed synagogue where we used to pray on the High Holidays. Take care of yourself, my son; you catch cold easily. When you leave home put on the sweater that your sister knitted, and the maroon scarf. I know they took it away from you in Dachau. It's a pity that you pleaded so much with the Germans. A maroon scarf is not the only thing that will keep a person warm. Your father and brother send their kisses too . . ."

Géza Seifert

On the Twenty-fifth Anniversary
of the Agreement
(Excerpts)

The two most difficult tasks facing the Jews of Hungary in the aftermath of the Second World War have been overcoming their petty bourgeois status, regarded as a source of social unsuitability by the architects of the new socialist order, and finding the most effective means for winning acceptance from a political system that treated professing members of religious denominations with suspicion and contempt. Though the relationship between the government of the Hungarian People's Republic and the Jewish community has been regulated since 1948 by an agreement whereby each pledged the other cooperation and respect, the National Representation of Hungarian Jews must see to it that members of the Jewish community fulfill the stipulations of the agreement and give no cause for friction between the state and the Jewish denomination. Dr. Géza Seifert (1906–76), a lawyer by profession, was the president of the Executive Committee of the National Representation and the Jewish Community of Budapest. Adopting the ideological stance that won him the authorities' trust while safeguarding the interests of the Jewish community, Seifert walked the political tightrope with skill and confidence. In his writings, which appeared mainly in Jewish publications, he was a dutiful reciter of the pledge of allegiance and the formulas of gratitude through which the leadership of the Hungarian Jews pays its dues of survival to the Hungarian State and the Soviet Union. The following article provides a good example of the ideologically acceptable perspective that the officials of the Jewish community are expected to display in their public speeches and writings. It is translated from "Az Egyezmény 25. évfordulójára," Évkönyv, ed. Sándor Scheiber (Budapest, A Magyar Izraeliták Országos Képviselete, 1973/74), pp. 3–37. By permission of A Magyar Izraeliták Országos Képviselete.

Twenty-five years ago, on 7 December 1948, our state signed the Agreement with our denomination. In accordance with the fundamental statute of the Agreement, our state, in the interest of guaranteeing the freedom of conscience and "on the basis of the principle of separation between state and church, on this occasion declares and with all possible and necessary means guarantees the free practice of religion. . . ."

Today as we reflect from a distance of twenty-five years on the period that passed since the signing of the Agreement, we may conclude that our state has faithfully and fully satisfied all of its obligations embodied in the Agreement. This Agreement has assured the freedom of our denominational life, the free exercise of our religion.

In the history of Hungarian Jewry the signing of the Agreement signifies a milestone and a celebration, inasmuch as with the liberation of the country, our denomination and its members—in contrast to the harmful discrimination and disfranchisement of the past—won full equality before the law, and, in the words of the Agreement, the peaceful and proper normalization of "relations between state and denomination, desired by both parties."

In the spirit of the Agreement we, the Hungarian Jews, are faithful to our socialist Hungarian fatherland, and as members of the national unity effectively and enthusiastically take part in the building of socialism, which aims at the economic, social, and cultural development of our nation.

Hungarian Jewry has strong reasons to greet the Agreement joyfully on the twenty-fifth anniversary of its inception. The pages of Hungary's thousand-year history clearly testify that until the liberation of our country in 1945, Hungarian Jewry had been the object of discrimination and prejudice, had never enjoyed true equality before the law, and could not exercise the rights of human dignity that are every person's due.

Hungarian Jewry received its freedom of conscience, in the true sense of the word, as well as its full freedom of religion, not only as stipulated by law but also as implemented, from the progressive socialist society founded on human truth that came into being in the aftermath of the liberation of our country in 1945.

The historical data should prove the validity of this thesis. . . .

As long as Christendom was at war in Hungary with pagan society, the Jews enjoyed unmolested the blessing of the freedom of religion. The Council of Szabolcs, held in 1092 during the reign of László the Saint, passed the first resolutions restricting the rights of Jews.[1] It decreed that Jewish men could not marry Christian women and annulled such marriages as were already made, so that the Christian women might regain their freedom. It forbade Jews to work on Sunday and Christian holidays under the penalty of severe punishment.

Ten years later Kálmán Könyves passed a new Jewish law that enacted the tithe, a special tax, and a penalty to be payed by Jews, and restricted their residence to episcopal estates.[2] This law also contained stipulations affecting court procedure. They nullified the equality of Jews before the law in litigations with members of other denominations. They declared, among other things, that a Jewish witness was not the equal of his Christian counterpart.

Thus the legal equality of Hungarian Jewry ceased with the Jewish laws of László the Saint and Kálmán Könyves.

In the succession of the kings of the House of Árpád, Kálmán Könyves was followed by the ambitious but weak and incompetent Endre II, whose rule brought much trouble to the country and had fatal consequences for the Jews as well.[3]

Article 24 of the Golden Bull, promulgated in 1222, declares that "money changers, salt officers, and toll collectors must be native-born noblemen. Ishmaelites [i.e., Muslims] and Jews must not be [holders of such offices]."

The Jewish Law of Béla IV, consisting of thirty-one articles, was promulgated in 1251, ten years after the Mongol invasion that took place soon after the issuance of the Golden Bull.[4] This law restored, with minor restrictions, the relationship that had existed between Jews and Magyars in the period before the issuance of the Golden Bull. . . .

The position of Jewry became extraordinarily precarious during the reign of Lajos the Great.[5] A zealous believer in and partisan of the Catholic Church, King Lajos the Great strove to put an end to the Jewish religion. He tried to the best of his ability to convert the Jews of the country to the Christian faith. Inasmuch as the "stubbornness of the Jewish heresy" thwarted his effort, he expelled all Jews from his realm in 1360.

Four years later, in 1364, Lajos the Great rescinded his decree and permitted the Jews to settle again in the country. During those four years, however, the expelled Jews found greater security in other European countries and returned to Hungary only in small numbers. Due to acts of disfranchisement following their return, the ghettoization of the Hungarian Jews was pursued more vigorously than before. . . .

In 1421, during the reign of King Zsigmond, the so-called Law of Buda was promulgated, which again prescribed the wearing of specific pieces of clothing for Jews: the pointed Jewish hat, the scarlet cape, and the palm-sized yellow patch on the most conspicuous part of the latter.[6]

The flames of anti-Semitism were resolutely fanned in this period. Trials of blood libels, well-poisoning, and profanation of the wafer, based on unfounded superstitions and prejudices, started in Hungary. Countless Jews fell victim to such trials, which were tolerated by the authorities. János Kapisztrán stood at the head of the persecutors, and at his instigation numerous Jewish martyrs suffered death at the stake. . . .[7]

Prior to the Battle of Mohács, uncontrollable agitation broke out against the Jews. Pogroms took place in Buda, Székesfehérvár, and Pozsony, and the royal guards that had been ordered out protected the lives and property of the Jews only slowly and reluctantly. . . .[8]

In the persecution of Jews, a leading role was played by the Palatine István Werbőczy, who in his *Tripartitum* codified the severely persecutory, disfranchising, and humiliating anti-Jewish laws. . . .[9]

In the sixteenth, seventeenth, and eighteenth centuries the kings placed the Jews under "the protective custody of nobles and burghers," who fulfilled their obligation to but a small degree or not at all. . . .

On the night of 19 February 1848 a massive anti-Jewish disturbance broke out. Its immediate cause was that János Bohus, the representative of Arad, moved to confer full civil rights on Jews.[10] The disturbance, within sight of the Diet, lasted for three days and spread to other cities as well. . . .

The law of emancipation, interpolated in Law 17 of 1867, declared the civil equality of Hungarian Jewry, though it did not confer on the Jewish community the rights enjoyed by other denominations. . . .

The emancipation and the *receptio* remained purely nominal.[11] The law stipulated resolutions affecting equality before the law, but in reality the Jews had not been granted equal rights. The stipulations of the law and actual practice were two different things. . . .

The struggle continued. Reactionary circles, in conflict with progressive ideas, could not acquiesce in the emancipation of the Jews.

It is known that the anti-Semitic leaders of the last century—Istóczy, Ónody, Verhovay, and their cohorts—wanted to bring back the spirit of the Middle Ages, and incited anti-Jewish feeling with lies and trumped-up charges.[12] They conspired with Rohling, the professor of Judaica-Hebraica at the University of Prague, and other Talmud falsifiers, engineered blood libels and anti-Jewish trials, and touched off the accusation of ritual murder at Tiszaeszlár, that inflammatory criminal procedure. . . .[13]

Such was the situation despite the freedom of religion guaranteed by the law. The dead letter of the law was one thing, practice was quite another. . . .

The [Hungarian] Soviet Republic put an end to this situation for a short time. The proletarian dictatorship triumphed on 21 March 1919, and the 133-day rule of the Soviet Republic followed. During this period Hungarian Jewry enjoyed full equality before the law, with guaranteed implementation, as well as freedom of religion and conscience.

Proclaiming the confusing tenets of the "Szeged Idea" and the "Christian Course," Miklós Horthy laid the foundations of a fascist political system that was characterized by a trampling on the rights to freedom, by anti-Semitism and the suppression of progressive ideas. Following its rise to power, Horthy's fascism initiated consciously persecutory and disfranchising activities against the Jews.[14]

For more than a decade and a half, a powerful and constant propaganda campaign advocated the repeal of the legal equality of Hungarian Jewry as well as the freedom of religion and conscience. The anti-Semites wanted to put an end to the emancipation of the Jews resulting from progressive middle-class ideals, even if it was a house of cards. Those who were filled with the fascist spirit, rabid anti-Jewish hatred, and subjectivity agitated and incited public opinion against the Jews in the press, in speeches, in other communications media, and in anti-Jewish plays and films, as well as by all other possible ways and means.

In the atmosphere that was the result of this decade-and-a-half-long blind and boisterous incitement, Prime Minister Kálmán Darányi, in a speech in Győr, announced "the lawful solution of the Jewish Question."[15] Soon after this speech he introduced his resolution, the so-called First Jewish Law, concerning "the more effective safeguarding of a balanced social and economic life." Parliament adopted it, and as Law 15 of 1938 it was put into effect on 29 March 1938.

In utter disregard for human rights and the laws of morality, this law exposed Hungarian Jewry to unjust, illegal, and prejudicial discrimination, by which it placed severe limitations on the Jews' means of livelihood.

The law was formulated in such a way that it gave the government broad powers to take appropriate action in providing a "more effective safekeeping of a balanced social and economic life," even if legislation was needed for such action. Thus the First Jewish Law became in effect a skeleton law that gave the government authority to pass disfranchising resolutions in the name of the "solution of the Jewish Question" by circumventing legislation.

It was on the basis of such legal authority that the government of Béla Imrédy revised the charters of the Press Club, the Stage and Film Actors' Union, the Bar Association, and the Medical Association, subjecting Jewish members of the press, Jewish stage and film actors, lawyers, and doctors to discrimination, and revoking their membership.[16]

Resolutions passed on the basis of this law deprived junior clerks and shop assistants of their sources of livelihood, removed them from their jobs, and revoked even their right to work.

Not even the unjust and inhuman Jewish Laws could put an end to the anti-Jewish agitation and the untrue slogans of the fascist propaganda. Nothing satisfied the fascist leaders. By resolution, Béla Imrédy tightened the Jewish Laws and made them more stringent after their promulgation. In a policy speech before his party, the Party of Hungarian Renewal, on 15 November 1938 he declared that "we must, to a certain extent, revise our philosophy in the Jewish Question."[17] Following this declaration he instructed his minister of justice to introduce a resolution calling for the Second Jewish Law, which took place on 23 December 1938, and was passed in Parliament. As Law 4 of 1939 it took effect on 4 May 1939.

The Second Jewish Law imposed on Hungarian Jewry additional discriminatory restrictions that further violated its life-sustaining rights to work.

The Second Jewish Law was soon followed by the Third, the so-called race-protecting law, which Prime Minister László Bárdossy introduced and which Parliament put into effect on 8 August 1941.[18] The race-protecting law was entered—shamefully—into the Corpus Juris Hungarici as Law 15 of 1941.

Aside from the fact that the three Jewish Laws and the orders implementing them (which were more rigorously anti-Jewish than the laws themselves) deprived the Jews of their human rights, Prime Minister Miklós Kállay, the well-known opportunistic politician, employed Machiavellian tactics in attempting to maintain the semblance of legality to a point that seemed almost ridiculous.[19] On his recommendation, on 19 July 1942 Parliament put into effect Law 8 of 1942, concerning the "normalization of the legal status of the Israelite denomination," which terminated the political equality of Jews as individuals and the religious equality of Judaism. By this time the law was of no great consequence. It was, however, symptomatic of the claptrap politics of the period.

In addition to the disfranchising Jewish Laws, countless orders restricting the rights of Jews were issued. In the *Budapesti Közlöny* alone, more than 130 "Jewish orders" were published.[20] The various ministries themselves issued disfranchising orders. Gradually but systematically, these orders contained provisions that led to the increasing restriction and eventual termination of the human rights of the Jews.

The provisions of these orders went so far as to forbid any Jew from being a telephone subscriber or a radio licensee, and put limitations on the Jews' use of public transportation and access to public streets, as well as to jobs requiring manual labor. Gradually the point was reached where a Jew could not engage in work of any kind to secure even the minimum standard of living.

Order 107.501/1944, relating to the Jewish houses, restricted Jews to living in only houses designated for that purpose. An order spelled out the compulsory wearing of the star. Orders 108.000 and 108.500/1944 regulated the supply of food for Jews; the maximum amount permitted was below subsistence level.

In the final analysis, these orders restricted the rights of the Jews so severely that they were left with only their lives—for the time being—but were given no opportunity to work or live in dignity.

On 19 March 1944 the Germans marched into Hungary. The German occupation marked the darkest age in Hungary. They immediately undertook to effect the *Endlösung der Judenfrage*, the solution of the Jewish Question, which by then all too obviously meant the complete destruction of Hungarian Jewry. The proponents of progressive ideals, the best Hungarian patriots, were jailed and deported. . . .

On 15 October 1944 the usurpation of power by Ferenc Szálasi signaled the start of the Arrow Cross's reign of terror.[21] It was characterized by suppression, murder, plunder, and uncontrollable terror. It had no system of law. In all of its manifestations it was characterized by lawlessness, trampling on laws, disregard for human rights, and unconditional service to the Germans. It was during the Arrow Cross's reign of terror that the capital's Jewry suffered the greatest tragedy of its persecution. With impunity and at will, young Arrow Cross men shot Jews to death even in the open street and in full view of everyone. The killing of Jews was a permissible act.

Szálasi's Arrow Cross henchmen concentrated numerous Jews in the brick factory at Újlak and from there on October 20 deported them through Hegyeshalom.[22] However, they were unable to liquidate the ghetto of Budapest, because the victorious Soviet army liberated it on 18 January 1945 and freed the capital's Jewry.

Hungarian Jewry thinks of the liberating Soviet heroes with eternal gratitude.

Six hundred thousand Hungarian Jews fell victim to the Nazi persecutions of the Second World War. Hungarian Jewry renders perpetual homage to their memory, which will never fade. . . .

Following the liberation of our country the Hungarian government abolished, with a stroke of the pen, all regulations of Horthy's fascism and the periods before it that were discriminatory to Jews.

In the Armistice Agreement, ratified as Law 5 of 1945, Hungary declared that it would void all anti-Jewish laws and any restrictions resulting from them. . . .

In accordance with the regulations that the Hungarian Republic enacted immediately after the liberation of the country, before any others were put into effect, Hungarian Jewry gained full equality before the law, freedom, and legal protection from harrassment. . . .

On 7 December 1948 the Agreement, regulating the legal status of Jewry, came into being between the government of the Hungarian Republic and the Hungarian-Jewish community, which had acquired its full freedom and freedom before the law.

"The government of the Hungarian Republic declares on this occasion also that it recognizes and guarantees by all possible and necessary means the full freedom of worship. The lawful representative organs of the Hungarian-Jewish community note on this occasion also that the legislation and government of the Hungarian Republic have even at this date guaranteed and protected the free exercise of religion, and significantly expanded (with the adoption of Law 33 of 1947) and facilitated, with aid provided to cover the personal and material expenditures of the community, the preservation of religious life.

"The government of the Hungarian Republic, in accordance with the existing laws, recognizes worship in temples and houses of prayer, family homes, and any other suitable buildings and places as being within the framework of the free exercise of religion; also the teaching of the Bible, and the Talmud, and other religious instruction in temples, houses of prayer, and family homes; the educational, pedagogical, and religious instruction in denominational journals and independent publications; the propagation of the Holy Scriptures and religious tenets; the holding of religious and denominational conferences and meetings; compulsory religious study in school, the establishment and maintenance of rabbinical schools, Talmud Torahs, and Yeshivas; the training of rabbis and Talmud Torah teachers; the performance of religious and charitable work. . . .

"The Jewish communities, in accordance with prescribed religious procedure, see to it that prayers are recited for the Hungarian Republic, the Head of State, the government, the well-being of the entire Hungarian people, and peace, and suitable religious services are held on national holidays. . . .

"The government of the Hungarian Republic recognizes and guarantees the right of the Jewish community to maintain compulsory religious instruction in all public schools. The government of the Hungarian Republic also guarantees to students of the Jewish faith the suitable celebration of Saturday in accordance with Jewish religious laws. In pursuance of the foregoing, students whose parents or guardians are certified by the appropriate community to be in the habit of observing Saturday are not obliged to attend instruction on Saturday. The number of such students may not exceed 20 percent of the students in any school. Students of the Jewish faith not observing Saturday are also exempted from writing, arithmetic, drawing, and handiwork and, in general, all such activities that according to the Jewish religious laws are forbidden on Saturday, provided that the parents or guardians of the students request it in writing from the principal of the school. All students of the Jewish faith are exempted from attending school on the following holidays: the two days of Rosh Hashana (New Year), Shabbat Shuvah (the Sabbath of Repentance), Yom Kippur (the Day of Atonement), Sukkot (Tabernacles), Hoshana Rabba (the seventh day of Tabernacles), Shemini Atzeret and Simchat Torah (the eighth and ninth days of Tabernacles), the first, second, seventh, and eighth days of Pesach (Passover), the first and second days of Shavuot (Pentecost). . . ."

It may undoubtedly be observed from the text of the Agreement quoted above that our state recognizes and by all possible and necessary means guarantees the full freedom of religion, and permits the free election and activity of the lawful representative organs of our denomination. In all respects it allows for the observance of the absolute Jewish traditions in the spirit of our sacred Torah. . . .

From the distance of twenty-five years we wish to declare that we Hungarian Jews are aware of the rights, the freedom of religion and conscience, the termination of past discrimination directed against us, and our equality before the law, all of which we have received from the progressive, socialism-building society of the Hungarian People's Republic. For that reason we, in addition to maintaining our Jewish traditions, are also faithful to our socialist Hungarian State, and participate as members of the Hungarian national unity in the work aimed at the economic, social, and cultural development of our country, the building of socialism.

Hungarian Jewry has found its place in the new society. We can well harmonize our adherence to our Jewish traditions with our love of our socialist fatherland and our civic allegiance. We remember with gratitude the faithful sons of our progressive society who labored to bring into existence and sign the freedom-inspiring Agreement. The twenty-fifth anniversary of the signing of the Agreement is a landmark in the life of Hungarian Jewry. May it be a pledge of faith and trust in the guaranteed future of a Hungarian Jewry that has suffered much, as well as a celebration of its sustained good relations with our state.

Notes

Introduction

1. Richard Wagner, *Richard Wagner's Prose Works*, trans. William Ashton Ellis, 8 vols. (London: K. Paul, Trench, Trübner 1895–1912), 3:85.

2. The most comprehensive and detailed accounts of the history of Jews in Hungary from the establishment of their national state by the Magyars until the end of the nineteenth century are Lajos Venetianer, *A magyar zsidóság története* [History of Hungarian Jewry] (Budapest, n.p., 1922); and Sándor Büchler, *A zsidók története Budapesten* [History of Jews in Budapest] (Budapest, n.p., 1901).

3. A leader of those opposing the emancipation of Jews was Count István Széchenyi (1791–1860), one of the most respected politicians of his time, who feared that the presence of German-speaking Jews in Hungary was a threat to the culture and political aspirations of the Magyars. George Barany, *Stephen Széchenyi and the Awakening of Hungarian Nationalism, 1791–1841* (Princeton: Princeton University Press, 1968), pp. 357–59.

4. For information on Kossuth's emergence as the leader of the 1848 Revolution, see István Deák, *The Lawful Revolution: Louis Kossuth and the Hungarians, 1848–1849* (New York: Columbia University Press, 1979).

5. Nearly half of the Jews living in Hungary were Orthodox. They had come from Austria and the German states, bringing "the closed system of rabbinism aiming at absolute authority," and had been settling on Hungarian soil since the middle of the seventeenth century. They retained their unswerving religious traditionalism and social exclusivism under the leadership of powerful rabbis such as Moses Sofer (1762–1839). The migration of Jews from Poland to Hungary, due to political uncertainties and fear of pogroms, began in the latter half of the eighteenth century, and gave rise to what has been called synthetic Hasidism. Inspired by their leader (*tzaddik*) in Sátoraljaújhely, the Polish-born Moses Teitelbaum (1759–1841), this novel religious trend aimed at reducing the differences between the Hasidim and their opponents, the Mitnaggedim. See Ernest (Ernő) Marton, "The Family Tree of Hungarian Jewry," in *Hungarian-Jewish Studies*, ed. Randolph L. Braham, 2 vols. (New York: World Federation of Hungarian Jews, 1966–69), 1:39–59.

Not all Orthodox leaders subscribed to the principle and practice of separation. Rabbi Eizik Taub (1751–1821), the legendary *tzaddik* of Kálló, spoke Hungarian, had friendly relations with non-Jews, and was a patriot. See László Szilágyi-Windt, *A kállói cádik: A nagykállói zsidóság története* [The Tzaddik of Kálló: the history of Nagykálló Jewry] (Tel Aviv: L. Szilágyi-Windt, 1959), pp. 16–39; Andrew Handler, trans., *Rabbi Eizik: Hasidic stories about the Zaddik of Kálló* (Rutherford, New Jersey: Fairleigh Dickinson University Press, 1978), pp. 13–19.

Among the Rabbinic leaders, Israel Hildesheimer (1820–99) was an indefatigable synthesizer of religious and secular learning and the founder of the so-called Cultural Orthodox, a group of thirty-five Jews who believed that it was possible to retain traditions while also acquiring the progressive spirit. He was a frequent target of attacks by extreme Orthodox rabbis. See Péter Ujvári, ed., *Magyar Zsidó Lexikon* [Hungarian-Jewish lexicon] (Budapest: A Magyar Zsidó Lexikon, 1929), s.v. "Hildesheimer Izrael Azriel."

Such efforts, however, had little, if any, effect on the strained relations between Orthodox and Progressive (Neolog) Jews. After irreconcilable differences surfaced in the course of an assembly of Jewish leaders, the Orthodox representatives broke with the Progressives and established an independent communal structure that stands to this day. Nathaniel Katzburg, "The Jewish Congress of Hungary, 1868–1869," in Braham, ed., *Hungarian-Jewish Studies*, 2:1–33.

6. Aron Moskovits describes the development and progressive secularization of the cultural institutions of Hungarian Jewry in *Jewish Education in Hungary, 1848–1948* (New York: Bloch Publishing Co., 1964).

7. Ujvári, ed., *Magyar Zsidó Lexikon*, s.v. "Magyarosítás" [Magyarization].

8. Though somewhat dated, Béla Bernstein's *Az 1848/49-iki magyar szabadságharc és a zsidók* [The 1848/49 Hungarian war of independence and the Jews] (Budapest: Franklin, 1898) is still the best source of information for the experiences of the Jews during this turbulent period in the history of Hungary.

9. For the events leading to this turning point in the history of the Jews in Hungary and for its long-range effects, see Nathaniel Katzburg, "Hungarian Jewry in Modern Times: Political and Social Aspects," in Braham, ed., *Hungarian-Jewish Studies*, 1:139–44.

10. Ujvári, ed., *Magyar Zsidó Lexikon*, s.v. "Nemesek" [nobles]. For a detailed study of the achievements of Jews in the modernization of Hungarian commerce and industry, see William O. McCagg, Jr., *Jewish Nobles and Geniuses in Modern Hungary* (New York: Columbia University Press, 1972).

11. Soon after he retired from active political life, Istóczy published a collection of his more memorable speeches, *Istóczy Győző országgyűlési beszédei, indítványai és törvényjavaslatai, 1872–1896* [Győző Istóczy's speeches, resolutions, and bills in the Diet, 1872–1896] (Budapest: Buschmann, 1904).

12. Judit Kubinszky provides a well-researched and documented account in her *Politikai antiszemitizmus Magyarországon, 1875–1890* [Political anti-Semitism in Hungary, 1875–1890] (Budapest: Kossuth, 1976) of the evolution, philosophy, political program, and literary activity of the Hungarian anti-Semites.

13. Ujvári, ed., *Magyar Zsidó Lexikon*, s.v. "Világháború" [World War I].

14. For the Communists' brief rule, see Rudolf L. Tőkés, *Béla Kun and the Hungarian Soviet Republic: The Origins and Role of the Communist Party in Hungary in the Revolutions of 1918–1919* (New York: Praeger, 1967). The precarious position of the Jews under Communist rule is well documented and explained in Ujvári, ed., *Magyar Zsidó Lexikon*, s.v. "Forradalom 1918–1919" [Revolution 1918–1919].

15. Predictably, the recollections of his widow contain not a single reference to his Jewish origin. Mme Béla Kun, *Kun Béla*, (Budapest: Magvető, 1969).

16. Ujvári, ed., *Magyar Zsidó Lexikon*, s.v. "Ellenforradalom" [Counterrevolution]; Katzburg, "Hungarian Jewry," pp. 153–55. Nicholas Horthy, *Memoirs* (New

York: Robert Speller & Sons, 1957), p. 109; Ferenc Pölöskei, *Horthy és hatalmi rendszere, 1919–1922* [Horthy and his system of power, 1919–1922] (Budapest: Kossuth, 1977), pp. 57–83; Erik Molnár, Ervin Pamlényi, and György Székely, eds., *Magyarország története* [History of Hungary], 2 vols. (Budapest: Gondolat, 1964), 2:376–85.

17. Though on the surface the Horthy-Bethlen partnership strove to achieve respectability at home and abroad, a retrospective analysis of their behind-the-scenes manipulations in particular clearly reveals the prevalence of "controlled" anti-Semitism and the "Christian course" of Hungary's militant irredentism. Miklós Szinai and László Szűcs, eds., *Horthy Miklós titkos iratai* [The secret papers of Miklós Horthy] (Budapest: Kossuth, 1965): and idem, *Bethlen István titkos iratai* [The secret papers of István Bethlen] (Budapest: Kossuth, 1972).

18. The achievements of these crowning years of Gömbös's political career stand in marked contrast also with his militant views and the embittered, yet defiant statements in the immediate aftermath of the fall of the Hungarian Soviet Republic that are found in his *Egy magyar vezérkari tiszt bíráló feljegyzései a forradalomról és ellenforradalomról* [The critical notes of a Hungarian staff officer of the revolution and counterrevolution] (Budapest: Budapesti Hirlap nyomdája, 1920). Awed by Horthy's unshakable conservatism and humbled by the full weight of his realization of Hungary's precarious political situation and economic vulnerability, he considerably softened his earlier anti-Jewish stance. István Deák, "Hungary," in *The European Right: A Historical Profile*, ed. Hans Rogger and Eugen Weber (London: Weidenfeld & Nicholson, 1965), p. 379.

19. For additional information on the multifaceted contributions of Jews to Hungarian economy, see István (Stephen) Végházi, "The Role of Jewry in the Economic Life of Hungary" in Braham, ed., *Hungarian-Jewish Studies*, 2:35–84; Robert A. Kann, "Hungarian Jewry during Austria-Hungary's Constitutional Period (1867–1918)," *Jewish Social Studies* 7 (1945): 366–73.

20. Ujvári, ed., *Magyar Zsidó Lexikon*, s.v. "Hitközségek" [Religious communities].

21. The *Magyar Zsidó Lexikon* is the sole source of information for the skills and achievements of Jewish athletes in Hungary for the period ending with the late 1920s.

22. For information in English about the Hungarian Fascists, see C. A. Macartney's classic *October Fifteenth: A History of Modern Hungary*, 2d ed., 2 vols. (Edinburgh: Edinburgh University Press, 1961); and Nicholas M. Nagy-Talavera's *The Green Shirts and the Others* (Stanford: Hoover Institution Press, 1970), which also examines Fascism in Romania. Three other studies deserve attention: István Deák, "Hungary;" György Ránki, "The Problem of Fascism in Hungary," in *Native Fascism in the Successor States, 1918–1945*, ed. Peter F. Sugar (Santa Barbara: ABC-Clio, Inc., 1971), pp. 65–72; George Barany, "The Dragon's Teeth: The Roots of Hungarian Fascism," in ibid., pp. 73–82.

23. In a speech delivered in 1924 Bethlen declared that in the work of national rebuilding there was a need for the contributions of honest and "hard-working" Jews. József Szekeres, ed., *Források Budapest történetéhez* [Sources for the history of Budapest], 4 vols. (Budapest: Budapest Székesfőváros Levéltára, 1972), 3:113.

24. In his memoirs Horthy made spirited attempts to portray himself as the paragon of Hungarian virtues and decency, the defender of Christianity and, indeed,

Western civilization against the Bolshevik menace. Contemporary Hungarian studies, such as Zoltán Vas's *Horthy, vagy a király* [Horthy; or, the King] (Budapest:
Szépirodalmi Könyvkiadó, 1971) and István Pintér's *Ki volt Horthy Miklós?* [Who
was Miklós Horthy?] (Budapest: Zrínyi, 1968) did much to discredit his contention.

25. Nagy-Talavera, *The Green Shirts*, p. 104n.

26. Y. Zvi Zahavi offers a sweeping narrative of the proto-Zionist and Zionist
thinkers and writers from 1799 to 1904 in his *Me-he-Chatam Sofer ve-'ad Herzl*
[From the Chatam Sofer to Herzl] (Jerusalem: Zionist Library, 1965).

27. Ujvári, ed., *Magyar Zsidó Lexikon*, s.v. "Magyar Cionista Szövetség" [Hun-
garian Zionist Federation].

28. Except for my *Blood Libel at Tiszaeszlár* (New York: Columbia University
Press, 1980), only sparse details of this shocking affair—the arrest, interrogation,
trial, and acquittal of a group of Tiszaeszlár Jews accused of murdering a Christian girl
in their synagogue—are available in English. The following works by Hungarian
writers provide adequate though incomplete information: József Bary, *A tiszaeszlári
bűnper* [The criminal case of Tiszaeszlár], 2d ed. (Budapest: Magyar Élet, 1941);
Károly Eötvös, *A nagy per* [The great trial], 3 vols., (Budapest: Révai Testvérek,
1904); Sándor Hegedüs, *A tiszaeszlári vérvád* [The blood libel of Tiszaeszlár]
(Budapest: Kossuth, 1966); Gyula Krúdy, *A tiszaeszlári Solymosi Eszter* [Eszter
Solymosi of Tiszaeszlár] (Budapest: Magvető, 1975); and Iván Sándor, *A vizsgálat
iratai: Tudósítás a tiszaeszlári per körülményeiről* [The documents of the investigation: report on the circumstances of the Tiszaeszlár case] (Budapest: Kozmosz, 1976).
By the time of the First Zionist Congress the affair had been largely hushed up.

29. "We, to whose joy this nation has acknowledged the legality of our religion,"
exulted Sámuel Kohn, one of the most distinguished Progressive rabbis and a leader
of the Magyarization of Hungarian Jewry, "not only feel but *know* that we are
Magyars. For us the word Israelite, even in our religious life that is Israelite as far as
the faith is concerned, is the adjective of the word Magyar. Let us proudly declare: it
signifies a Jewish Magyar." "Elnöki megnyitó" [Presidential opening speech], in
Évkönyv [Yearbook], ed. Vilmos Bacher and József Bánóczi (Budapest: Az Izraelita
Magyar Irodalmi Társulat, 1897), p. 8.

30. "A Cionizmus" [Zionism], in *Évkönyv*, ed. József Bánóczi (Budapest: Az
Izraelita Magyar Irodalmi Társulat, 1908), p. 237.

31. Ujvári, ed., *Magyar Zsidó Lexikon*, s.v. "Magyar Zsidók Pro Palesztina
Szövetsége" [The Pro-Palestine Federation of Hungarian Jews].

32. Most Hungarian Jews felt that the philosophy and goals of Herzlian Zionism
affected the lives of only their less fortunate, homeless coreligionists. When Nordau's
pamphlet, *Zionism*, was published in Hungary in Hungarian, the translator felt
compelled to add an explanatory codicil clarifying the position of the Hungarian Jews
on Zionism. Though he admitted that there indeed were Hungarian Zionists, he
described them as "happy, emancipated citizens of a chivalrous nation." The majority
of Hungarian Jews, he declared proudly, "are not and cannot be in need of the good
deeds of Zionism." Miksa Nordau, *A Czionizmus* [Zionism], trans. Gyula Gábel
(Budapest: Gross & Grünhut, 1902), pp. 19–22.

33. The lengthy article devoted to him in the *Magyar Zsidó Lexikon*, s.v. "Herzl
Tivadar" was indicative of the slowly changing stance of the Hungarian Jews on the
Zionist issue.

34. Palestine was thought of as "our trust in the future and source of hope."

Bertalan Édelstein, "A külföldi zsidóság az 5691 évben" [Foreign Jewry in the year 5691] in *Évkönyv*, ed. Samu Szemere (Budapest: Az Izraelita Magyar Irodalmi Társulat, 1932), p. 279.

35. Built between 1929 and 1931, it is one of the most impressive and modern synagogues in Hungary. Architecturally it forms a unit with the Jewish Museum and the much larger and older Dohány Street Synagogue, where, incidentally, Herzl celebrated his bar mitzva in 1873. Fülöp Grünwald and Ernő Naményi, "Budapesti zsinagógák" [The synagogues of Budapest] in *A 90 éves Dohány-utcai templom* [The ninety-year-old Dohány Street Temple], ed. József Katona (Budapest: Az Országos Magyar Zsidó Múzeum, 1949), pp. 29–30.

36. Nagy-Talavera, *The Green Shirts*, pp. 182–83.

37. Paul Lendvai, *Anti-Semitism without Jews* (New York: Doubleday, 1971), p. 322.

38. Nicholas Kállay, *Hungarian Premier* (Westport, Connecticut: Greenwood Press, 1970), p. 433.

39. As late as 1943 Ottó Komoly, then president of the Hungarian Zionist Federation, still believed that the establishment of the independent Jewish national home in Palestine would make possible the assimilation of those staying behind. Others, however, struck a more realistic and pessimistic note. Aladár Komlós ("Zsidóság, magyarság, Európa" [Jewry, Magyardom, Europe] in *Ararát*, ed. Aladár Komlós [Budapest: Országos Izraelita Leányárváház, 1943], pp. 24–27) sadly admitted to the "cooling relationship between Jews and Magyars" and cautioned his coreligionists "not to try to be more Magyar" than those who had already learned that Jews would have to "relinquish voluntarily some things that are the natural rights of trueborn Magyars."

40. An increasing number of scholarly works dealing with the persecution of Jews in Hungary are available in both English and Hungarian. Of those in English, the following offer comprehensive and detailed accounts: Randolph L. Braham, *The Destruction of Hungarian Jewry: A Documentary Account*, 2 vols. (New York: World Federation of Hungarian Jews, 1963); idem, *The Hungarian Jewish Catastrophe: A Selected and Annotated Bibliography* (New York: Yivo Institute for Jewish Research, 1962); and Jenő Lévai, *Black Book on the Martyrdom of Hungarian Jewry* (Zürich, n.p., 1948).

Readers familiar with Hungarian may find the following works instructive: Jenő Lévai, *Zsidósors Magyarországon* [Jewish fate in Hungary], 2d ed. (Budapest: Magyar Téka, 1948) and Márton Himler, *Így néztek ki a magyar nemzet sírásói* [That is what the gravediggers of the Hungarian nation looked like] (New York: St. Marks Printing, 1958).

In addition, important details of the condition and mood of Hungarian Jewry and individual Jews during the war years may be found in articles published in the *Évkönyv* [Yearbook] of the Hungarian-Jewish Literary Society, 1939–43 and 1948, and the *Évkönyv* of the National Representation of the Hungarian Jews, a current series edited by Sándor Scheiber, the well-known Hungarian-Jewish scholar and director of the National Rabbinical Institute. Their readership, however, is limited to Jews. A much wider circle of readers was shocked by the gradual realization in the 1970s of the extent of the Jews' suffering and the bestiality of their torturers with the publication of a number of novels and monographs dealing with the Holocaust. György Moldova, *A Szent Imre-induló* [The St. Imre march] (Budapest: Magvető,

1975) and Mária Ember, *Hajtűkanyar* [Hairpin bend], 2 vols. (Budapest: Szépirodalmi Könyvkiadó, 1977) chronicle the saga of Hungary's doomed Jewry; Kálmán Vargha, *Gelléri Andor Endre* (Budapest: Szépirodalmi Könyvkiadó, 1973) and Béla Pomogáts, *Radnóti Miklós* (Budapest: Gondolat, 1977) document the works and tragic fates of the famed Hungarian Jewish novelist and the equally famous poet; Ödön Gáti et al., eds., *Mementó: Magyarország, 1944* [Memento: Hungary, 1944] (Budapest: Kossuth, 1975) contains the recollections of some of the best-known contemporary Hungarian poets, writers, and publicists of the tragedy-filled months of the German occupation and Arrow Cross rule; József Debreczeni's *Hideg krematórium* [Cold crematorium] (Budapest: Fórum, 1975) is probably the only novel published in Hungary that describes the horrors of Auschwitz; and the cynical callousness of the politically and morally bankrupt Arrow Cross leaders, their trials, and executions are described and documented in László Frank, *Zöld ár* [Green tide] (Budapest: Zrínyi, 1974) and in Elek Karsai, *Itél a nép* [The people pass judgment] (Budapest: Kossuth, 1977).

41. For additional information on the promulgation and implementation of the anti-Jewish laws, see Katzburg, "Hungarian Jewry," pp. 158–60.

42. Some bravely compassionate—or easily bribable—doctors gave injections to induce local and temporary paralysis. Such practices were common among Jews with ample financial resources and social connections. I am indebted to my late father for information about examples of desperate individual efforts to retain the last vestiges of solvency and to postpone what then appeared, at least to some, a journey of no return.

43. For two excellent analyses of the Kállay years, see Béla Vágó, "Germany and the Jewish Policy of the Kállay Government," in Braham, ed., *Hungarian-Jewish Studies*, 2:183–210 and Mario D. Fenyő, *Hitler, Horthy, and Hungary: German-Hungarian Relations, 1941–1944* (New Haven: Yale University Press, 1972).

44. Lenke Steiner "Az év magyar-zsidó irodalma" [Hungarian-Jewish literature of the year], in *Ararát*, ed. Aladár Komlós (Budapest: Országos Izraelita Leányárvaház, 1944), pp. 148–56. For a detailed, though not comprehensive, review of Hungarian-Jewish culture, see Erzsébet Balla, "The Jews of Hungary: A Cultural Overview," in Braham, ed., *Hungarian-Jewish Studies*, 2:85–136.

45. *Hungarian Premier*, p. 39.

46. Szinai and Szűcs, eds., *Horthy Miklós titkos iratai*, p. 261.

47. In a dramatic contrast to the nearly 500,000 Jews who lived in Hungary during the 1920s, once Southern Slovakia, Sub-Carpathia, and Northern Transylvania were reannexed, Hungary's Jewish population swelled to over 700,000. For additional statistical data, see Ernő László, "Hungary's Jewry: A Demographic Overview, 1918–1945," in Braham, ed., *Hungarian-Jewish Studies*, 2:137–82.

48. Szinai and Szűcs, ed., *Horthy Miklós titkos iratai*, p. 262.

49. Joseph Goebbels, *The Goebbels Diaries*, ed. and trans. Louis P. Lochner (New York: Popular Library, Eagle Books, 1965), p. 87.

50. Joseph Goebbels, *Final Entries, 1945: The Diaries of Joseph Goebbels*, ed. Hugh Trevor-Roper and trans. Richard Barry (New York: G. P. Putnam's Sons, 1978), p. 173. One of the most remarkable features of German-Hungarian relations was Hitler's reluctance, well before 19 March 1944, to occupy Hungary, even though (a) the Hungarian forces were regarded as the worst of Germany's allies (p. 407); (b) Prime Minister Kállay and Horthy's son and heir, István, were considered hostile to Germany (p. 185); and (c) Horthy was thought to be "badly tangled up with the Jews

through his family" and always resorting to "humanitarian counterarguments" at a time when the Nazis believed that one "just cannot talk humanitarianism when dealing with Jews" (p. 185).

51. Goebbels, *The Goebbels Diaries*, p. 576.

52. Ibid., p. 545.

53. For the last months of the Horthy era, see György Ránki, *1944. március 19.: Magyarország német megszállása* [19 March 1944: the German occupation of Hungary] (Budapest: Kossuth, 1978).

54. He was also German Foreign Minister Joachim von Ribbentrop's principal informer of the developments in Hungary. The Veesenmayer correspondence is reproduced in György Ránki et al., eds., *A Wilhelmstrasse és Magyarország: Német diplomáciai iratok magyarországról, 1933–1944* [Wilhelmstrasse and Hungary: German diplomatic documents on Hungary, 1933–1944] (Budapest: Kossuth, 1968).

55. Eichmann's activities in Hungary are described and documented in detail in Jenő Lévai, ed., *Eichmann in Hungary: Documents* (Budapest: Pannonia, 1961).

56. Lévai, *Zsidósors Magyarországon*, p. 110.

57. Ibid., pp. 87–121, 239–52. A small number of Jews in the countryside eluded deportation by taking one of three circuitous avenues of escape. They either slipped across the border into Slovakia or Romania after paying off Hungarian and German soldiers, hid out on farms or in cellars with the help of compassionate or enterprising neighbors, or traveled to Budapest by using documents which the Jewish Council had issued. In Budapest, the rescue work was greatly hampered by the lack of cooperation and trust among the leaders of various organizations. Kasztner, in particular, was accused of directing the so-called *Blut für Ware* (blood for goods) plan in an authoritarian manner. He was tried in Israel in 1955 on charges of collaborating with the Nazis. Though acquitted, he was assassinated in 1957. Komoly was murdered by Arrow Cross militiamen, and Brand, rendered inoperative by the British, who mistook him for a Nazi agent and arrested him in Syria in May 1944, spent the rest of his life after the war helping track down Nazi war criminals. He also testified at the trial of Eichmann in Jerusalem and at the trials of his subordinates in Germany.

58. The author of the memorandum gave a full description of the pertinent details of the deportation procedures in the countryside. It was a sweeping indictment of both the German supervisors and the Hungarian gendarmerie *(csendőrség)* and state police. "We must remember, with a profound, painful feeling, the treatment, utterly humiliating to human dignity and humanity, to which the unfortunate Jews were subjected in some places." Szinai and Szűcs, eds., *Horthy Miklós titkos iratai*, pp. 445–49. For the text of Horthy's rescript to Sztójay, instructing the prime minister to put a stop to the handling of the Jewish Question by methods irreconcilable with the "Magyar way of thinking," see ibid., pp. 450–55.

59. Rather naïvely, Horthy informed Hitler not only of his intention to fire Sztójay but also requested that the German occupational forces, the SS formations, and the Gestapo be recalled, lest his position as well as German-Hungarian friendship be undermined. Ibid., pp. 466–68.

60. Horthy, *Memoirs*, pp. 227–28.

61. For the events of the final three weeks culminating in Horthy's abdication and Szálasi's appointment, see Macartney, *October Fifteenth*, 2:356–443; Ránki, *1944. március 19.*, pp. 302–16; Ágnes Rozsnyói, *A Szálasi-puccs* [The Szálasi coup] (Budapest: Kossuth, 1977).

62. Jenő Szemák, the last president of the Supreme Court of Hungary in the

Arrow Cross era, offers a legalistic argument in an attempt to prove the legitimacy and morality of Szálasi's government in *Living History of Hungary* (McIntosh, Florida: Danubian Research and Information Center, 1969).

63. *Út és cél* [Way and goal], 3d ed. (Buenos Aires: n.p., 1955), p. 10.

64. Ibid., p. 21.

65. Goebbels, *Final Entries,* p. 173.

66. Macartney, *October Fifteenth,* 2:447–48.

67. The most prominent Hungarist chroniclers of the Arrow Cross movement and Szálasi's brief rule are Ferenc Fiala, *Zavaros évek* [Troubled years] (Munich: Mikes Kelemen Kör, 1976); Ödön Málnási, *A magyar nemzet őszinte története* [The honest history of the Hungarian nation], 2d ed. (Munich: n.p., 1959); Lajos Marschalkó, the Hungarists' "expert" on Jewish affairs, *Világhódítók: Az igazi háborús bűnösök* [World-conquerors: the real war criminals], 5th ed. (Munich: József Süli, 1958); and idem, *Országhódítók: Az emancipációtól Rákosi Mátyásig* [Nation-conquerors: from the emancipation to Mátyás Rákosi] (Munich: Mikes Kelemen Kör, 1975).

Of the many books based either on scholarly research or personal experience that have been published in Hungary about the rise of the Arrow Cross party and Szálasi to national prominence the following, in addition to the ones already cited, may be consulted: Elek Karsai, *"Szálasi naplója": A nyilasmozgalom a II. világháború idején* ["Szálasi's diary": the Arrow Cross movement at the time of the Second World War] (Budapest: Kossuth, 1978); Miklós Lackó, *Nyilasok és nemzetiszocialisták, 1935–1944* [Arrow Cross men and National Socialists, 1935–1944] (Budapest: Kossuth, 1966); Éva Teleki, *Nyilas uralom Magyarországon, 1944 október 16. / 1945 április 4.* [Arrow Cross rule in Hungary, 16 October 1944 – 4 April 1945] (Budapest: Kossuth, 1974).

68. Deák, "Hungary," p. 395.

69. For the various attempts by the representatives of neutral nations, the International Red Cross, and some Hungarian priests and nuns to save Jews by issuing official documents or hiding them, see Jenő Lévai, *Szürke könyv: Magyar zsidók megmentéséről* [Gray book: on the rescue of Hungarian Jews] (Budapest: Officina, 1946). For the activities of the Hungarian anti-Fascist organizations, see Dezső Nemes, *Magyarország felszabadulása* [The liberation of Hungary] (Budapest: Szikra, 1955).

70. Lévai, ed., *Eichmann in Budapest,* p. 145.

71. Ibid.

72. "Arrow-cross men, among them hooligans of 13 and 14 with sub-machine guns, lay in wait everywhere like wolves and jackals. They robbed the Jews of all their belongings . . . and divided the spoils among themselves. There was simply nobody who could protect the Jews obliged to move into the protected area from robbery, theft, and plunder, from being carried off to the brickyard and in many cases from deportation." Ibid., p. 154.

73. An excellent account of the bitter fighting for the control of the Hungarian capital may be found in Sándor Tóth, *Budapest felszabadítása, 1944–1945* [The liberation of Budapest, 1944–1945] (Budapest: Zrínyi, 1975).

74. Szekeres, ed., *Források Budapest történetéhez,* 3:570–71.

75. For the most detailed description and documentation of the ghettoization of Budapest's Jewry and the fate of the thousands of deportees and labor service men, see Lévai, *Zsidósors Magyarországon;* Randolph L. Braham, *The Hungarian Labor Service System, 1939–1945* (New York: Columbia University Press, 1977).

76. Lévai, ed., *Eichmann in Budapest*, pp. 163–64.

77. Lévai, *Zsidósors Magyarországon*, pp. 390–98.

78. Macartney, *October Fifteenth*, p. 461 (n. 1); Nagy-Talavera, *The Green Shirts*, pp. 236–37.

79. Notwithstanding the insistence of Hungarist historians to the contrary, the military operations conducted by the Germans were singularly self-serving. Nor did the Germans respect the land and property of their last, hapless ally. They looted not only the deserted homes and stores of deported Jews, but those of Christian Magyars as well. Automobiles, horse-drawn wagons, and cattle were confiscated as Arrow Cross law-enforcement officials watched helplessly. Béla Esti, ed., *Dokumentumok Magyarország felszabadulásáról, 1944–1945* [Documents on the liberation of Hungary, 1944–1945] (Budapest: Corvina, 1975), pp. 45–46.

80. For information on the atrocities of retreating Arrow Cross militiamen and German soldiers, see István Fehér, *Politikai küzdelmek Dél-Dunántúlon 1944–1946 között* [Political struggles in Southern Transdanubia between 1944 and 1946]. (Budapest: Akadémiai Kiadó, 1972), pp. 46–53.

81. Displaying an astonishingly skewed logic, the Hungarist historian Marschalkó even makes an attempt, indiscriminately using statistical data, to prove that the number of Hungarian Jews found alive after the war was actually greater than those who perished. *Országhódítók*, pp. 236–53.

82. *Zavaros évek*, p. 142. Fiala also reports (p. 143) that in early November 1944, at a news conference, Szálasi expressed regrets over the atrocities and promised that he would see to it that they ceased.

83. Lévai, *Zsidósors Magyarországon*, p. 398.

Aladár Komlós

1. József Kiss (1843–1921) was the only Hungarian-Jewish poet who acquired national reputation based solely on the literary excellencies of poems devoted to Jewish subjects. His *Zsidó dalok* [Jewish songs] was published in 1868. Though best known as a compassionate chronicler of some of the most pressing problems that hampered the assimilation of Jews into Hungarian society, such as the infamous blood libel of Tiszaeszlár ("Az ár ellen" [Against the tide], 1882) and the unfavorable reaction which the influx of poor Galician Jews evoked ("Legendák a nagyapámról" [Legends about my grandfather], 1910–16), he was also an acute observer of the everyday problems of the Hungarian petit bourgeoisie ("Mese a varrógépről" [Tale of the sewing machine] 1883), the plight of the oppressed peasants ("Dózsa György" 1883), and revolution-prone Russia ("Knyaz Potemkin" 1906). Kiss was also the founder (1890) and editor of *A Hét* [The Week], the first Hungarian-Jewish literary magazine. On his seventieth birthday, in recognition of his literary contributions, Kiss was elected to the Kisfaludy Society, the prestigious and exclusivist stronghold of the Hungarian literati.

Sándor Bródy (1863–1924), one of the most popular novelists and playwrights of the Hungarian fin de siècle, successfully combined his love of everything Hungarian with his devotion to Judaism. Bródy was a restless, rebellious man with an unmistakably unpredictable, often strangely uneven literary style. He often borrowed his characters from the Jewish life he knew so well, and held the distinction of having been the first writer in Hungarian literature to deal with the problems of the Jewish worker (*Nyomor* [Misery] 1884). He was also a sometime journalist (*Magyar Hirlap* and *Újság*), editor (*Fehér Könyv* and *Jövendő*), and theater critic.

The famed editor-in-chief of *Nyugat*, Ignotus (Hugó Veigelsberg, 1869–1949) started his career as a poet (*A slemil keservei* [The schlemiel's grievances] 1891) before he turned his attention to literary criticism. He was a spirited champion of artistic freedom and a bitter critic of the proponents of the so-called theory of imperialist Magyardom and its extension, epigone literature. A man of great intellect, a voracious reader, and one of Freud's earliest disciples in Hungary, Ignotus was a sharp-eyed discoverer of literary talent and gave many of Hungary's most famous poets and writers their first exposure to the general public.

Ferenc Molnár (Neumann, 1878–1952), the author of such popular plays as *Carousel* (adopted from *Liliom* [Lily]) and *Testőr* [Guardsman] (1910), was the most celebrated Hungarian playwright before he left his native country in the late 1930s. Molnár is best remembered for the flighty plots, romantic characters, and witty dialogues of his plays that were staged in the West. In Hungary his name is inevitably associated with the immensely popular children's story *A Pál utcai fiúk* [The Paul Street boys] (1907). There was, however, a lesser-known, serious side to his literary career as well. *Egy haditudósító emlékei* [Memories of a war correspondent] (1916) is a brilliant though glorifying portrait of the brave Hungarian soldier in the bloody battles of the First World War. Though his familiarity with the socioeconomic peculiarities of the class-conscious Hungary of his time allowed him to create credible characters, Molnár never quite succeeded in capturing the real meaning of Jewish life and the complexities of assimilation. In comparison with the standard characters of his novels and plays—romanticized workers, middle-class upstarts, eccentric aristocrats—his Jewish figures are rarely representative of the mainstream of Hungarian Jewry. Some make themselves pitifully ridiculous by going overboard in their attempts to assimilate fully, others are trapped in a limbo of self-criticism and rejection (*Andor*, 1918).

Dezső Szomory (1869–1944), after abandoning a promising career in music—he had been a pupil of Franz Liszt—became one of the most prolific Hungarian novelists and playwrights. He often portrayed such subjects as the outcasts of society and people oppressed by psychological problems, and did so with dramatic skill and understanding. Though Jewish characters often crop up in his work, only one of his plays, *Péntek este* [Friday evening], is based on a Jewish theme.

2. Though he completed his legal studies, Tamás Kóbor (Adolf Bermann, 1867–1942) capitulated to the lure of literature when his brother-in-law, József Kiss, founded *A Hét* [The Week] in 1890. His feuilletons and political editorials, written with great eloquence and irrefutable logic, along with his novels and collections of short stories earned him a national reputation. A judicious analyst of the assimilationist attempts of the Hungarian Jews, Kóbor conducted a spirited fight against the demagogic proponents of racial anti-Semitism, and was an outspoken defender of Jewish rights. He is remembered for such works as *Ki a gettóból* [Out of the ghetto] (1911), *Halál* [Death] (1918), and *Pók Ádám hetvenhét élete* [The seventy-seven lives of Ádám Pók] (1923). One of his plays, *Egy test, egy lélek* [One body, one soul] (1910), was staged in the National Theater. Perhaps his most memorable political work was *Bolsevizmusról a bolsevizmus alatt* [About Bolshevism during Bolshevism] (1919).

3. For biographical information, see the introduction to Zsolt's "Letter to a Well-Meaning Person" in this volume.

4. The son of Mihály Pollák, Chief Rabbi of Sopron, Károly Pap (1897–1944) was jailed for eighteen months for his activities in the short-lived Hungarian Soviet Republic. Following his release he spent some time in exile before returning to Hungary. Despite his political convictions, Pap remained deeply committed to Jewish causes and became a tireless investigator and interpreter of the position and role of Jews in society. The best known among his works are *Megszabadítottál a haláltól* [Thou hast delivered me from death] (1932) and *Nyolcadik stáció* [The eighth station] (1933)—novels about Jesus, whom he called the "leader of the Jewish proletariat"— and the autobiographical *Azriel* (1933). Two of his plays, *Bászséba [Bathsheba] (1940)* and *Mózes* (1944), were staged in the Jewish Theater of Budapest. In May 1944 he was called up for military labor service, and is believed to have died subsequently in Bergen-Belsen.

5. One of the most popular Hungarian poets, János Arany (1817–82) was an uncompromising exponent of the true Magyar spirit (*Buda halála* [The death of Buda], 1863), a moderate follower of the revolutionaries of 1848 (*Elveszett alkotmány* [The lost constitution], 1845), and an eloquent memorializer of the knightly virtues of medieval Hungary (*Toldi*, 1847).

Lajos Dénes

1. Count Gyula Andrássy the Elder (1823–90) was chairman of the committee that prepared the groundwork of Hungarian participation in the negotiations with the Austrian authorities which were to lead to the *Ausgleich* (Compromise) of 1867, and was subsequently a prime minister. The arrow-straight Andrássy Avenue, a popular promenade renamed Avenue of the People's Republic after the Second World War, has been one of the most noteworthy features of Budapest since its completion in the 1870s. The Kőrút is a main circular thoroughfare on the Pest side of the capital.

Ottó Komoly

1. Hebrew for "exile."

László Gömöri

1. In 1235 Batu, the second son of the Mongol chieftain Juchi, was charged with the conquest of Eastern Europe. His armies devastated Hungary in 1241–42.

2. King of Moravia, he was killed in battle against the invading Magyar tribes (884–95).

"The Crisis of Jewish Life"

1. *The author of this article, one of the outstanding figures of Hungarian-Jewish cultural life, does not wish to be identified by name.*

Sándor Scheiber

1. *Delivered at the memorial services for martyrs on the Hungarian Radio on 31 December 1946.*

2. 3:6.
3. *Genesis, 1:31.*
4. *Job, 3:22.*
5. *Jonah, 4:3.*
6. Excerpted from a poem by the famous Hungarian poet Endre Ady (1877–1919).
7. Excerpted from a poem by the famous Hungarian poet János Arany (1817–82).

Samu Szemere

1. Read before the general assembly of the Hungarian-Jewish Literary Society on 30 December 1947.
2. Lipót Lőw (1811–75) was rabbi of Szeged, editor of the influential journal *Ben Chananja,* and a tireless champion of both the Emancipation and the Magyarization of Hungarian Jewry, serving as its first historian. Immánuel Lőw (1854–1944) followed closely in his father's footsteps. In addition to being rabbi of Szeged as of 1878 and the planner in his native city of the architecturally most impressive synagogue in Hungary (completed in 1903), Lőw was an internationally known botanist (*Die Flora der Juden,* 4 vols. [1924–1934]), a Talmudic and Rabbinic lexicographer, and a frequent contributor to Hungarian and foreign scholarly publications. He was also the permanent representative of Progressive (Neolog) Jewry in the Upper House of Parliament.

Béla Bernstein (1868–1944) attended the National Rabbinical Institute in Budapest and the Jüdisch Theologisches Seminar in Breslau. He was ordained in 1892 and became rabbi in Szombathely (1892) and later in Nyíregyháza (1909). A prolific writer and meticulous researcher, Bernstein was the author of a number of books covering a wide spectrum of Jewish history. He is, however, best known for his pioneering work in the history of the Hungarian Jews during the Revolution of 1848 (*Az 1848/49-iki magyar szabadságharc és a zsidók* [The 1848/49 war of independence and the Jews], 1898).
3. Hebrew for "the Land of Israel."

Pál Kardos

1. A town in eastern Hungary.
2. A city in southern Hungary.
3. A car manufactured in East Germany.
4. *Lager* is German for "camp"; Bükkszállás and Zombor are villages in northern Hungary.

Dezső Kellér

1. A town in southern Hungary.

Sándor Schwartz

1. A city in eastern Hungary.
2. The infamous doctor of the Auschwitz extermination camp between 1943 and 1945, Josef Mengele (b. 1911) conducted insidious experiments on selected inmates

and earned the name "the Auschwitz monster" from those whose agony he would prolong, sometimes terminating it by sending them into the gas chambers, literally by a movement of his hand. Incredibly, he lived under his own name in Bavaria until 1951, moving later to Argentina and Paraguay. He has been the target of an intensive search by Jewish and non-Jewish groups for more than twenty-five years.

3. Selected by extermination-camp officials, the *Kapo*, himself an internee, received certain privileges in return for overseeing groups of prisoners. Many *Kapos*, fearing for their lives, were given to outbursts of brutality, although some were known to have been men of secret compassion. *Kapos* in charge of groups of Jewish inmates were usually Jews.

4. A town in eastern Hungary.

5. One of the districts in the southern part of Budapest.

László Gerend

1. A town formerly in northeastern Hungary. Today it is part of the Soviet Union, and has been renamed Mukačevo.

2. A steppe in eastern Hungary, near the city of Debrecen. A popular place among tourists visiting Hungary, the Hortobágy, with its romantic inn (the *hortobágyi csárda*, by the Hortobágy River), pipe-smoking shepherds, whip-cracking horse-herds, and fierce horses, is often described as the last surviving relic of the Magyars' nomadic way of life, a place where one may experience the "real" Hungary.

3. Known as "The Hangman," Reinhard Heydrich (1904–42) was chief of the Security Police of the Gestapo before his appointment as Gauleiter of Bohemia-Moravia. Outraged by his brutal methods, a group of Czechs assassinated him in May 1942.

4. Though accurate statistical data are still not available for the number of Jews who served in the Hungarian armed forces in the First World War, a number of high-ranking Jewish officers, army doctors, industrialists, and philanthropists received decorations of various classes, some of which, after the outbreak of the Second World War, provided temporary exemption from the anti-Jewish laws.

5. Actually, the invading Magyar tribes were under the command of another chief, Kuszán (d. 904), after whose death the leadership passed into the hands of Árpád (d. 907), the progenitor of the Magyars' first native dynasty. The House of Árpád ruled Hungary until 1301.

6. Often compared with some expansive green sea, the Alföld is a plain that stretches from south to northeast across the region between the Danube and Tisza rivers and the Tiszantúl, territory east of the Tisza. In its northernmost section are Szabolcs-Szatmár and Borsod-Abaúj-Zemplén, counties with the greatest concentration of Hasidic Jews before the Second World War.

7. An aristocratic Transylvanian family, the Rákóczis owned huge estates in northern and eastern Hungary.

8. The wife of two princes of Transylvania, Ferenc Rákóczi I (1645–76) and Imre Thököly (1657–1705), Ilona Zrínyi (1643–1703) was a heroic defender of the fortress of Munkács in 1685, during the last stage of the Hungarians' successful struggle to throw off the yoke of the Ottoman Turks.

Ferenc Rákóczi II (1676–1735) was the leader of an anti-Habsburg war of liberation (1703–11) that was aimed at the establishment of an independent Hungarian state.

Despite some early military victories and the formation of a nobles-dominated confederation at the Diet of Szécsény (1705), which, however, stopped short of declaring him king, Rákóczi's forces, weakened by a fratricidal leadership, were defeated by the Habsburgs. The Hungarians' struggle ended with the signing of the Peace of Szatmár (1 May 1711). Rákóczi died as an exile in the Turkish town of Rodosto (Tekirdagi). The *kurucok* were soldiers fighting in the armies of Imre Thököly and Ferenc Rákóczi II.

9. The powerful leader of the armies of the Holy Roman emperor Leopold I (1640–1705) in Hungary, General Anton Caraffa (1646–93) was as successful in fighting the Turks as he was brutal in suppressing an anti-Habsburg conspiracy at Eperjes in 1687.

10. Villages in northeastern Hungary.

11. A town formerly in northern Hungary. Today it is the Czechoslovakian Košice.

12. A town formerly in northern Hungary. Today it is the Czechoslovakian Presov.

13. Hebrew for "holy brotherhood," the Chevra Kaddisha is a charitable society of volunteer members among Ashkenazi Jews, responsible for the burial of the dead.

István Tamás

1. A town in western Hungary.

2. The largest lake in Hungary. Wines made from grapes grown on the hills on its shores are world famous.

3. A hill and village near Lake Balaton.

Ernő Szép

1. Named after the famous Hungarian poet, Mihály Vörösmarty (1800–1855), the square is located in the center of Budapest.

2. Arrow Cross militiamen were assigned to supervise the deportation of Jews following the formation of Hungary's last wartime government by their leader, Ferenc Szálasi (1897–1946), on 15 October 1944.

László Bárdos

1. Hungarian-speaking people living in Moldavia (Romania).

2. Once Hungarian, the town is now the Czechoslovakian Košice.

3. The plain bounded by the Danube and Tisza rivers and the Tiszantúl.

Sándor Sásdi

1. A city formerly in northwestern Hungary. Today it is the Czechoslovakian Bratislava.

2. A *Todtist* is a soldier belonging to the 2d SS Field Division, the *Totenkopf* (death's-head). *Oberscharführer* is German for "technical sergeant."

3. Pécs is a city in southwestern Hungary.

Géza Seifert

1. László I was king of Hungary from 1077 to 1095. A devout Catholic and a fierce defender of the Church who was canonized for his piety and zeal, László introduced

anti-Jewish laws similar to the ones that had already been in effect elsewhere in Christendom. His conquest of Croatia in 1091 gave Hungary access to the Adriatic Sea.

2. Kálmán I ruled Hungary from 1095 to 1116. A physically weak but intellectually and spiritually strong nephew of László I, Kálmán was an able administrator, an astute politician, and a circumspect lawgiver. His laws, though strict in both secular and ecclesiastical matters, are thought to have been generally less harsh than those of his predecessor. However, laws relating to Jews were severely discriminatory.

3. The House of Árpád was Hungary's first dynasty. It started with Árpád (d. 907), the conquering tribal chief, and came to an end with the death of András III in 1301. Endre II was the king of Hungary from 1205 to 1235, and was also known as András II. An inept administrator and a recklessly ambitious participant in the Fifth Crusade, Endre caused grave hardships to his people by his excessive dependence on foreigners and gross mismanagement in financial matters. Free Hungarians, apprehensive of the unchecked growth of royal and aristocratic power, forced the king to sign the Golden Bull, which was to protect their privileges. The Golden Bull also contained anti-Jewish stipulations which, however, were not implemented until 1233, when the king swore an oath before an emissary of Pope Gregory IX to put them into effect.

4. Soon after succeeding his father, Endre II, Béla IV (r. 1235–70) faced the mighty Mongol army of Batu. In the Battle of Mohács on 11 April 1241 the Mongols decisively defeated Béla's forces and ravaged Hungary. The king spent the rest of his reign directing the recovery of his realm. He protected the Jews, whom he regarded as his servants, and relied on their services in rebuilding Hungary's economy despite being admonished for it by Pope Urban IV in 1262.

5. The French-born Lajos I (r. 1342–82) of Anjou was king of both Hungary and Poland. His numerous wars, which put a constant strain on the royal treasury, forced the king to devise a sound economic policy and strengthen the nobles' privileges. He was also a generous patron of artists and scholars. Though tradition describes him as a kind and compassionate monarch, Lajos had no qualms about expelling the Jews, an act that won him words of praise from Pope Innocent III.

6. Zsigmond (Sigismund) I (r. 1387–1437) was Holy Roman emperor and king of Hungary and Bohemia. The son of Emperor Charles IV and the husband of Maria, daughter of the French-born Hungarian king, Lajos I, Zsigmond's European policies, unsuccessful struggle against the Ottoman Turks, and inability to placate rebellious Hungarian peasants left Hungary in socioeconomic shambles. Notwithstanding the humiliating stipulations of the Law of Buda, Zsigmond permitted Hungarian nobles to settle Jews on their estates and profit financially by the Jews' economic activity.

7. A Catholic monk, Kapisztrán was a leader of anti-Semitic agitators in the late fifteenth century.

8. Székesfehérvár is a city in northwestern Hungary; Pozsony, formerly in northwestern Hungary, is today the Czechoslovakian Bratislava.

9. In the aftermath of the ill-fated revolt of the Hungarian peasants led by György Dózsa (ca. 1470–1514), the *Tripartitum* of István Werbőczy (ca. 1458/60–1541) declared that the nobles had an inalienable right to land and that the peasantry (*jobbágyság*), aside from wages earned, had rights neither to land nor freedom. Werbőczy, a man of excessive greed and self-interest, was one of the chief instigators against the Jews.

10. Arad was formerly in southeastern Hungary. Today the Romanian city bears the same name.

11. On 15 May 1895, following nearly two years of impassioned debates in both houses of Parliament, the Upper House, by a majority of one, voted to admit the Jewish denomination to the status of the *religiones receptae* (accepted religions), putting the Jews on an equal footing with Catholics, Calvinists, and the Eastern Orthodox.

12. A representative in the Diet and one of the earliest proponents of political anti-Semitism in Europe, Győző Istóczy (1842–1915) founded the National Anti-Semitic Party on 6 October 1883 and became a lifelong advocate of the removal of Jews from Hungary to Palestine. One of Istóczy's most faithful followers, Géza Ónody (b. 1848), dedicated his political career to the anti-Semitic cause. He was a resident of the village of Tiszaeszlár, whose district he represented in the Diet; he was thus to play a leading role in the infamous ritual murder case of Tiszaeszlár. Gyula Verhovay (1848–1906) was the anti-Semites' propaganda expert. An able journalist, Verhovay in 1879 became the editor of *Függetlenség* (Independence), a newspaper he put at the disposal of the anti-Semitic movement.

13. August Rohling (1839–1931) was the author of *Der Talmudjude*, a quasi-scholarly book, in which he attempted to substantiate, mostly by falsifying Talmudic excerpts, allegations about the depravity of Jews and their hatred of non-Jews.

On 1 April 1882 Eszter Solymosi, a young Christian girl, disappeared from Tiszaeszlár, a village in northeastern Hungary. Rumors of foul play, soon snowballing into a nationwide hysteria, indicted the Jews of the village, accusing them of having killed her and having used her blood for the preparation of unleavened bread for Passover. Károly Eötvös (1842–1916), a well-known lawyer and politician, was hired to defend them. The trial of the Tiszaeszlár Jews (19 July to 3 August 1883) was held in the nearby town of Nyíregyháza. Though the body of the girl had been found and a team of famous forensic pathologists established suicide as the cause of death, the anti-Semitic presiding judge turned the trial into a theatrical event, dragging through the maze of court procedures the misguided son of one of the principal defendants, who testified against his father; the impassioned defense lawyer; a reluctant prosecutor who gave no credence to the charge; a multitude of witnesses; and the unruly, often screaming, spectators. The defendants were eventually acquitted, yet the memory of the blood libel of Tiszaeszlár still evokes conflicting opinions.

14. Born in the French-held city of Szeged during the counterrevolution of 1919, the "Szeged Idea" was an ill-defined political program principally aimed at the restoration of historic Hungary, espoused by a variety of chauvinistic and conservative fascist associations. The supporters of the "Szeged Idea" were also the chief protagonists of the "Christian Course," which related more to their anti-Semitism than to Christian exclusivism. They claimed that the Judeo-Bolshevist ideas of the Hungarian Soviet Republic and international Communism were a menace to and irreconcilable with the true Hungarian conception of life and nation.

In 1919 Admiral Miklós Horthy (1868–1957), a former commander-in-chief of the Adriatic Fleet of the Austro-Hungarian Navy, assumed command of the anti-Communist National Army. It consisted mainly of Hungarian officers who gathered around the leaders of the Szeged Movement. His subsequent election as Regent of Hungary initiated nearly a quarter-century of authoritarian rule, characterized by conservative politics, a nobles-dominated society, and a capitalist economy. Forced out of office by Ferenc Szálasi's Arrow Cross coup on 15 October 1944, Horthy was placed in "protective custody" by the Germans. Following the end of the Second World War, Horthy spent the rest of his life in exile in Estoril, Portugal.

15. A man of inconspicuous personality and modest administrative talents, Kálmán Darányi (1886–1939) gave free reign to right-wing political opposition groups, allied Hungary with Nazi Germany—his visit to Hitler in November 1937 led to the participation of Hungarian forces in the occupation of Czechoslovakia—and introduced anti-Jewish legislation during his brief (1936–38) tenure as prime minister. Győr is a city in northwestern Hungary.

16. A former director of the National Bank, a respected financial expert, and a reputedly devout Catholic, Béla Imrédy (1891–1946) performed a surprising political turnabout as prime minister (1938–39). Once known for his polished pro-British views, he suddenly became a rabid pro-Nazi. As a reward for servile support of Nazi Germany, some territories that had been annexed to Czechoslovakia on the northern border after the First World War were returned to Hungary. Imrédy introduced compulsory military service and withdrew Hungary from the League of Nations. His severe, racially oriented Jewish Law victimized not only Jews but thousands of converts as well. Ironically, that was to be his undoing. Embarrassed and humiliated by rumors that one of his great-grandparents was of Jewish descent, Imrédy resigned in February 1939. He was captured by the Americans in Germany at the end of the war and flown to Hungary. The People's Court sentenced him to death, and he was executed on 1 March 1946.

17. The author is in error. It was not until October 1940 that a group of extreme right-wing representatives in Parliament, led by Béla Imrédy, left the Government party and formed the Party of Hungarian Renewal (Magyar Megújulás Pártja). Philosophically and politically it followed Nazi Germany in the hope of establishing Hungarian National Socialism, and advocated the solution of the Jewish Question, the promulgation of a fascist constitution, and the nationalization of banking and heavy industry.

18. An able diplomat and conservative politician who was convinced that only a firm alliance with Hitler would result in the rectification of injustice committed against Hungary by the Treaty of Trianon, László Bárdossy (1890–1946) used his brief premiership (3 April 1941 to 9 March 1942) to make the future of his country totally dependent on the success of the German war effort. Consequently, he committed Hungarian forces in a shameful, brutal attack on Yugoslavia, joined Hitler's invasion of the Soviet Union, sent thousands of Jewish labor servicemen to the eastern front, and pushed through Parliament the Third Jewish Law, which forbade marriages between Jews and Christians as a means of safeguarding the racial purity of the Magyars. Following his capture by the Americans in Germany and extradition to Hungary, the People's Court sentenced him to death. As he stood before the firing squad he shouted, "Lord, save the country from these scum!"

19. Though numerous conflicting closing arguments have already been heard, the verdict of history is yet to be pronounced on Miklós Kállay (1887–1967), Hungary's prime minister from 9 March 1942 to 19 March 1944. Present-day Hungarian historians view him as an incorrigible anti-Communist and a two-faced opportunist, who in the spring of 1942 sent the Second Hungarian Army and nearly 40,000 Jewish labor servicemen to certain death on the eastern front. Western analysts of modern Hungarian history describe him as an anti-Nazi, antifascist, and anti-Communist

conservative politician whose sole objective was to save Hungary from the debacle that was awaiting Nazi Germany. Only Horthy's support kept Kállay aloft in the hateful atmosphere generated by the Germans and the Hungarian fascists, who regarded the prime minister as the principal obstacle to the fulfillment of the "common Hungarian-German destiny" and the destruction of Hungarian Jewry. Following the German occupation of Hungary on 19 March 1944 Kállay sought asylum in the Turkish embassy. He spent the rest of his life in exile.

20. The *Budapesti Közlöny* is a government publication containing laws, decrees, and regulations.

21. An army officer who had fought in the First World War, Ferenc Szálasi (1897–1946) began to develop the political ideology of Hungarism in the late 1920s. The Arrow Cross Party, which he founded in the mid-1930s, became the best-known and most popular of the fascist political organizations by 1937. Yet it was only after the German occupation of Hungary on 19 March 1944, and as a last desperate measure to stop the steadily advancing Soviet forces, that Szálasi acceded to power on 15 October 1944. The bloody rule of the Arrow Cross, however, merely postponed the inevitable by a few months. Szálasi was captured in Germany. Extradited by the Americans, he was tried and sentenced to death. He was hanged on 12 March 1946.

22. Újlak is one of the districts of Budapest; Hegyeshalom is a town in northwestern Hungary, near the Austrian border.

Bibliography

Balla, Erzsébet. "The Jews of Hungary: A Cultural Overview." In *Hungarian-Jewish Studies*. Edited by Randolph L. Braham. 2 vols. 2:85–136. New York: World Federation of Hungarian Jews, 1966–69.

Barany, George. "The Dragon's Teeth: The Roots of Hungarian Fascism." In *Native Fascism in the Successor States, 1918–1945*. Edited by Peter F. Sugar, pp. 73–82. Santa Barbara: ABC-Clio, Inc., 1971.

———. *Stephen Széchenyi and the Awakening of Hungarian Nationalism, 1791–1841*. Princeton: Princeton University Press, 1968.

Bary, József. *A tiszaeszlári bűnper* [The criminal case of Tiszaeszlár]. 2d ed. Budapest: Magyar Élet, 1941.

Bernstein, Béla. *Az 1848/49-iki magyar szabadságharc és a zsidók* [The 1848/49 Hungarian war of independence and the Jews]. Budapest: Franklin, 1898.

Braham, Randolph L. *The Destruction of Hungarian Jewry: A Documentary Account*. 2 vols. New York: World Federation of Hungarian Jews, 1963.

———. *The Hungarian Jewish Catastrophe: A Selected and Annotated Bibliography*. New York: Yivo Institute for Jewish Research, 1962.

———. *The Hungarian Labor Service System, 1939–1945*. New York: Columbia University Press, 1977.

Büchler, Sándor. *A zsidók története Budapesten* [History of Jews in Budapest]. Budapest, n.p., 1901.

Deák, István. "Hungary." In *The European Right: A Historical Profile*, edited by Hans Rogger and Eugen Weber, pp. 364–407. London: Weidenfeld & Nicholson, 1965.

———. *The Lawful Revolution: Louis Kossuth and the Hungarians, 1848–1849*. New York: Columbia University Press, 1979.

Debreczeni, József. *Hideg krematórium* [Cold crematorium]. Budapest: Fórum, 1975.

Édelstein, Bertalan. "A külföldi zsidóság az 5691 évben" [Foreign Jewry in the year 5691]. In *Évkönyv* [Yearbook]. Edited by Samu Szemere, pp. 279–99. Budapest: Az Izraelita Magyar Irodalmi Társulat, 1932.

Ember, Mária. *Hajtűkanyar* [Hairpin bend]. 2 vols. Budapest: Szépirodalmi Könyvkiadó, 1977.

Eötvös, Károly. *A nagy per* [The great trial]. 3 vols. Budapest: Révai Testvérek, 1904.

Esti, Béla, ed. *Dokumentumok Magyarország felszabadulásáról, 1944–1945* [Documents on the liberation of Hungary, 1944–1945]. Budapest: Corvina, 1975.

Fehér, István. *Politikai küzdelmek Dél-Dunántúlon 1944–1946 között* [Political struggles in southern Transdanubia between 1944 and 1946]. Budapest: Akadémiai Kiadó. 1972.

Fenyő, Mario D. *Hitler, Horthy, and Hungary: German-Hungarian Relations, 1941–1944*. New Haven: Yale University Press, 1972.

Fiala, Ferenc. *Zavaros évek* [Troubled years]. Munich: Mikes Kelemen Kör, 1976.

Frank, László. *Zöld ár* [Green tide]. Budapest: Zrínyi, 1974.

Gáti, Ödön, et al., eds. *Mementó: Magyarország, 1944* [Memento: Hungary, 1944]. Budapest: Kossuth, 1975.

Goebbels, Joseph. *Final Entries, 1945: The Diaries of Joseph Goebbels*. Edited by Hugh Trevor-Roper and translated by Richard Barry. New York: G. P. Putnam's Sons, 1978.

————. *The Goebbels Diaries*. Edited and translated by Louis P. Lochner. New York: Popular Library, Eagle Books, 1965.

Gömbös, Gyula. *Egy magyar vezérkari tiszt bíráló feljegyzései a forradalomról és ellenforradalomról* [The critical notes of a Hungarian staff officer of the revolution and counterrevolution]. Budapest: Budapesti Hirlap nyomdája, 1920.

Grünwald, Fülöp, and Ernő Naményi. "Budapesti zsinagógák" [The synagogues of Budapest]. In *A 90 éves Dohány-utcai templom* [The ninety-year-old Dohány Street Temple]. Edited by József Katona, pp. 19–31. Budapest: Az Országos Magyar Zsidó Múzeum, 1949.

Handler, Andrew. *Blood Libel at Tiszaeszlár*. New York: Columbia University Press, 1980.

————. trans. *Rabbi Eizik: Hasidic Stories about the Zaddik of Kálló*. Rutherford, New Jersey: Fairleigh Dickinson University Press, 1978.

Hegedüs, Sándor. *A tiszaeszlári vérvád* [The blood libel of Tiszaeszlár]. Budapest: Kossuth, 1966.

Horthy, Nicholas. *Memoirs*. New York: Robert Speller & Sons, 1957.

Himler, Márton. *Így néztek ki a magyar nemzet sírásói* [That is what the gravediggers of the Hungarian nation looked like]. New York: St. Marks Printing, 1958.

Istóczy, Győző. *Istóczy Győző országgyűlési beszédei, indítványai és törvényjavaslatai, 1872–1896* [Győző Istóczy's Speeches, Resolutions, and Bills in the Diet, 1872–1896]. Budapest: Buschmann, 1904.

Kállay, Nicholas. *Hungarian Premier*. Westport, Connecticut: Greenwood Press, 1970.

Kann, Robert A. "Hungarian Jewry during Austria-Hungary's Constitutional Period (1867–1918)." In *Jewish Social Studies* 7 (1945):357–86.

Karsai, Elek. *Itél a nép* [The people pass judgment]. Budapest: Kossuth, 1977.

————. "Szálasi naplója": *A nyilasmozgalom a II. világháború idején* ["Szálasi's diary": The Arrow Cross movement at the time of the Second World War]. Budapest: Kossuth, 1978.

Katzburg, Nathaniel. "Hungarian Jewry in Modern Times: Political and Social Aspects." In Hungarian-Jewish Studies. Edited by Randolph L. Braham. 2 vols. 1:137–70. New York: World Federation of Hungarian Jews, 1966–69.

————. "The Jewish Congress of Hungary, 1868–1869." In *Hungarian-Jewish Studies*. Edited by Randolph L. Braham. 2 vols. 2:1–33. New York: World Federation of Hungarian Jews, 1966–69.

Kecskeméti, Lipót. "A Cionizmus" [Zionism]. In *Évkönyv* [Yearbook]. Edited by József Bánóczi, pp. 221–39. Budapest: Az Izraelita Magyar Irodalmi Társulat, 1908.

Kohn, Sámuel. "Elnöki megnyitó" [Presidential opening speech]. In *Évkönyv* [Yearbook]. Edited by Vilmos Bacher and József Bánóczi, pp. 7–8. Budapest: Az Izraelita Magyar Irodalmi Társulat, 1897.

Komlós, Aladár. "Zsidóság, magyarság, Európa" [Jewry, Magyardom, Europe]. In *Ararát*. Edited by Aladár Komlós, pp. 24–27. Budapest: Országos Izraelita Leányárvaház, 1943.

Krúdy, Gyula. *A tiszaeszlári Solymosi Eszter* [Eszter Solymosi of Tiszaeszlár]. Budapest: Magvető, 1975.

Kubinszky, Judit. *Politikai antiszemitizmus Magyarországon, 1875–1890* [Political anti-Semitism in Hungary]. Budapest: Kossuth, 1976.

Kun, Mme Béla. *Kun Béla*. Budapest: Magvető, 1969.

Lackó, Miklós. *Nyilasok és nemzetiszocialisták, 1935–1944* [Arrow Cross men and National Socialists, 1935–1944]. Budapest: Kossuth, 1966.

László, Ernő. "Hungary's Jewry: A Demographic Overview, 1918–1945." In *Hungarian-Jewish Studies*. Edited by Randolph L. Braham. 2 vols. 2:137–82. New York: World Federation of Hungarian Jews, 1966–69.

Lendvai, Paul. *Anti-Semitism without Jews*. New York: Doubleday, 1971.

Lévai, Jenő. *Black Book on the Martyrdom of Hungarian Jewry*. Zürich, n.p., 1948.

————. *Szürke könyv: Magyar zsidók megmentéséről* [Gray book: on the rescue of Hungarian Jews]. Budapest: Officina, 1946.

————. *Zsidósors Magyarországon* [Jewish fate in Hungary]. 2d ed. Budapest: Magyar Téka, 1948.

————. ed. *Eichmann in Hungary: Documents*. Budapest: Pannonia, 1961.

McCagg, William O., Jr. *Jewish Nobles and Geniuses in Modern Hungary*. New York: Columbia University Press, 1972.

Macartney, C. A. *October Fifteenth: A History of Modern Hungary*. 2d ed. 2 vols. Edinburgh: Edinburgh University Press, 1961.

Málnási, Ödön. *A magyar nemzet őszinte története* [The honest history of the Hungarian nation]. 2d ed. Munich, n.p., 1959.

Marschalkó, Lajos. *Országhódítók: Az emancipációtól Rákosi Mátyásig* [Nation-conquerors: from the emancipation to Mátyás Rákosi]. Munich: Mikes Kelemen Kör, 1975.

————. *Világhódítók: Az igazi háborús bűnösök* [World-conquerors: the real war criminals]. 5th ed. Munich: József Süli, 1958.

Marton, Ernest (Ernő). "The Family Tree of Hungarian Jewry." In *Hungarian-Jewish Studies*. Edited by Randolph L. Braham. 2 vols. 1:1–59. New York: World Federation of Hungarian Jews, 1966–69.

Moldova, György. *A Szent Imre-induló* [The St. Imre march]. Budapest: Magvető, 1975.

Molnár, Erik, Ervin Pamlényi, and György Székely, eds. *Magyarország története* [History of Hungary]. 2 vols. Budapest: Gondolat, 1964.

Moskovits, Aron. *Jewish Education in Hungary, 1848–1948*. New York: Bloch Publishing Co., 1964.

Nagy-Talavera, Nicholas M. *The Green Shirts and the Others*. Stanford: Hoover Institution Press, 1970.

Nemes, Dezső. *Magyarország felszabadulása* [The liberation of Hungary]. Budapest: Szikra, 1955.

Nordau, Miksa. *A Czionizmus* [Zionism]. Translated by Gyula Gábel. Budapest: Gross & Grünhut, 1902.

Pintér, István. *Ki volt Horthy Miklós?* [Who was Miklós Horthy?]. Budapest: Zrínyi, 1968.

Pölöskei, Ferenc. *Horthy és hatalmi rendszere, 1919–1922* [Horthy and his system of power, 1919–1922]. Budapest: Kossuth, 1977.

Pomogáts, Béla. *Radnóti Miklós*. Budapest: Gondolat, 1977.

Ránki, György. *1944. március 19.: Magyarország német megszállása* [19 March 1944: the German occupation of Hungary]. Budapest: Kossuth, 1978.

———. "The Problem of Fascism in Hungary." In *Native Fascism in the Successor States, 1918–1945*. Edited by Peter F. Sugar, pp. 65–72. Santa Barbara: AFC-Clio, Inc., 1971.

——— et al., eds. *A Wilhelmstrasse és Magyarország: Német diplomáciai iratok Magyarországról, 1933–1944* [Wilhelmstrasse and Hungary: German diplomatic documents on Hungary, 1933–1944]. Budapest: Kossuth, 1968.

Rozsnyói, Ágnes. *A Szálasi-puccs* [The Szálasi coup] Budapest: Kossuth, 1977.

Sándor, Iván. *A vizsgálat iratai: Tudósítás a tiszaeszlári per körülményeiről* [The documents of the investigation: report on the circumstances of the Tiszaeszlár case]. Budapest: Kozmosz, 1976.

Steiner, Lenke. "Az év magyar-zsidó irodalma" [Hungarian-Jewish literature of the year]. In *Ararát*. Edited by Aladár Komlós, pp. 148–56. Budapest: Országos Izraelita Leányárvaház, 1944.

Szálasi, Ferenc. *Út és cél* [Way and goal]. 3d ed. Buenos Aires: n.p., 1955.

Szekeres, József, ed. *Források Budapest történetéhez* [Sources for the history of Budapest]. 4 vols. Budapest: Budapest Székesfőváros Levéltára, 1976.

Szemák, Jenő. *Living History of Hungary*. McIntosh, Florida: Danubian Research and Information Center, 1969.

Szilágyi-Windt, László. *A kállói cádik: A nagykállói zsidóság története* [The Tzaddik of Kálló: the history of Nagykálló Jewry]. Tel Aviv: L. Szilágyi-Windt, 1959.

Szinai, Miklós, and László Szűcs, eds. *Bethlen István titkos iratai* [The secret papers of István Bethlen]. Budapest: Kossuth, 1972.

———. *Horthy Miklós titkos iratai* [The secret papers of Miklós Horthy]. Budapest: Kossuth, 1965.

Teleki, Éva. *Nyilas uralom Magyarországon, 1944 október 16. / 1945 április 4.* [Arrow Cross Rule in Hungary, 16 October 1944 – 4 April 1945]. Budapest: Kossuth, 1974.

Tóth, Sándor. *Budapest felszabadítása, 1944–1945* [The liberation of Budapest, 1944–1945]. Budapest: Zrínyi, 1975.

Tőkés, Rudolf L. *Béla Kun and the Hungarian Soviet Republic: The Origins and Role of the Communist Party in Hungary in the Revolutions of 1918–1919*. New York: Praeger, 1967.

Ujvári, Péter, ed. *Magyar Zsidó Lexikon* [Hungarian-Jewish lexicon]. Budapest: A Magyar Zsidó Lexikon, 1929.

Vágó, Béla. "Germany and the Jewish Policy of the Kállay Government." In *Hungarian-Jewish Studies*. Edited by Randolph L. Braham. 2 vols. 2:183–210. New York: World Federation of Hungarian Jews, 1966–69.

Vargha, Kálmán. *Gelléri Andor Endre*. Budapest: Szépirodalmi Könyvkiadó, 1973.

Vas, Zoltán. *Horthy, vagy a király* (Horthy; or, the King]. Budapest: Szèpirodalmi Könyvkiadó, 1971.

Végházi, István (Stephen). "The Role of Jewry in the Economic Life of Hungary." In

Hungarian-Jewish Studies. Edited by Randolph L. Braham. 2 vols. 2:35–84. New York: World Federation of Hungarian Jews, 1966–69.

Venetianer, Lajos. *A magyar zsidóság története* [History of Hungarian Jewry]. Budapest, n.p., 1922.

Wagner, Richard. *Richard Wagner's Prose Works*. Translated by William Ashton Ellis. 8 vols. London: K. Paul, Trench, Trübner, 1895–1912.

Zahavi, Zvi Y. *Me-he-Chatam Sofer ve-'ad Herzl* [From the Chatam Sofer to Herzl]. Jerusalem: Zionist Library, 1965.

Index